Friedrich Kiel

DIARY OF A JOURNEY
TO ENGLAND

IN THE YEARS 1761-1762

Elibron Classics
www.elibron.com

Elibron Classics series.

© 2005 Adamant Media Corporation.

ISBN 1-4212-3315-0 (paperback)
ISBN 1-4212-3314-2 (hardcover)

This Elibron Classics Replica Edition is an unabridged facsimile
of the edition published in 1902 by Longmans, Green, and Co.,
London, New York and Bombay.

DIARY OF A JOURNEY TO ENGLAND IN 1761–1762

GRAF FRIEDRICH VON KIELMANSEGGE, LANDDROST IN RATZEBURG.

DIARY OF A JOURNEY
TO ENGLAND

IN THE YEARS 1761–1762

BY

COUNT FREDERICK KIELMANSEGGE

TRANSLATED

BY

COUNTESS KIELMANSEGG

WITH ILLUSTRATIONS

LONGMANS, GREEN, AND CO.

39 PATERNOSTER ROW, LONDON

NEW YORK AND BOMBAY

1902

All rights reserved

PREFACE

ONE day, on looking through the library at my German home, I came upon a manuscript written by my husband's great-grandfather, containing a diary of his journey to England in the years 1761 –1762, in which he describes—for the benefit of his German family and friends—the Coronation of George III.—which he witnessed—London and its sights, the society of that day, and his visits to various towns and country places in England. It appeared to me that some of the impressions of a foreigner in England in those days would be of interest to my own country-people, as they were to myself; I therefore determined to translate them.

In this work I am much indebted to Mr. A. Llewelyn Roberts for his kind assistance in revising this translation.

Philippa Kielmansegg
(*née* Sidney).

Gülzow,
July, 1902.

LIST OF ILLUSTRATIONS

DIARY OF A JOURNEY TO ENGLAND IN 1761–1762

AFTER several delays, my brother[1] and I[2] started on the 4th of September on our intended journey to England, in order to be present at the Coronation of King George III. and Queen Sophia Charlotte, Princess of Mecklenburg Strelitz, which was to take place on the 22nd of September.

We left Hanover, at last, at seven o'clock in the evening, but did not arrive at our first station, *Neustadt am Rübenberge*, until midnight, as our postillion lost his way ; thus we only reached *Nienburg* at six in the morning. We started off at once, with fresh horses, to Suhlingen, a journey of about three hours, where we met Herr Privy

---

[1] Count Carl Kielmansegge (so spelt at that time, but originally spelt without the " e.' The family has latterly reverted to the original spelling). He became later President of the Chamber (Prime Minister) of Hanover. B. 1731, d. 1810.

[2] Count Frederick Kielmansegge, later Hanoverian Landdrost of the Duchy of Lauenburg. B. 1728, d. 1800.

eat, but we noticed that six spokes were broken off one of the hind wheels of our brand new carriage, which we had only received from the coach-builders the moment before our departure from Hanover. So we had to have new spokes put in, which delayed us until four o'clock, when we started with fresh post-horses for *Mohrburg*, a village in the district of Oldenburg.

As this place was in the vicinity of the East Friesland boundary, we were not allowed to take the Mohrburg horses more than half a mile on, to the Prussian village of *Grossen Sander*. As a matter of fact, travellers are only allowed to take Oldenburg horses right through to this place in cases of necessity, probably in order that the Grossen Sander people may not lose their profit. The delay which ensues on so short a stage of course seriously inconveniences travellers.

The Prussian postmaster in Grossen Sander, who is also the village innkeeper, was one of the rudest fellows in the world. When we arrived, he was making a great disturbance with an English courier of the name of Collins, and a servant of Prince Ludwig of Brunswick[1] at the Hague, whom the Prince had sent, so he said, to

---

[1] Third brother of Prince Ferdinand.

Prince Ferdinand,[1] and who was travelling in the same direction as we were. Both parties were probably at fault, as neither the Englishman nor the rough East Frieslander understood each other. After their departure, we tried to get off as quietly and as fast as possible, so as to arrive as early as we could on the morning of the 7th at *Lehr*, 2½ hours distant, a pretty place, very much like a Dutch town. We attained our wish so far as to arrive at *Nieuwe Schantz*, about two hours further on, towards midday, this being the first place we reached in Holland. We passed through beautiful country by Lehrort, half an hour from Lehr, which we reached after we had passed over the River Ems in a ferry-boat. As our post-house was situated outside the Schanze, or Redoubt, and as we had no time to spare, we could not see the inside of the place, but had to hurry on in order to get fresh post-horses at *Sudlaren*, a borough in the province of Gröningen, five hours distant from there, and to travel thence to *Beylen*, in the province of Oberissel, three hours off, which we reached about midday on the 8th. After

[1] Ferdinand, Duke of Brunswick, distinguished General in the Seven Years' War in Germany, so celebrated for his victory of Minden. B. 1721, d. 1797.

changing horses only at *Wiesck*, a small town
three hours from *Beylen*, we reached *Zwoll*, another
three hours distant, at midnight of the same day.

We had been forced to take five horses at
Grossen Sander, but we sent them back from
Lehr, as we found it unnecessary to take them
any further. Zwoll is a large, well-built town
in Guelderland, where there is a great deal of
traffic, and whence carts travel such a distance
that a great many of them are to be met
throughout the Empire.

The next morning we drove right on, as, the
gates being shut, it was not possible for us to
change horses or to get rid of the ones we had ;
so we continued with the same horses to *Amersfort*,
seven hours further, through a district which can
compete with our country about Lüneburg for
barrenness and sand, with not a tree to be seen,
much less a house, for more than 2 to $2\frac{1}{2}$ German
miles. This, coupled with the necessary stoppages,
the chattering of the drivers at all the different
inns, a storm, heavy rain, and darkness, prevented
us from arriving at Amersfort until two o'clock
in the morning, and from reaching *Utrecht*, two
hours further on, until nine o'clock.

Although we had looked forward to seeing the

sights of this renowned town, and its universities, we had to relinquish the idea, as we were obliged to take the Saturday's packet-boat for England. We had to curb our curiosity, therefore, as we were obliged to go to the Hague, in order to see some of our relations, and to get the necessary passport for the packet from the English Ambassador, General Yorke.

We contented ourselves by going to the English resident, Pouchoud, to whom we had been directed, in order to arrange the necessary storage of our carriage ; then, at four o'clock in the afternoon, after we had dined, we went to the ordinary Dutch towing-barge, which starts every Thursday at that hour, and arrives on Friday morning at six at Leyden without changing, as do the other barges from Utrecht, which are not allowed to go further. The charge for the so-called little keep or cabin is 10 florins, when you hire it for yourself, and you have a comfortable couch ; by this means we were able to recover somewhat from the fatigues of the last six nights' journey.

The owner and skipper of the barge is one of the beadles of the University, a German by birth, who earns a little extra by this means.

The charge for each servant is 24 to 25 stiver,[1] and for luggage in proportion ; so that for these thirteen hours, or 6½ German miles, as far as the Hague, it cost us about 20 florins of Dutch money, including the tips ; a small sum compared with the cost of posting in Holland.

As we passed through Leyden at two o'clock in the night, I cannot describe the beauty of the town or its buildings ; but from what I could see by the moonlight, it is a large place, situated in a beautiful country. On the road from Utrecht you see nothing but beautiful gardens and houses, which the Dutch call "buyten" places.

On our arrival at the Hague, we inquired, first of all, for the lodgings of Hofgericht Assessor von Lenthe from Hanover, and for Hofrath von Leyser from Celle, but without success, as they had preceded us by twenty-four hours at each place we had passed through. We put up at the Marshal de Turenne, one of the principal hotels, and then went as soon as possible to see our mother's brother, the Hanoverian Chamberlain, and Envoyé Baron von Spörcken, whose sister, the Landräthin von Weyhe, was paying him a short visit. But before doing this, we had to call

---

[1] Worth about a penny (Dutch money).

upon the Hanoverian resident, Herr Laurentzi, in order to obtain our necessary passports. Our uncle at once thought of taking us with him to call upon these gentlemen, but not till we had visited the Ambassador Yorke, who lived in the so-called Printzen Haus, situated outside the Hague, and who presented us to the Duke Ludwig of Brunswick [1] and to the Hereditary Stadtholder.

The former is so well known that it is not necessary to describe him. The latter is a young prince of thirteen,[2] of whom much cannot yet be said, save that the Duke of Brunswick takes great trouble with his education, with the result, so it is said, that a great difference can already be detected in his progress. The future only will show whether all the trouble spent by his guardian has been successful ; at present it is impossible to judge.

---

[1] Brother of Prince Ferdinand, and tutor to the Hereditary Stadtholder.

[2] William V., Prince of Orange, born 1748, son of William, Prince of Orange, and Anna, eldest daughter of George II. Succeeded his father in 1751, under the regency of his mother, and, after her death, under that of the Prince of Brunswick. He assumed the reins of government in 1766, but the long-continued discontent of the people necessitated his dismissal in 1782 ; he died in Brunswick, 1806. His son became, in 1814, King of the Netherlands as William I.

The rest of the day we spent with our uncle,
whilst our two travelling companions went without us to the French play.   In the evening we
made the acquaintance of the wife of Herr Treuer,
who acts as Resident at two German courts, and
had been formerly secretary to the Envoyé
Spörcken.   As we had to be at Helvoetsluys at
noon on the following day, we forwarded all our
luggage during the night to Maassluis, four hours'
journey, and four of us, who had clubbed together,
followed our belongings the next morning before
four o'clock, in two Dutch phaetons.   At Maassluis everything had been ferried over an arm of
the Maas to the Island of Rosenberg ; from there
we drove in two short hours towards Briel, and
had to cross in a boat again in order to reach that
place.   All the luggage was then taken in wheel-
barrows to the town before the house of the
Posting Commissioners, from whom we obtained
other carriages, which had to take us a drive of
two good hours to Helvoetsluys.

The English agent, Leyning, is staying in the
pretty little town of Briel, where all passengers
for England have to call and pay a certain passage-
money ; for this they receive another passport to
deliver to the captain of the packet.   Each person

pays 7 florins, and we had to pay, in all, for ourselves, our servants and luggage, 49 Dutch florins.

We noticed the existence of a very curious custom here with regard to the ordering of post-horses. As soon as any travellers arrive, the post-master rings a bell three times, which hangs high up before his house; after the third peal a peculiar game-board is brought out and placed before the doors. This board is similar in shape to those used by the ancient Romans; the dice fall round and round through a large funnel on to the board. Each driver has one throw with two dice, and the one who throws the highest number gets the fare. This game of hazard causes much inequality, and it frequently happens that one driver, if he throws unluckily, earns nothing for several weeks, while the lucky ones are continually making money, especially as they are paid pretty highly.

At Helvoetsluys we dined at an English inn, and then went on board the packet, called the *Prince of Orange*, Captain Hund. We found such a crowd of fellow-travellers of all nations on board, that it was impossible for them all to get berths, although there were sixteen;

many had to lie on the floors of the large and small cabins, and on deck. I belonged to the latter, and although the captain had assigned to me one of the best berths, I preferred the deck to the closeness down below, feeling well in the fresh air.

It was the identical ship, with the same captain, in which my brother and father crossed over in 1752. About a year, or a year and a half ago, when the captain was not on board, on account of illness, the French took the ship and sold it to the Dutch, from whom Captain Hund rebought it with the King's money. It must not, however, be supposed that the packet-boat belonged to the King or the Crown ; it is the property of the captain, who receives a sum of money for each voyage, and gets a guinea from each traveller for a berth in his cabin, and half a guinea for servants and others, who are in the large cabin ; this must bring in a pretty considerable sum in the course of the year, particularly on occasions like the present, when so many people are going over to England in order to see the Coronation.

There are usually four packets weekly between Holland and England, two every Wednesday

and two every Saturday, sailing respectively from
Harwich and Helvoetsluis. In times of peace,
there are only fourteen men on board, but in
times of war there must be twenty-one men, and
the ship is armed with six to eight cannons,
besides several swivel guns (a sort of movable
small cannon, which is held on a kind of fork,
by which means it can be fired off in all
directions).

Among our numerous travellers were some
rich Portuguese Jews from Amsterdam, one of
whom, named Cappadoci, was a real epicure.
Others, with whom we made great friends, and
who subsequently joined us from Harwich to
London, were Captain Egerton, one of the Duke
Ferdinand of Brunswick's aide-de-camps, whom
he was sending over to London, with two
standards of the French regiments of Vierset,
which the Hereditary Duke of Brunswick had
taken at Dorsten ; a certain rich merchant from
Rotterdam, named Schlemmer, the eldest son
of the Hanoverian Ober Amtmann at Harste,
and brother of the present Ober Amtmann at
Rotenkirchen : he is head manager of the commercial business of the Hanoverian Government
mines, and is married to a rich French lady who

was with him ; also a merchant from Smyrna, with
his unmarried sister, of the name of Annesley.
The last two were really Scots, and their father is
a clergyman of the Scottish church at Rotterdam.

Miss Annesley is rather a good-looking young
lady, who is very clever and lively in addition.
Her brother, who is in the prime of life, is also a
very accomplished man, who has already lived ten
years at Smyrna with a friend in the same commercial business.   He has only just come back to
Holland, in order to see his family, by way of
Constantinople, through Poland and Upper and
Lower Saxony, and returns later on, so as to give
his partner an opportunity to leave Smyrna for
three years.   It was most agreeable to us to have
such pleasant travelling companions.

Immediately after the post-bag had arrived, at
three o'clock in the afternoon, we weighed anchor
and set sail, and though the wind was not quite
favourable, we were able to get through the sand-
banks out of the Meuse into the sea.   To the
post-bag, which was lying next the rudder and
above it, large pieces of stone or iron were fastened
with stout ropes, so that the bag could be thrown
overboard, this being the duty of the captain
should the packet-boat have to surrender.

We were not far distant from the island of
Goeree, situated at the mouth of Meuse, when we
sighted a large three-masted vessel under full sail
lying in our path, which at first occasioned us
some anxiety ; more particularly as we observed
that it was not an English vessel or man-of-war.
As she did not answer our signal (a large English
flag), and as our ship's company could not recog-
nize what nation she belonged to, our anxiety lest
she might be a French privateer did not seem
quite unfounded, for notice had been given us
that a ship of this nature had been seen recently
in these waters. Notwithstanding this, our captain soon changed his mind, and passed within a
short distance of her ; which I think he was
induced to do owing to the vessel having furled
all her sails and dropped her anchor. We, too,
anchored and remained in the vicinity overnight
for six hours, as the wind had dropped nearly to
a perfect calm, and we did not sail again until next
morning at half-past six. Very soon afterwards
we saw a vessel much like ours, which gave us to
understand, by hoisting a large flag, that she had
come to meet us, for our protection ; she also
was armed with six or ten guns, but had a larger
complement than ours. This enabled us to sail

securely in her company, as no privateer would be likely to attack two armed vessels.

At last, towards evening, we sighted the English coast, and as the wind had freshened during the whole day, we were able to put on shore at Harwich at nine o'clock ; but before doing so, our pockets and clothes were examined by a custom-house officer, who had come on board to ascertain whether we carried any contraband about us. We had to leave all our luggage behind, so that it might be examined in the daytime ; for this reason, we left all our servants on board, and went to the inn called the Three Cups, the host being one of those who had met us on shore and had taken pains to persuade each passenger to come with him. He tried to make sure of success by actually taking possession of an overcoat, which one of the company allowed him to carry, thus securing those of us who did not wish to separate. At his house we found everything we could wish for ; a good cup of tea, bread and butter, and well-aired and clean beds, which my brother and I were very glad to occupy, this being the first of ten nights on which we were able to undress and lie between two sheets.

Harwich is not a big town ; it consists partly

of wooden houses, and is situated close to the sea-shore, so that you step from the boat on shore into the town. Our first care, next morning, was to get our luggage through the custom-house, where, in the presence of my brother, our boxes, portmanteaus, and writing-desks were opened and thoroughly examined. Consequently everything ·was mixed up together. According to a strict rule, the importation of newly made clothes, linen, and lace which has never been worn is prohibited ; it is possible, however, with the aid of a guinea or two, to avoid too strict an examination, if the officers are assured that the things are for your own use. Thus we had no trouble at all, although some new clothes, silk stockings, etc., might have been found.

The quantity of carriages which had been hired this day by travellers to London obliged us four countrymen to undertake the journey in a landau, with only two servants and one box ; we left the other servants and luggage to follow next day in a specially ordered stage-coach, hired for six guineas. We paid five guineas altogether for our landau, and as we were able to keep it open in fine weather, it was possible for us to enjoy and admire the fine scenery in comfort; it

c

was invariably splendid the whole way, and was a source of delight to us owing to its novelty. It is seventy-two English miles to London, each of which is marked by a large stone, on which the figures of the distance from London are cut.

At Colchester and Ingatestone we got fresh horses, which are ready when you arrive ; no country is so well arranged for comfort and rapid travelling as this. At Colchester, a pretty town twenty-two miles from Harwich, we dined ; and although this delayed us two hours, owing to the quantity of guests dining on that day, we nevertheless made the fifty miles to Ingatestone in 10½ hours. We left Harwich at eleven, and reached Ingatestone soon after nine in the evening, remaining there the night.

The whole of this country is not unlike a well-kept garden ; you pass a succession of towns, boroughs, country houses, meadows between hedges, and fields in which all kinds of cattle are grazing. The broad road along which we drove is as even and as well kept as our Herrenhausen Allée. All this keeps the attention of the traveller occupied without intermission, and adds considerably to the pleasure of the journey, while the somewhat hilly country gives you the impression of so many green amphitheatres. The roads are always kept in good order with coarse or fine gravel or sand, and the slightest unevenness is mended at once ; the broad wheels of the carts and vans, which measure nine inches wide, act as rollers to level the ruts cut by the other carriages. Ingatestone, in which we spent a very comfortable night, although only a borough, contains very neat houses.

We arrived at the extensive town of London on the 15th, at one o'clock in the afternoon ; and as the hired carriages from Harwich do not go further than the King's Arms in Leadenhall, an inn in the city, we four, who had to go to the vicinity of St. James's, got a hackney-coach, which took two of us to our father's sister, my Lady Howe,[1] and the Herren von Lenthe and von Leyser to the Private Secretary von Hinüber, in order to hear where our lodgings were.

We found my Lady Howe at home, and went from there to our lodging in the same neighbourhood, in Little Ryder Street, kept by an old spinster named Ridley. The arrival in London

[1] Viscountess Howe, eldest daughter of the Hanoverian Baron Kielmansegge, widow of Emmanuel Scrope, second Viscount Howe. She died 1782, and he died 1735.

of so many foreigners, as well as people from all parts of England, had raised the price of lodgings a little, especially in this district, and we had to pay for one room, not over large, consisting of a bedroom and dressing-room combined, with common mahogany furniture, which is found in most houses here, and for a room for the servant, 35s. a week, or $1\frac{3}{4}$ pounds sterling; our two fellow-travellers, for a somewhat bigger room, paid $3\frac{1}{2}$ guineas.

The present number of visitors has increased the price of everything so much that foreigners, without exception, have to give their servants half a guinea board wages per week, instead of, as formerly, a third of a guinea (seven shillings), which was the usual sum. We noticed the same thing with carriages; it proved so difficult to find a "carosse de remise," that we were obliged, in the end, to get the horses from one place for 10 guineas without the pourboire, and the carriage from another for $3\frac{1}{2}$ guineas. These "carosses de remise" consist principally of four-wheeled post-chaises, upon which a seat for the coachman is placed, just as in the country people's chaises.

We dined at Whitehall with the greater part of

the Howe family at the house of my Lord Howe,[1] our aunt's eldest son, and a captain in the Navy, who has acquired fame and distinction on several occasions, notably at the beginning of this war, in 1755, when he took the French warship *L'Alcide* in America. He has been married for several years to a charming wife,[2] who is very popular with everybody. In the evening we visited our Privy Councillor, Baron von Münchhausen,[3] and his wife, also Lady Yarmouth,[4] who was going next day for some weeks to the Duchess of Newcastle's,[5] until her new house was ready, in order to avoid the discomfort entailed in changing her residence.

On Wednesday, the 16th, at two o'clock in the afternoon, we were presented to the King by the Privy Councillor, Baron von Münchhausen, and

[1] Richard, fourth Viscount (the celebrated Admiral). B. 1725, d. 1799. His monument, executed by Flaxman at the national expense, is in St. Paul's Cathedral.

[2] Mary, daughter of Chiverton Hartopp.

[3] Philip Adolph, Baron von Münchhausen, Hanoverian Prime Minister in London.

[4] The Countess of Yarmouth was the daughter of von Wendt, General in Hanover in George I.'s time; she married Herr von Walmoden, and was created Countess of Yarmouth by George II. She was a cousin once removed to the author and Lady Howe.

[5] Wife of the Duke of Newcastle, Prime Minister of England and Secretary of State in Pitt's time, daughter of Earl of Godolphin.

the Duke of Ancaster.[1] There is a *levée du Roi* every Monday, Wednesday, and Friday. This gave us an opportunity of being present at the ceremony of the presentation of an address to the King by the University of Oxford, congratulating him on his marriage. The Chancellor of the University, accompanied by the members of the Senate, and a number of the students, who assist at such ceremonies, two hundred and fifty in all, in their University robes, was led by the Master of the Ceremonies before the King's throne, where he read an address from a large parchment. He was very old, and, even with the help of spectacles, could not read well, so it took rather a long time. The King answered, without reading, with grace and fluency. They were then all allowed to kiss his hand.

In the evening we went first to the Dutch Minister, Hop, and his family, whom we knew formerly in Hanover, and who receive company on Wednesdays and Saturdays; from there we went to Ranelagh.

This famous place, a mile from London, is principally intended for winter performances,[2]

---

[1] Lord High Chamberlain ; third Duke.
[2] A mistake, which the author corrected later on. See p. 166.

and consists of a large circular hall, 150 feet in
diameter, besides the entrance, orchestra, and
amphitheatre. Round the hall are forty-eight
recesses, in which a table and benches which ac-
commodate twelve to fourteen people comfortably
are placed, for the purpose of refreshment. Above
the recesses are the same number of boxes, which
are rarely used except for large parties, or on
exceptional occasions. In the centre is a large
open fireplace, serving to give the necessary
warmth as well as to supply hot water, and round
it are placed tables and benches. The whole
hall is lighted with a great many chandeliers and
candles. Everybody has to pay half a crown
entrance; for this you have from eight o'clock
to half-past ten some pretty good instrumental
and vocal music, and you may drink as much tea
with bread and butter as you like, without any
further charge, except, perhaps, a shilling to the
waiter. The numbers of people who are generally
assembled here, and who are walking round and
round, present a curious sight, which, together
with the quantity of lights and music, astonishes
people who see it for the first time, much more
even than Vauxhall.

Vauxhall is a large garden used for the same

purpose in summer. As there is more space,
the crowd is not so conspicuous ; it is preferred
by most people who have often visited both
places, but as Vauxhall is not opened in winter,
I cannot form an opinion.

The large and pretty garden belonging to Ranelagh is seldom used, except for fireworks, the
place, as I have already said, being open only
during the winter ; but, notwithstanding this, you
occasionally come across couples there, as it is
always lighted up. Everybody here can choose
the society he prefers, as, contrary to the custom
which generally prevails in England, no distinction is made between the several classes ; so that
you never know, unless you actually come across
them, whether the Duke of York[1] (who is seldom
absent), or any other member of the royal family,
is present or not ; and you are not expected to
take off your hat to them.

On the 17th we were presented to the Queen
(in the absence of my Lord Chamberlain of Manchester[2]) by the Queen's Vice-Chamberlain, my
Lord Cantelupe,[3] who was, in the year 1759,

[1] Brother to George III. B. 1739, d. 1767.
[2] Fourth Duke of Manchester.
[3] First Earl of De La Warr.

aide-de-camp to the Duke of Cumberland, under the name of West. As the rest of the royal family do not at present give any audiences, we have not been able to pay our court to the widowed Princess of Wales, nor to the Duke of York, the Duke of Cumberland,[1] and the other princes and princesses.

The Queen was so gracious as to thank us for the letter given us by her brother, Prince Charles, the Hanoverian Colonel, and to inquire the day of the wedding of my youngest sister to the High Chamberlain, Count von Bülow.

The same evening, at Drury Lane Theatre, we saw the English comedy called *The Careless Husband*, a pantomime, *Harlequin Ranger*, and, as after-piece, a ballet. Of the actors and actresses performing on that day, I particularly admired one of the name of O'Brian, who acted "Lord Foppington," and Mistress Clive, who acted the part of a soubrette. The Covent Garden Theatre is larger and handsomer than Drury Lane, but the company is not so good ; a place in the first row of the boxes costs 5s.

On the morning of the 18th we went into St. James's and Hyde Parks, where we saw a number

---

[1] Uncle of George III. B. 1721, d. 1765. Hero of Culloden.

of deer, which were grazing among the tame cattle
close to the passers-by.   In fine weather you
meet a number of people on foot, especially in
St. James's Park, which is the usual promenade
of all who live in this part of the town.   In
the evening we went to see the rehearsal of the
illumination of Westminster Hall, as well as the
four riding-horses which they intend to use at
the ceremony in the Hall, and which were led
about to get accustomed to it.   We also saw the
champion try on his coat of mail.   After that, we
drove to Ranelagh, as we had got our carriage
in order at last, and in the forenoon of the 19th
we began to pay some visits ; amongst others to
Herr von Borcel, Dutch Ambassador Extraordinary to the Court of St. James's.

In the evening we saw the comedy, *The Beau's
Stratagem*, acted at Drury Lane ; in this piece
the famous actor and chief of this company,
Garrick,[1] represented "Scrub," a stupid valet,
amidst general applause.   The second piece was
called *Polly Honeycomb*, in which, amongst others,
Miss Pope distinguished herself.   In general,

---

[1] David Garrick, celebrated actor.   B. 1716.   Joint patentee
with Fleetwood, of Drury Lane Theatre.   D. 1779.   Interred in
Westminster Abbey.

the English theatre has the advantage of a good
cast for every piece, and the faces of the actors
look as if they are cut out for the characters
they represent.

On Sunday we went to Court again, as every
Thursday and Sunday a large reception of both
ladies and gentlemen is held by the Queen, at
which the King is also present. The Court was
exceptionally full, as everybody had come to
town, and it was with great difficulty that we
at last succeeded in getting through the first
rooms into the drawing-room, where the crowd
was no less. We saw the Duke of Cumberland
for the first time during our visit, and were very
much astonished to notice how much the prince
had increased in size since 1757.

After the Court, we proceeded to pay our other
visits, and in the evening went to a reception
at Mme. Hop's—a very pleasant and sociable
gathering, where you are not obliged to play
at cards ; so I have taken this opportunity to
decline once for all. In this house, and in that
of Privy Councillor Baron von Münchhausen,
very few English, but all the ministers and
foreigners of note, are to be met.

On the morning of Monday, the 21st, we went

to the City, principally for the purpose of making the acquaintance of our banker, Solomon Levi, to whom we had a letter of credit from Michel David in Hanover. He was not at home, but we found him at Tom's Coffee House, close to the Royal Exchange. This gave us an opportunity of seeing something of the extent of London on foot. So far, all we had seen had been from our carriage, as, entering from the Harwich side, we drove through the whole length of the town, from Whitechapel to St. James's.

To-day we sent for our dinner from the tavern. In the evening we went to the reception at Privy Councillor Baron von Münchhausen's. People never dine in London before four o'clock, and take very little before that hour—a very good thing for business men, who can thus have their long mornings to themselves. As you breakfast here late and well, you easily accustom yourself to this way of living, especially if you do as I did. I did not deny myself the early cup of coffee to which I was accustomed, and this I followed by a good breakfast at ten o'clock, consisting of tea, bread and butter, and toast.

This evening we received from Privy Councillor Münchhausen our tickets for the Coronation, which was to take place the next day ; they had been sent to him from the Lord Chamberlain's office, but they were only for Westminster Abbey, and not for Westminster Hall. This did not matter to us, as we had already got tickets for the Hall, through the interest of my Lady Howe and her two youngest daughters and their friends ; but several of our countrymen had to give up all hope of getting into the Hall.

So as to arrive in good time, and to avoid being hustled in the crowd, we intended to get through the streets about four o'clock on the morning of the 22nd ; but we found the streets everywhere full of carriages, and it took us an hour and a half to get from Pall Mall to Charing Cross, which was not really halfway to the Abbey. Making up our minds, therefore, to get into the first hired sedan chair returning empty, we both got into one at first, until a second came up, and we arrived at last at the Abbey, at six o'clock.

It is not my intention to give a full description of the Coronation, or of all the ceremonies, as accounts of them have appeared in print, either at the present time or on former occasions. These descriptions I intend to translate, as good practice

in the English language, adding them as a
supplement to this journal.[1] I will therefore
only mention what does not appear in such a
description.

The whole of the large church (the altar of
which is easily distinguished by its Gothic architecture) was entirely altered, quantities of benches
being arranged in tiers for the lookers-on in the
gallery, with others below all covered with red
cloth, for the members of the procession. The
whole of the altar, as well as the raised daïs of
five steps before the King's throne, and three
steps before the Queen's, was covered with new
cloth of gold, without any design upon it.
Neither thrones nor stools could be more
splendid, or in better taste. The Princess of
Wales, with the younger princes and princesses,
occupied a box to the right of the altar (as it
were *incognito*) ; above was a reserved place for
the foreign ministers, and, above again, another
for other foreigners.

As this was a ceremony of some hours, arrangements were made enabling you to purchase all
sorts of refreshments, such as cold meat, chocolate
wine, etc., at a certain place set apart for the

[1] Not to be found

purpose in the Abbey. The Princess of Wales and the foreign ministers had extra tables prepared for them during the interval when the procession went from the Abbey to the Hall.

It is impossible to imagine anything more magnificent and beautiful than the procession was. The dress of the fashionable world was nothing but velvet and cloth of gold ; very little cloth of silver. The dress of the Knights of the Bath is beautiful, and the hats, with the high white ostrich feathers, considerably increase the effect.

Besides the privy councillors (amongst whom was the old General Ligonier[1]) and the Court officials, viz. grooms-in-waiting and gentlemen of the bedchamber, etc., who are not peers, every class has its special dress and badges and marks of distinction, which consist chiefly of red or black cloaks.

The most beautiful part of the cortège was the procession of peers and peeresses, all in their robes of cloth of gold and cloth of silver, and wearing quantities of jewels. If the Crown possessed the value of all these jewels, added to that of those

[1] John, Earl of Ligonier, Field-Marshal of the English Army ; served in the wars of Queen Anne under the Duke of Marlborough ; became Commander-in-Chief. D. 1770, aged 92.

worn on this occasion by the spectators in the
Abbey, it might certainly continue the war for
some considerable time! Over these rich robes
they wore purple velvet mantles and long trains
lined with ermine.

Before the coronation took place they carried
their coronets, consisting of gold, diamonds, and
red velvet, and did not put them upon their
heads until the moment when the Queen's crown
was placed on hers.

All the peers were in cloth of gold and cloth of
silver, with white shoes and silk stockings. The
dress consists of a kind of *juste-au-corps*, provided with facings and flaps, like a sort of riding-
jacket, over which the rich sword-belt, with gilt
sword in an old-fashioned sheath, is buckled. All
of them wore purple velvet cloaks, with long
trains lined with ermine, and coronets of red
velvet and gold, set with large pearls. Each
class of peers and peeresses (of which there are
five, viz. dukes, marquesses, earls, viscounts, and
barons) has its special kind of coronet. The
number of these peers and peeresses gave the
ceremony and procession a majestic appearance,
and I believe that its like could not be seen
anywhere else.

The Princess Augusta,[1] the King's sister, carried the Queen's train ; her own train was not carried, but was only kept in order on the ground by a gentleman of the Court. As she is not a peeress, she wore neither the same style of dress as the peeresses, nor a real coronet, but only a kind of wreath, like a bride's, and without any velvet. The Duke of York, dressed as a peer, held the King's train.

The procession did not arrive at the Abbey until half-past twelve, so we had plenty of time to get bored beforehand. As we wished to avoid the great crush, we did not remain until the end of the ceremony in the Abbey ; but, in order to get a good and comfortable seat, we went in good time to Westminster Hall, where the King and all the peers were to dine in great splendour. We found this enormous hall already so full of people, the majority of whom had had no tickets for the Abbey, that no more room could be found on the galleries and stands which had been erected. We witnessed the arrival of the procession, however, from below, but as the crush became so

---

[1] Princess Augusta. Married, 1764, Duke Charles William Ferdinand of Brunswick ; was mother to Queen Caroline, and grandmother to Princess Charlotte.

great after the arrival of the King, we went into
one of the boxes, prepared for the foreign ministers
and their suites, where we found enough room to
witness the ceremonies of the table and the
champion. The reason which led us to leave the
Abbey so early also induced us to leave the Hall
before the King, and we went home on foot with
the help of a musketeer whom we took with us
in return for a pourboire, as there seemed no
chance of finding our carriage.

As soon as the King and Queen, accompanied
by their suites, had left the Hall, everything
remaining on the table was given to the public.
After the coronation, medals were thrown from
the Abbey, but not far enough for us to catch
any.

The Duke of York, and after him the Duke of
Cumberland, first did homage to the King ; then
the bishops (who precede all the other dukes)
touched the crown, as a sign that they will do all
in their power to keep it on the King's head, and
kissed him on the left cheek. One of the finest
sights which I saw whilst the King was still in
the Abbey, was when I went with a few others
and a naval officer down the streets, which were
lined by regiments of the Horse Guards and

Dragoons in full dress, with their banners and standards flying. Throughout the ten different streets along which the whole procession now passed, the stands, which were erected in several tiers for the sightseers, were covered with blue cloth ; in addition to the stands, the roofs of the houses, and the streets, as well as the large bridge at Westminster, which is not far off, were so crammed full of people that you could see nothing but a sea of heads and faces. Somebody made the not improbable calculation that the total number of those who were present at the procession, including the onlookers and those inside and outside the Abbey and Hall who took part in the ceremony, must almost have reached the figure of 250,000. Westminster Bridge presented such a vast sea of human faces that some one conceived the funny idea that the simplest way of counting the people would be to calculate the number of acres there were—*en faisant le calcul combien d'arpens* [1] *de visages il y avait.* As nobody was allowed to move from the stands during the procession, we had a full view of this mass of people.

It is not easy to imagine or realize the beauty

[1] French acres.

of the sight, to the magnificence of which the
crowds of well-dressed people at the windows
and on the stands, as well as in the Abbey and
Hall, and the full dress of the ladies, added not
a little. In the evening a great part of the town
was illuminated, but this did not make much
show, as only a small number of the houses were
lighted up.

On the 23rd we dined at my Lord Howe's,
and spent the evening at Ranelagh. On the
24th we dined at Privy Councillor Baron von
Münchhausen's, and remained the evening there,
having spent the morning in company with six
other Hanoverians, viewing the royal palace
of Kensington, which is situated about a mile
from London.

Kensington Palace is somewhat nearer to
London than the small town of that name,
and was formerly the seat of Chancellor Finch,
afterwards Earl of Nottingham. It was bought
by King William III., who was very fond of it,
and who made a road, lighted by a great many
lamps, through St. James's and Hyde Parks for
the benefit of the royal family. Queen Mary
extended the grounds considerably. Queen Anne
continued this, and liked the place so much

that she often had supper in the summer in the Orangery.

The late Queen Caroline of Anspach improved the grounds by enlarging them towards the high-road to Acton, so as to be able to make a lake[1] in them. With the earth, which was dug out for this purpose, was formed a hillock, on which a covered seat was so arranged that it could be turned round according to the direction of the wind. The mound is surrounded by a small wood of evergreen trees, and has a fine view towards the south and west; in short, the park of three and a half English miles in circumference is kept in very good order, and in the summer is visited by a great many people.

The house has neither the size nor the appearance of an English King's palace, and is very irregularly built, but its nearness to the town makes it very convenient. The royal apartments are large, and contain a great many fine pictures. The entrance from the courtyard is through a large portico into an entrance-hall, with a stone floor; this leads to a fine staircase, which consists of several flights of black marble steps, with iron banisters of artistic workmanship. In the

[1] The Round Pond.

room which was inhabited by the late Queen
Caroline hangs a fine piece of tapestry by Vander-
branck, representing a Dutch winter-piece, and
showing the peculiar variations of type in that
nation.   Over the mantelpiece is a splendid
Vandyck, representing King Charles II., King
James II., and their sister, the Princess of Orange,
as children.   The gallery is decorated with many
fine paintings, and at one end of it hangs a
picture of King Charles I. on a white horse, with
the Duc d'Epernon holding his helmet ; the
king has a noble and majestic appearance, but
a melancholy expression.   The perspective of the
triumphal arch, the drapery, and other parts, are
perfect, and painted in such a striking manner
that the king, who is in the background, appears
so lifelike that you feel quite ready to make way
for the horse, and bow to his Majesty.   Opposite,
at the other end of the gallery, is another picture
of the king and his consort, and two sons,
Charles II. and James II. when children, the latter
on the queen's lap.   The king's fatherly tender-
ness is well portrayed (his eldest son stands by
his knee) ; and so is the expression of the queen,
which shows a loving devotion to her liege lord
and her efforts to draw his eyes down upon the

child, who is especially well painted. The usual want of thought is noticeable about the child's face, and it does not know what to do with its hands. These two excellent pictures are by Vandyck.

We remained at home alone on the 25th until evening, as my brother was not quite well ; we then drove to Ranelagh, where some fine fireworks were let off in the garden, in honour of the coronation. This gave us another opportunity for witnessing the crowd of people, which, before and after the fireworks, filled both the lower and upper boxes as well as the hall, which also was so crammed that it was difficult to get through the crowd, although many people remained in the garden. After the fireworks, from nine to ten, there was no tea, sugar, bread and butter, or hot water to be had, the caterers apologizing, on the ground that they had only expected two thousand people instead of the four thousand who were present.

On the 26th we drove with my Lady Howe to the City, to several shops, and bought a few things in mahogany, close to St. Paul's church. In the evening we went to Drury Lane, and saw the *Tragedy of Richard III.*, by Cibber, which is quite in the English tragic style—very bloody.

Garrick, the great actor, did not act himself, and
" Richard " was played by a man called Holland,
while Mistress Pritchard acted the part of the
mother to young Edward V. and his younger
brother, the Duke of York (whom their uncle
Richard caused to be killed in the Tower) ; these
two actors were the only ones who could be
called good ; the others were only indifferent or
bad, and better qualified for comedy than tragedy.
Between the first and second, and again between
the third and fourth act, there was a good ballet,
in which the principal dancer, Vincent, who was
said to appear for the first time, displayed wonderful strength in his legs.   The after-piece, *Polly
Honeycomb*, we had seen before.   On the 27th we
went to Court, and dined and spent the rest of
the day at the house of the Dutch Minister, Hop,
where we made the acquaintance of Schütz,
equerry to the Queen, and nephew of the late
August Schütz.

On the 28th we dined with the Danish
Minister, Count von Bothmer, subsequently
going to a reception at Privy Councillor von
Münchhausen's, and, as Ranelagh was open that
evening for the last time this winter, we went
on there, accompanied by two gentlemen, Herr

von Bülow, and his brother-in-law, von Beaulieu, who had just arrived the day before, and wished to see the place. When I came home in the evening, I heard that Major von Schulenburg was prevented by illness from going next day to Cambridge, a journey which he had intended taking with Dean (Domdechant) von Vincke, so I went in his place.

At half-past six in the morning of the 29th we started in a four-wheeled post-chaise, with two horses and a servant on horseback, and drove through Enfield, Hoddesdon, and Hockerell, to Audley End, the country place of General Griffen, who had met Herr von Vincke in last year's campaign at Minden, and had asked him to dine with him on his road to Newmarket.

I was glad to avail myself of this opportunity to make his acquaintance, especially as he had known my father when in the army in Germany. He has the reputation of being an agreeable man ; he was wounded at Zierenberg, near Kloster camp, and has now left the service and retired to his country place.

The house at Audley End was in former times the largest place in all England, and, although a great part of it has been pulled down, it remains one of the most perfect pieces of architecture in the kingdom. It was built from the ruins of an old convent by Thomas, the second son of Thomas, fourth Duke of Norfolk, who had married the only daughter and heiress of Thomas, Lord Audley of Walden, Chancellor to King Henry VIII. This Thomas, second son of the Duke of Norfolk, was called to Parliament in Queen Elizabeth's time as Lord Audley of Walden, and was afterwards made Earl of Suffolk, Earl Marshal of England, and Lord High Treasurer of England, by King James I. ; he was first Chamberlain, and afterwards Chancellor of the Exchequer.

The building was at first intended for a regal palace, and when it had been built with great care and beauty, and in the best taste of those days, and was ready, the King was asked to come and see it. He passed the night there on his road to Newmarket, and was so astonished that, when he was asked how he liked it, he answered that it was too big for a king, and only appropriate for a Chancellor of the Exchequer, to whom it was thereupon given. In those days the owner was supposed to have £50,000 a year, but at the present time the property, including its various rents, brings in about £3000 a year. King Charles II.[1] took the house over, so it returned to its original destination. He mortgaged the house-tax to the seller as security for the purchase-money, and made the Earl of Suffolk of that day Keeper of the Castle, with a salary of £1000 a year. So it remained until the time of the Revolution, when this tax was abolished, and King William gave the property back to the family,[2] and, owing to the want of means, the owner pulled down a great part of it.

The entrance is through large iron gates, into a big courtyard, where the offices formerly were, but now only a low wall is left standing there. On passing through part of the house, you come to an extensive quadrangle, surrounded on all sides by large apartments, all of which are fine and roomy, more especially the gallery, which is at the back and runs the whole length of the house, and which is supposed to be the largest in England.

The grounds are not remarkable, and will be improved by the changes which the owner is now very busy making.

---

[1] The third Earl alienated the property to Charles II.
[2] The property was reconveyed to Henry, the fifth Earl, in 1701.

Behind the house is a good park, reaching as far as the small town of Saffron Walden, which derives its name from the quantity of saffron which used formerly to grow in the neighbourhood. The park is well stocked with deer, but has not much fine timber. In it is a low hill, and if the house had been built on this, instead of in its present low situation, it would have had a much better view. The soil is as unproductive as the position is unhealthy.

Beautiful and splendid as it all is, it has one blot, if the rumour be true, that it was built with Spanish gold, after the fall of the great and learned Raleigh, caused by the revenge of Spain, the wiles of Gondomar, the avarice of Suffolk, and the unjustifiable weakness of his king.

The estate came to Sir C. Griffen, through my Lady Portsmouth,[1] but the circumstances of the transfer, whether through relationship or by purchase, are unknown to me. His wife is the daughter of Colonel Schütz, who is still alive, and whose son I have already mentioned.

After we had seen the house and the garden, which is still comparatively new, and had dined,

---

[1] Daughter of Lord Griffen. Elizabeth, Countess of Portsmouth, bought the estate in 1747 for £10,000.

we drove by Chesterford to Cambridge, where
we remained the night. On the morning of the
13th we went to see some of the colleges—King's,
Queens', Trinity, Jesus, etc., also King's College
chapel ; but as we had nobody with us to show
us round and explain everything inside, we had
to put up with an external view only.

Trinity is the largest, and consists, in addition
to its outbuildings, of a large quadrangle, in the
middle of which is a roomy square. It is said to
have a large and fine library, and is also famous
for having educated Newton, Barrow, Lord Bacon
of Verulam, Ray, and Bentley, each of whom laid
the foundation of his scientific work there.

Jesus College, although not large, is built in
modern style and in good taste, and the pillars all
round it are in the so-called Composite style, which
gives this building a fine appearance.

King's College is an equally large and handsome building of cut stone, 236 feet long and 40
feet wide ; but the most remarkable part of this
college is the chapel, celebrated for its artistic
Gothic architecture. Both internally and externally it is supposed to be the finest specimen of its
kind in the whole world. Some slight idea of its
internal beauty can be derived from an existing

print ; but you must previously have seen several other Gothic buildings (which are not rare in England, as many of the old churches are built in that style) in order thoroughly to appreciate the beauty of this college.

The chapel is 304 feet long and 73 feet wide, the height to the pinnacle of the roof being 91 feet. I am told that there are no pillars inside, although the whole vaulting of the roof consists of a vast amount of stonework.   The painted windows, the carving, and other ornaments, I hear, cannot be surpassed.

Behind Queens' College I saw a wooden bridge for foot-passengers, lightly built without piles, and it appeared to me to be jointed together very cleverly ; but later on I saw several bridges of this kind in England, and some even for carriages.

The Duke of Newcastle [1] is Chancellor of the University, which, however, cannot be compared with Oxford as regards its buildings and libraries, etc.

As soon as we had finished this sight-seeing, we drove on without further delay to Newmarket, where we dined, and in the afternoon saw several

---

[1] Thomas Holles Pelham, Duke of Newcastle. Prime Minister of England ; Secretary of State in Pitt's time. B. 1693, d. 1768.

races, both on the straight and the round course ; the latter is said to be four English miles long.

The small town of Newmarket must gain considerably by these races, which take place twice a year—spring and autumn. For a small room the usual charge is one guinea a day, without food and the attendance, etc., which the majority of people need.

The arrangement which provides that all bets must be settled before and not during the races is noticeable. A thousand people or more, perhaps, are to be seen on horseback, who crowd together like a drove of sheep and bet pell-mell together, so that the offerer of odds can see by the raising of hands that his odds have been accepted, but most frequently does not know by whom. You would think that fifty or more of such bets, when made at the same time, would cause frequent occasion for quarrels ; but these never occur, as every one is convinced that he will be paid in case he wins, even if the sum should be a large one. An Englishman, who would have no compunction about taking in his neighbours in other things, will never be found a defaulter in this respect ; such bets are much too sacred for him not to act with the utmost sincerity in their settlement, as his credit depends upon this.

On the evening before our arrival, the bets in advance in the coffee-house had already reached 6000 guineas. Everybody bets here, down to the smallest boys, who wager their pennies, just as the lords their two to three hundred guineas or more.

The races last through a week. As the jockeys and their saddles, etc., must scale a certain weight, which is fixed beforehand, and which also depends upon the age of the horse, they are weighed together, and any deficiency there may be is made up by stones, or the like, put into the riders' pockets. As soon as they have reached the winning-post, they are weighed again, so as to ascertain if they have lightened themselves in any way. The private races, or those where two or more private gentlemen race their own horses one against another, with special prizes, are generally run on the long course, and are decided in one heat. But where the prizes are given by the King, or by others, the races are run on the round course, where the starting and finishing post are one, and they are decided in the same way as a rubber of whist, viz. by winning two out of three.

On the day of our visit, the first race was run on the long course between seven geldings, amongst which was a horse of the Duke of Cumberland's ; each owner of these seven horses had subscribed 200 guineas as sweepstakes, so that my Lord Waldegrave won 1400 guineas, the Duke of Cumberland's horse coming in last. The second and third races consisted in each case of a match between two horses. In the first race a gelding belonging to the Duke of Bridgewater was matched against Lord Scarsdale's for 500 guineas, which the latter won ; but in the second, a mare belonging to Mr. Ofley, and matched against the Duke of Grafton's mare, won 200 guineas. On the round course, a fine roan, belonging to my Lord Northumberland, won the two first races, so that the third race was given up. He had a humpbacked jockey, who seemed to make up for this deformity in skilfulness.

The whole dress of the jockeys consists of a short silk jacket, over which leather breeches are fastened, and, instead of boots or shoes, they have a piece of leather, buckled round with a strap, to which the spur is fastened, and a little cap on their heads. In order that I might be able to say I had betted at Newmarket, I put a guinea

E

on the Duke of Grafton's mare against Mr. Ofley's, which a Dutchman had backed who knew both horses as little as I did.

Fair dealings may not always go on at these races, and many a horse wins through bribing the jockeys; nevertheless, I believe that the author of a certain book goes too far in his description of Newmarket, which I give as a matter of curiosity.

"As I arrived at Newmarket in October, I had an opportunity of witnessing the races, and met a great number of the nobility and of every class from London and all England. They were all so eager, so busy, and so intent upon what one may call fleecing one another over their bets in a polite way, that they really appeared to me to be more like horse-dealers from Smithfield than like gentlemen, lowering themselves in such a manner. I could hardly believe that people of the highest nobility, whose word of honour is their bond, and is accepted in the law courts, as is the oath of men of lower station, could condescend to place themselves on a par with flunkeys and stable-boys, and leave their honour and credit in the hands of men who take bribes and cheat the masters who trust them, and

yet pretend to remain honest people. It is certain
(to the undeniable disgrace of the high-born in
particular, and to the reproach of the nation in
general) that the best horse frequently does not
win, but the one whose victory has been assured
by prearranged plans. Before I became aware
of this so-called secret, which obviously is only
a trick for defrauding people, these races gave
me great pleasure. But after I had come to know
of this trickery (for this pastime had become a
general nuisance, and a quantity of smaller races
of the same kind had arisen all over the kingdom),
the law took the matter in hand, and in the
thirteenth year of King George II.'s reign a statute
was passed, which enacted—

"' 1. Nobody but the owners of horses should
be permitted to run a horse, and each person
should run one horse only.

"' 2. No prize under £50 is to be allowed,
and a penalty of £200 is to be incurred by
anybody who publishes or advertizes any at a
lower price.

"' 3. A five-year-old must not carry more than
10 stone, a six-year-old more than 11 stone, a
seven-year-old more than 12 stone, under a
penalty of the confiscation of the horse, as well

as a fine of £200; provided that the race be begun and ended on the same day.

"'4. That only at Newmarket and Black Hambleton in Yorkshire should it be lawful to hold similar meetings under a penalty of £200. (This was not to affect the appointed yearly prizes.)

"'6. The penalties in Somersetshire to be given to the hospital at Bath.

"'7. The entrance fee to be given ultimately to the best horse.'"

Newmarket is a fine, well-built town, which derives considerable advantages both from the quantity of people who are always passing through, and from the horse-racing. It consists principally of one long street, of which the north side is in Suffolk and the south side in Cambridgeshire. The King has his own house there, where he resides when he attends the races. The town has two churches, and one public school founded by King Charles II.

We drove back to Cambridge directly after the end of the races, as we were due in London next day to dine with the Duke of Newcastle, and as our curiosity had been fully satisfied in one day, we remained there the night, and arrived the following day, the 1st of October, at half-past two p.m., in London.

At the Duke of Newcastle's [1] we found a party of twelve Germans, headed by Privy Councillor von Münchhausen ; so the host and my Lord Barrington [2] were the only foreigners amongst us. I never saw such a quantity of food ; several tables might have been furnished from our over-abundance without noticing any difference at our board.

The quantity of gold and silver plate, and vessels on the sideboards, was such that it would be hard to find the like in the houses of many German princes. At one time we had silver, at another gold, and at another china plates ; according to the different courses. At least ten to twelve servants out of livery waited upon us, of whom the majority wore long wigs, which would naturally make it difficult for a stranger to distinguish between guests and servants. Now, all these people, in spite of their fine clothing, expect their tips when you leave, but to a gold-laced coat you cannot offer a solitary shilling ; you must slip

[1] The Duke of Newcastle's house was in Lincoln's Inn Fields.
[2] Second Viscount. Was Secretary for War, Chancellor of the Exchequer, etc., etc. B. 1717, d. 1793.

two shillings and sixpence into his hand. Luckily,
when we left, they were not all in attendance, so
that we got off with half a guinea each.

As the Countess of Yarmouth had come to
town for the day, but intended leaving again the
next morning for some other country house, we
all went to see her, and from there went on to
Mme. de Münchhausen.

On the 2nd of October my brother and I, as
well as Herren von Werpup, von Bülow, and
von Beaulieu, dined with Colonel Schütz at his
country place at Sion Hill, not far from Richmond. We renewed our acquaintance there with
Stanhope, who formerly resided in Hamburg, and
the whole party went to see the house of my
Lord Holdernesse in the vicinity, which is well
worth seeing, if only for its valuable tapestry,
some of which cost vast sums of money.

In the principal room is a mantelpiece of white
Carrara marble, with yellow pillars of the same,
the workmanship of which cannot be surpassed.

Towards evening we crossed the Thames in a
boat to my Lady Howe's little villa, which she
had hired at Richmond, where we spent a few
days with her and her two unmarried daughters,
and availed ourselves of the opportunity of seeing

VISCOUNTESS HOWE.

From a painting by Sir Godfrey Kneller.

the surrounding country houses and gardens at leisure. The next day, the 3rd, we drove with our ladies to Painshill, near Cobham, about ten English miles from Richmond. It belongs to Charles Hamilton, and its garden is decidedly worth a visit. The grounds are five English miles in circumference, and the soil is said to have grown nothing but heather and scrub in former times, but it has now been brought to a high state of perfection. The garden, like all of English design, is arranged according to modern ideas of an improvement on the beauty of Nature.

The principal features of all English gardens are gravel or grass walks, between irregular high trees, or through wild growth consisting of all kinds of trees, shrubs, and flowers, native and foreign, summer-houses, seats and benches of all shapes and forms, placed in high or otherwise convenient places, and heathen temples, ruins, colonnades, hermitages, mosques, etc. An effort is frequently made to bring in a natural water-course, or, failing that, to dig out one artificially with many windings and turnings, waterfalls, and bridges, so as to please the eye. Pretty views are the principal aim in gardens here, and an

Englishman thinks nothing of a garden without water.

The fact that the country about here, as I have mentioned before, is very undulating, adds greatly to the natural beauty of the gardens; the fine views giving the Englishman every opportunity of conveniently carrying out his ideas in this respect, so that you are sometimes in doubt whether you are looking at a garden or at an ordinary landscape.

The finest part of this Hamilton garden is the lake, very carefully made, at the foot of the hill, where the water falls over large and irregularly placed rocks, and runs into a deep pool, in the middle of which is an island, covered with a shrubbery and walks, which lead to small bridges of artistic construction. The water is brought from the River Mole (which lies much lower) by an artificial wheel of thirty-six feet in diameter; on the outer circumference of this enormous wheel are four leather pipes or hose, with openings at the side, which carry the water, by the turning of the wheel, into a narrow channel, which leads to the waterfall.

All this part of the garden is hilly, and is covered with high trees, thick shrubbery, etc., leaving space only for narrow walks ; and it is difficult to believe how art has been able to copy Nature to the extent done here. The fruit and kitchen gardens are always quite separate, and frequently so well hidden that you cannot discover them without help.

We were home by dinner-time, and spent that evening, as well as the following evenings, at Richmond, playing a game of tresset amongst ourselves.

On the morning of the 4th my Lady Howe drove to London, to go into waiting for six weeks at the Princess of Wales's, or rather to show herself in that capacity, as the princess's ladies do not see her, except at the courts and on Sundays. So our aunt was back again at 3 p.m. to dine with us, and we had meantime taken a walk on the banks of the Thames, through the meadows.

On the 5th of October we all drove to Windsor, fourteen to fifteen miles from Richmond, to see the large royal castle. This castle is the grandest of all the royal residences.

The town, which derives its name from its low winding banks, is bright, and has a considerable population ; it is twenty-three miles from London, and is situated on the southern bank of the Thames, amidst beautiful valleys. The church is a large, venerable building, and the Town Hall, of the date of 1686, is a well-built house, with pillars and arches of Portland stone (the best stone for building in England). At one end a statue of Queen Anne is to be seen in a niche, with a gilt inscription, and at the other end Prince George of Denmark, her consort, in Roman armour.

Several of the nobility live about here ; amongst others, the Duke of St. Albans, and Sir Edward Walpole, in whose house the Marshal of Belleisle [1] lived some time as a prisoner.

This castle of Windsor is the most convenient and the finest royal palace in England. It was built by William the Conqueror, immediately after he ascended the throne, on account of the beautiful situation and the security of its position as a fortress. Henry I. improved and enlarged it, by adding several buildings, and surrounded it with a strong wall. The succeeding kings resided in it, until Edward III. pulled down the old building, and built the present splendid castle, as well as St. George's Chapel, surrounding

---

[1] Charles Louis Auguste Fouquet, Count of Belleisle, Marshal of France. B. 1684, d. 1761.

the whole with a stone wall, and founding the Order of the Garter. William of Wykeham, afterwards Bishop of Winchester, was principally employed in building it, and, when the building was finished, he had these words of double meaning cut in the stone, "This made Wykeham." When the style of the inscription, bearing the interpretation that the bishop wished to assume to himself the honour of having built the castle, was brought to the notice of the King, Wykeham would have fallen entirely into disgrace if he had not assured the King that the sense of the words was, "This building had made him great, and had brought him into his master's favour by giving him a bishopric."

In later times the castle was considerably enlarged by different monarchs, especially by Edward IV., Henry VII., Henry VIII., Elizabeth, and Charles II. The last monarch repaired it thoroughly, after his restoration to the throne, as it had suffered severely during the disturbed times preceding his restoration, and he restored it to its former splendour. As the King usually spent the summer there, he spared no expense in giving it the appearance of a royal residence. He entirely altered the shape of the upper court, enlarging

the windows and making them symmetrical, and
furnished the rooms with valuable furniture and
fine pictures, to which he added a collection of
armour.   In short, King Charles II. left nothing
incomplete, so that the kings James II. and
William III. had only to add a few pictures in
order to make everything perfect.

This beautiful and venerable castle is divided
into two courts by a large round tower.   The
middle court is called a square, as it was formerly
separated from the lower part by a strong wall
and drawbridge.

The whole extends over twelve acres, and has
several towers and batteries for its defence, but
length of time has much reduced their strength,
and the good understanding between the King
and his people makes such improvements unnecessary.   The castle stands on a high mound,
which rises gradually from the plain, and presents
fine views in all directions.

In front stretches a large valley of cornfields,
meadows, and copses, along one side of which the
Thames flows ; behind it lies a hill covered with
wood, as though intended by nature for the chase
and enjoyment.   On the slope of the hill is a fine
terrace, surrounded by a stone wall, 1870 feet long.

This terrace one is justified in calling the finest walk in the world, both on account of the strength and grandeur of the work, and of the fine view in every direction ; the Thames and the many surrounding villages give you an impression that nature and art have vied with one another to produce perfection.

From this terrace you descend into a park surrounding the castle ; the so-called Home Park, to distinguish it from another and larger one. This small park is four miles in circumference, and is surrounded by a brick wall. The grass is of the most beautiful green, and adorned with many shady walks, amongst others Queen Elizabeth's walk, which in summer-time is filled with the best society. On the top of the hill King Charles laid out a pretty bowling-green, whence there is a fine view over the Thames and the well-cultivated country around. In the park is a good deal of game, and the forester's house at the furthest end makes a charming residence.

Among other rare things in the King's room is a large piece of tapestry, which Queen Mary of Scotland is supposed to have worked while she was a prisoner in Fotheringay Castle. She is represented, amongst other figures, begging the

Virgin Mary to release her and do justice to her
and her son, the future King James I. On a
shield is written in Latin, "I love wisdom, and
have tried diligently to acquire it from my youth
up." This tapestry, which had been put away in
a cupboard, was hung up long after by Queen
Anne.

From the King's guard-room you enter St.
George's Hall, which is especially arranged for
the Order of the Knights of the Garter, and
which is perhaps one of the finest and noblest
rooms in Europe, both as regards the shape and
the paintings, the latter being in remarkably good
taste. This fine room is 108 feet long, and the
entire north side is taken up with a representation of the triumphal procession of Edward, the
Black Prince, in old Roman style.

At the lower end of the Hall is a fine music-
gallery, and close by is St. George's, or King's
Chapel, which is no less splendid. The carving
and panelling of lime-wood are by Gibbons, and,
owing to the variety of subject depicted, such as
pelicans, pigeons, palm-leaves, and other devices
from the Bible, they merit the notice of lovers of
such allegories. The large chapel or church of St.
George is quite separate, and is situated in the

middle of the lower court. This antique building, in the purest and most beautiful Gothic
architecture, was originally erected by King
Edward III., in the year 1337, immediately after
the building of the colleges, in honour of the
Garter and the patron saint of England, St.
George. King Edward IV., finding it not sufficiently complete, increased and extended it, and
planned the present building, including the houses
of the deans and canons, situated on the north
and west side of the chapel. Henry VII. finished
the work, and in completing the decorations of
the chapel and the vault, availed himself of the
help of his favourite Knight of the Order,
Reginald Bray.[1]

The architecture of the interior has always been
admired for its beauty and elegance ; the arching
of the stone vault especially is said to be a masterpiece in its way. It is elliptic in shape, upheld by
Gothic pillars, the arches of which support the
entire ceiling.

On the north side is a chapel dedicated to St.
Stephen, in which scenes from his life are painted
on wood, and which is well preserved.

---

[1] Sir Reginald Bray. An English statesman ; favourite of
Henry VII. ; finished St. George's Chapel. D. 1503.

The choir is more remarkable still. Both sides are lined by stalls of beautiful old carving for the members of the Order of the Garter; on a canopy above his stall each knight places his helmet, mantle, plumes, and sword, and over these hangs his armorial standard. At the backs of each of the stalls the names of the deceased knights are inscribed on copper plates. A new member receives the last vacant stall, and you probably see on one stall about twenty plates, and on another only three or four. This was pointed out to us as something remarkable, and as showing how more or less changes have taken place with every seat, and with some more frequently than with others.

After James II. held his Roman Catholic services and had mass publicly read there, the chapel was entirely neglected, and suffered very much from the action of time. It is said that the present King has decided upon having the necessary repairs executed.

Besides the twenty-five Knights of the Garter, not including the King, the Royal College of St. George at Windsor consists of a dean, eleven clerks, one organist, one beadle, and two door-keepers, also of eighteen poor knights, of whom thirteen were created by the King, and five others by Peter le Maire in the time of James I.

We drove from there three English miles further, to the Grand Lodge, the Duke of Cumberland's residence, which is situated on a hill, and is reached by a broad and beautiful road along a continuous avenue through Windsor Forest. The garden is said to contain some remarkable things, especially in the way of water scenery. The house also appears to be fine ; but, as the duke had returned this very morning from Newmarket, nobody was allowed in, so, before driving home, we had to content ourselves with seeing it only from a distance.

The park measures fourteen miles in circumference, and contains a quantity of all kinds of game. In the large forest there are a few fine stags, which are rather rare in England. This Grand Lodge is really the house of the Ranger of the Windsor forests and parks.

On the 6th of October we went to see Hampton Court, which is pleasantly situated on the north bank of the Thames, about two miles from Kingston, and close to the little town of Hampton. It was sumptuously built in brick by Cardinal Wolsey, who, amongst other things, put in 108

beds, with silk hangings, ornamented with gold
and silver, for guests.

In order to silence the great envy which all this
magnificence created, he gave the palace to King
Henry VIII., who allowed him in return to live
in the palace at Richmond. The King afterwards greatly enlarged it, adding five spacious
courts, surrounded by buildings, which were so
much admired by both natives and foreigners in
those days, that the celebrated Grotius wrote in
Latin verses, " Any one who was so ignorant as
not to know of the riches of England, would only
have to look at Hampton Court and compare it
with every other palace in the world, when he
would be sure to exclaim, ' In these lived kings,
but in the first they must have been gods.' "

You have only to read Hentzner's description
of his journey to England to be convinced of the
truth of these words.

The palace became afterwards the prison of
King Charles I.

The Thames encloses palace and park in a half-
circle. William and Mary were so attached to
the place, on account of its beautiful situation,
which justified the conversion of the palace into
one of the finest in Europe, that he pulled down

nearly the whole of it, and rebuilt it in its present form. Not being inclined to leave it during the time of reconstruction, he had a temporary building called the Water Gallery erected close to the river, so that he could stay there until the palace was finished.

Since the demolition of this gallery, the south-west side has been much improved, and has been protected from the strong winds by high hedges, and small parterres have been laid out for the purpose of planting out exotic plants during the summer. In the vicinity are two ponds, for watering these plants, which can be seen from most of the windows. On this west side, not far away, there stood a large hothouse, in which Queen Mary had a fine collection of plants ; being very fond of gardening, she kept a clever botanist, Dr. Plukenet, who received the high salary of £200 a year as head manager. After the queen's death, most of these plants died, so that very few of them now remain.

The park and gardens, with the site on which the palace stands, are three miles in circumference.

The garden is not in the present English style, being far too regular with its cut hedges and an artificial labyrinth, etc. The labyrinth, with high, close-cropped hedges, quite tired us and our cousins, as we failed for a long time to find the way out—not an easy thing to do, without following a certain plan which you must know.

On the north side of the palace is the bath-house, behind a door leading into what is called the Wilderness, and further on is the large stone gate of the garden, with the lion and unicorn on the top.

On the left side of the second court is the large old hall, in which, by order of the late queen, a theatre was built, where she intended to have performances twice a week, when the Court was there; but only seven pieces are said to have been performed there, by actors from Drury Lane, some during the summer of its completion, others in the following year for the Duke of Lorraine, afterwards Emperor Francis.

In the Queen's Gallery, which is about seventy feet long and twenty-five feet wide, hang seven very fine pieces of tapestry, which represent incidents in the life of Alexander the Great, from celebrated drawings by Charles Le Brun.

Queen Anne's state-room is hung with green damask, and on the wall are nine pictures. In former times they were all in one panoramic

frame, as can clearly be seen, for several have
been cut and so separated ; the whole nine represent the Triumph of Julius Cæsar. After a long
procession of soldiers, priests, and officials, etc.,
the dictator appears in a triumphal chariot, with
Victory holding a laurel wreath over his head.
The work is painted in water-colours, on linen, by
Andreas Mantegna.

In the cartoon room hang the famous cartoons
of Raphael Urbino, which are so called because
they are painted on paper. There are seven,
representing subjects from the New Testament,
which are said to have been originally intended as
designs or sketches for tapestry, and it is stated
that King Louis XIV. offered 100,000 louis d'or
for them. These cartoons might properly be
called full-sized sketches in colours, having been
painted with much skill and beauty in water-
colours. In the first, which represents the
miraculous draught of fishes, Christ is painted
sitting in Godlike majesty in a boat ; the second
is the presentation of the keys to Peter after the
resurrection of Christ ; the third the healing of
the lame before the beautiful gate of the Temple ;
the fourth is the death of Ananias ; the fifth
Elymas the sorcerer being struck blind ; the sixth

the sacrifice at Lystra to Paul and Barnabas ; the seventh Paul preaching to the Athenians. All these cartoons are executed with much feeling and art, according to their different characters and meanings, and though each merits a separate description, it is not easy to give a preference to any one of them. There were really twelve altogether ; two are in the possession of the King of France, and two are the property of the King of Sardinia. The twelfth had been in the hands of a private person in England, who had mortgaged it. When the mortgagee was informed that the owner wanted to reclaim it, he was so furious at having to give it back that he damaged it to such an extent that he was sued for damages in Westminster Hall by the owner, and the picture was brought into court. It represented the slaughter of the Innocents.[1]

From the palace we drove to the town of Hampton, where the famous English actor of the present day, Garrick, owns a pretty country house and garden, near the Thames. The finest feature in this garden is a temple which Garrick has

[1] This cartoon was originally in three compartments, and it was one of these compartments only which was purchased by a Mr. Prince Hoare.

dedicated to his patron, Shakespeare ; opposite the
door, in a niche, is his life-size statue in alabaster,
or white marble. Holding in his right hand a pen,
he leans his whole body on a table, on which are
lying all kinds of books and other things, while
the left hand supports his cheek, as if in deep
thought. Close to this niche is a mahogany arm-
chair, finely carved, with a footstool attached to
it, like a throne, and at the top is Shakespeare's
bust.

A certain Englishman of the name of Churchill [1]
printed, some time ago, some pretty little verses
called *The Rosciad*, which lately happened to fall
into my hands. In these he describes how the
English theatre was very much upset by the death
of the famous Roman actor, Roscius, and how all
the living actors and actresses applied for his place
as first actor ; at last Shakespeare and Jonson
were selected as judges to allot the vacant appointment to the most deserving. The former, with
the assent of his colleague, accorded the place to
Garrick, with commendation in the following
words : " Garrick, take this chair ; nor quit it,
till thou place an equal there." So Garrick was
not wrong in choosing for his patron saint this

---

[1] Charles Churchill. He published his *Rosciad* in 1761.

favourable judge, who was also prince of the English theatre.

On the 7th we went to see Richmond and Kew ; the former is the favourite resort of the present King, to which he goes with the Queen for a few hours every Saturday morning. Their house is not unlike an indifferent private house, therefore it was not worth the trouble of going to see it.

The small town of Richmond is situated twelve miles from London, and is considered to be the prettiest suburb of England, and a real Frascati. In former times the kings frequently resided there. Edward III. died there of grief at the death of his son, Edward the gallant Black Prince, as also did Queen Anne of Bohemia, consort of Richard II., who was the first person to show English women the use of the side-saddle, as they had previously ridden astride. Her death was such a grief to the King, and made him dislike the place so much, that he dismantled the castle. But it was afterwards restored and refurnished with great splendour by Henry V., and, being burnt down in the year 1497, was again rebuilt by Henry VII., who gave the palace the name of Richmond, after the earldom he had borne before he came to the throne.

The site on which this palace stood is now the property of a private gentleman. The present palace was built by the Duke of Ormond, who received this piece of land near Richmond from William III. for his services during the war. In the beginning of King George I.'s reign it was reclaimed by the Crown, because the duke had sided with the opposite party ; so the late King gave it to Queen Caroline as dowry, and as the King liked the place, he made great improvements in the palace, whilst the Queen found pleasure in improving and laying out the garden and park.

The present King has decided to begin the building of an entirely new palace in February next, but it has not been definitely settled on what site it is to stand ; but in all probability it will be placed on the terrace above the Thames. As nature has been in no way restricted here, the whole pleasure-garden consists of a wilderness and a pleasing irregularity which cannot find its equal, but which is all the more to the English taste.

On entering, you come first to the dairy, which is a pretty little brick building, ornamented inside with stucco ; the furniture is worthy of the owner, and the milk-pans are of beautifully fine china.

Next to it is the Temple, situated on a hill ; it has
a round dome and Tuscan columns, with a round
altar in the middle. The first thing you see in
the wood is the Queen's pavilion, a pretty building with a remarkably handsome chimney-piece,
copied from Palladio's drawings, with a model of
the palace which was intended to have been built on
this site ; further on is the duke's summer-house,
which has a large vaulted entrance-hall, and ends
in a point with a ball at the top. On emerging
from the wood, you come to the summer-house
on the terrace, with large side-windows from which
to see the view as well as Lord Northumberland's fine building, Sion House. In this little
building are two good paintings, representing the
taking of Vigo by the Duke of Ormond.

After passing through a labyrinth, you come to
the cave of Merlin near a pond ; a Gothic building, thatched with straw. The late Queen built
it as her favourite reading-place. Merlin was a
prophet who, several centuries ago, predicted that
our Hanoverian house would ascend the English
throne. In the centre of three niches in the wall
this old prophet sits at a writing-table, with his
wand in his hand, dictating his prophecies to a
small boy, who is his clerk, and who sits opposite

him ; these lifelike figures are in wax-work, as are those on each side, one of which represents Queen Elizabeth with her old nurse, and the other a Queen of the Amazons with another person. I must not omit to mention that they are all dressed in real and suitable clothes. Here also the library of the late Queen is preserved.

After leaving this old and venerable cave, you come to a large oval ground, measuring five hundred feet in diameter, and further on is the Hermitage, a grotesque house, which looks as if it had stood there for several centuries. It has three doors ; all the stones of the middle one, which has a kind of ruined portico, look as if they had been roughly put one upon the other. The dense wood behind, and a small tower with a bell at the top, which is reached by a winding staircase, give to the whole a venerable appearance. From here you pass through grass, corn-fields, and waste lands, with pines and bushes, where there were formerly quantities of hares and tame pheasants, which the present King has done away with ; the Duke of Cumberland had hundreds of the former taken to Windsor Park in carts. The other walks and improvements are equally extensive and pleasant. At the end of the

pleasure-ground is another house belonging to the
Queen, and close to it that of the late Prince
of Wales, and opposite, that of Princess Amelia.

The small town has a large and pleasant bowling-green, and many people from London live
here, some of whom have their own houses and
gardens, while others have hired ones.

Besides the small park, in which there is a
good deal of game, is the large new one, situated
on the top of the hill, as the town rises a mile
along the slope of the hill, below which the
Thames flows. On the side of the hill are
springs of a good mineral water, which many
people are said to visit in summer. From the
top of the hill is a very distant and grand view
of fields, hedges, and meadows, intermixed with
many beautiful country seats, and the Thames
flowing by, with its numerous boats and barges.
It is without doubt one of the finest views
imaginable, and for this reason has often appeared
in prints.

The new park is situated really between Richmond and Kingston. It is one of the finest in
England, is surrounded by a brick wall built by
Charles I., and is said to measure eleven miles
in circumference. From a small hillock, called

King Henry's Mount, you can see London and
Windsor Castle in the distance and six counties
of England. New Lodge, or the new house of
the overseer of the park, has been prettily laid out
by Robert Walpole, Earl of Orford, but nobody
inhabits it, as Princess Amelia lives in the old one.

Kew is a small town not far from Richmond.
Here the Princess of Wales has a house and
garden, which the late prince bought. A narrow
drive serves only as a communication between
Richmond and Kew Gardens. The house is not
large, nor is the garden, in comparison with
others, but there is much to see in it in the way
of summer-houses, some of which are being built.
There are close upon twenty such little buildings.
In these gardens are also fine hothouses and
orangeries; an enclosure of wooden lattice-work
for pheasants and other rare birds; a large
aviary; a temple dedicated to the Sun, after the
plans of the ruins of the temple in Baalbec; a
Turkish mosque; a Moorish temple; a Chinese
pagoda in the form of a round pointed tower, to
the summit of which a winding staircase of 235
steps leads, having ten resting-places with windows
on all four sides; an old ruin in stone; a colonnade; and a "tourniquet," or house which turns

round and round on a pivot. All these buildings
consist of wood only, but are so cleverly covered
with plaster, and painted in oil colours, that you
would swear they were solid buildings of quarry
stone, unless by knocking them you discovered
the truth from the sound. The large number of
columns which are disposed about all these buildings add much to the illusion. I can well believe
that these wooden structures will not last long,
but it appears that this was not the princess's
object. The house and garden have been bought
from my Lord Essex for ninety-nine years, after
which they will revert to his family; therefore no
one can find fault with her because she does not
have such pleasure-houses built in a costly manner
with stone. Lord Essex is the only one of the
late King's Chamberlains who was not reappointed
after the accession of the present King, and the
reason is supposed to be that he has not behaved
very well about this garden.

On the 8th we did not go to see anything, on
account of the bad weather, but had to content
ourselves with admiring the incomparable view
from the top of Richmond Hill, and with taking
a turn in Richmond Park afterwards.

On the 9th of October we went to see my

Lord Harrington's garden, which is well situated
on the top of Richmond Hill; the views from
it are surpassingly beautiful, especially when looking towards the Thames. It consists, like all
English gardens, only of wild trees and grass hills
and valleys, with here and there a seat, where the
view is finest. The house, which we only saw
from the outside, has not a remarkable frontage,
but it has a good appearance from the garden side,
where it is very regularly ornamented, so that I
preferred it to many others I had seen.

From here we took a walk along the Thames,
and rowed about in a boat, returning home the
same way as we had come. While boating, we
saw a country house, near which quite a new
Gothic building with a tower stood. I took it
for a church, but heard afterwards that it was a
barn which had been built in that style, to look
better; just as if such a useful building could
be disfiguring!

On the morning of the 10th we went to see my
Lord Lincoln's gardens, called Oatlands, near
Weybridge, about ten miles from Richmond.

The park measures four miles round, and the
house is situated in the middle of it. From the
large terrace, consisting of sward of the freshest

green, with alternate high trees, and partly natural, partly artificial, windings on the hill, you get a view quite equal to that from Richmond, or even sur-passing it, since art has helped nature in beauti-fying it. Below flows a broad and long artificial river. Beyond this, the Thames is visible, and, at some distance, another smaller sheet of water.

Not far from this park and near his house a cer-tain nobleman has built, for his own amusement, and at a great expense, a fine large wooden bridge over the Thames, of remarkable construction, without any piles, which looks as if it belonged to the park with the river and the ground beyond. This *point de vue* adds greatly to the beauty of the aspect, which in itself is very fine and ex-tensive, so that, taking it altogether, its charm cannot easily be surpassed. In the afternoon we drove back to London.

At noon of the 11th we went to Court; we then dined with my Lady Howe, and in the evening paid a visit to the Countess of Yarmouth and my Lady Harrington. Here we met Captain Lockhart, R.N., who has made a name for himself, principally by taking thirteen French armed vessels, some of them more powerful than his own.

On Monday, the 12th, we paid several visits
still owing to foreign ministers, and one to my
Lady Northumberland, and dined at my Lord
Howe's with Lieutenant-Colonel Clark, whose
name has become prominent during the war by
several projects of attack on strong places such as
Rochefort, Belle Isle, etc. In the evening we
went to the reception of Privy Councillor von
Münchhausen.

I may mention here, by the way, the six ladies-
in-waiting to the Queen : first, the Duchess of
Hamilton ; second, Lady Effingham ; third, Lady
Egremont ; fourth, Lady Northumberland ; fifth,
Lady Weymouth ; sixth, Lady Bolingbroke.
The Duchess of Ancaster is the Mistress of the
Robes, whose place of precedence is immediately
after the lady-in-waiting on duty. Besides the
ladies-in-waiting, the Queen has six maids of
honour, who must not be the daughters of lords.
The only ones amongst them who can be called
good looking are Miss Bishop and Miss Cates,
especially Miss Bishop. The rest, namely, Miss
Wrottesley, Miss Beauclerk, Miss Meadows, and
Miss Tyron, cannot lay claim to the title of
beauty.

On the 13th a Court was held for the first

G

time by the Dowager Princess of Wales. We
were therefore presented with many others ; the
gentlemen by the Chamberlain, my Lord Boston,
and the ladies by my Lady Howe, who happened
to be there in waiting. Amongst the latter was
Lady Chatham, wife of the famous Mr. Pitt.
The King made her Lady Chatham when her
husband retired from office, and she received a
pension of £3000 for the lives of her husband,
herself, and one son.

We dined at my Lady Howe's, and in the
evening I accompanied her to Drury Lane to
see the celebrated tragedy, *Hamlet*, by Shakespeare, which is essentially English ; but as I had
seen the second piece twice before, I went on
to Covent Garden, where a pretty pantomime was
being given, and my brother went to see the
new opera at the Haymarket, *Alessandro nelle
Indie*. I forgot to mention that, although it was
said in the morning that the presentations to
Princess Augusta would not take place, as the
Duke of York was away (presentations taking
place according to precedence in the royal family),
the announcement was not correct ; the report
probably originating because the Duke of York
was likely to remain absent some time longer.

COUNTESS OF YARMOUTH.

Therefore we were all presented by her maid of honour, Lady Susanna Stuart.

This princess is very like her brothers, and has, in common with her brother, the King, and the whole family, a tendency to become rather stout; but it is said that the Princess of Wales has become much thinner during the last few years. They all speak very good German.

The 14th of October. We dined with my Lady Yarmouth, the company consisting of Hanoverians only, excepting my Lady Howe, and as neither of us is in the habit of playing cards, we went to Covent Garden, and, although we arrived rather late, we saw a pretty pantomime, called *The Fair*.

On the 15th my brother dined with the Dutch Minister Extraordinary, Borcel; illness prevented me from going, and kept me at home on the 16th, 17th, and 18th, whilst my brother went with the Howe family to Badlestone, a country place forty miles from London, belonging to Mr. Page—a brother-in-law of my Lady Howe, as his wife was a sister of the late my Lord Howe.

On Monday, the 19th, feeling better, I took a drive in a hackney-coach, which seemed to do me

good, and went with some friends to see the
Foundling Hospital. The usefulness of this institution is so great, and the arrangements are so
perfect, as to merit a detailed description.

As far back as Queen Anne's time several great
merchants interested themselves in the number of
innocent children who were daily exposed to ruin
and misery ; they proposed therefore to found a
hospital for the reception of such children among
the lower classes as were deprived by misfortune
or cruelty of the support of their parents, and to
bring them up to work and to be useful. To
this laudable end they proposed a public subscription, and solicited an Act of Parliament, but in
vain, as people believed that such a convenient
institution for children would only serve to increase
immorality. However, some of these charitable
people were not discouraged, but gave considerable
sums of money towards the erection of such a
building, and when this came to the knowledge of
a certain merchant captain of a trading company,
Thomas Coram, he was so moved by mere benevolence and compassion for the fate of so many
innocent children, who were daily exposed in the
streets, or even murdered, that he did not rest
until, in consequence of a petition supported by

over twenty of the greatest ladies in the kingdom, and by a large number of men of the most influential classes, he obtained, on the 17th of October, 1739, the royal assent to the founding of such a hospital.

Eventually this charity was started at a meeting held in the house of the Duke of Bedford, who became the first president of the institution. Subscriptions were opened, and a plot of land was bought on which to build the house, and an Act of Parliament was at last obtained. As, from the first, the funds rapidly increased, children were received in increasing numbers even before the house was built, and for want of sufficient wet-nurses other nurses were engaged to bring up the children by hand. It soon became evident that fewer deaths occurred amongst the children who had been nursed than amongst those who were brought up by hand, and also that those who were sent into the country throve more than those who were retained in the Hospital; so it was decided to send all the children with their wet-nurses into the country until they had passed their third year. When they returned, they were all vaccinated, with good results.

The house is built of brick on regular lines,

without much external decoration, and is comfortably arranged with two wings ; an appropriate plan
for a hospital. The chapel is in the centre of the
building, and communicates with the wings by
arched passages. Before the house is a large open
courtyard. In this court are small stone pillars,
with a good many lanterns, right up to the great
gateway ; between them are paths for the benefit
of the children, and on each side are two large
gardens. A high wall encloses the whole.
Although it was intended to avoid all unnecessary
decorations, several good painters, sculptors, and
other artists were found who wished to leave
memorials of their skill and benevolence in the
great hall, and who gave four masterpieces, em-
bracing subjects from the history of the Bible,
which were very appropriate to this foundation.
The fine organ was presented by the famous
Handel, who arranged that once every year the
oratorio *Messiah* should be played in this chapel,
every person paying half a guinea entrance for the
benefit of the Hospital. This brought in from £400
to £500 yearly so long as he lived, as he always
played himself; but, after his death, this amount
decreased considerably. As the sum which came
in every year from this source was considered a

bequest, it was entered in gold numbers on a huge blackboard, upon which amounts given or bequeathed were also written, with the names of the givers. With the exception of a private gentleman, who had partly given, partly bequeathed, a sum of £15,000, and another who gave in his lifetime £12,000 in one sum, Handel was the greatest benefactor of the charity. The chapel is richly ornamented through these great gifts.

As regards the domestic arrangements, it soon became evident that the restriction as to taking in children under two months was not sufficient to prevent the inconvenience which arose from every mother wanting her particular child to be admitted to the exclusion of all others ; so it was resolved that the number of children to be received should be chosen from all those presented, at an appointed time, by impartially drawing lots. This was continued until Parliament voted a considerable sum, on condition that all children under two months old should be accepted, who were not suffering from any infectious diseases.

On their arrival, all therefore were thoroughly examined in the presence of a doctor and surgeon. Each child at once receives a distinguishing letter, which is tied to its hand, and the overseer and

clerk each write down on a slip of paper this
letter, the probable age, sex, dress, marks (if any)
on the body, the year and date of entry, and
whatever else may have been stated to them verb-
ally or in writing. This paper is sealed, and the
letter marked outside. After this, the child at
once receives the usual dress, and is sent to a wet-
nurse in the country, to whom a corresponding
letter is given, and remains under the special care
of a respectable person in the vicinity. The children
are dressed and fed according to the instructions
given by Dr. Cadogan, in a book which he had
printed for the convenience of the Hospital.

From their third to their sixth year, the children
learn to read and are taught their catechism, and
in the intermediate hours they are taught to be
quick and agile, and are made fit for work, as far
as their health and strength permit. Later on
they are given harder tasks, and are made to dig,
hoe, plough, plant, cut wood, and to carry loads, so
as to accustom them especially for farm work and
service at sea. Some help in the garden, others
in the kitchen, and so qualify themselves to go
out to service. The girls, when they are six years
old, learn to spin, sew, and knit, to serve in the
kitchen, do washing, and to be useful in the

household, so as to be able to go out to service as maids ; excepting those who are wanted in the Hospital itself, as, according to the rules, no maid is appointed to the Hospital but from among those who have been reared there.

Their food is simple and good of its kind : coffee, tea, tobacco, butter, and strong drinks are not allowed. Their recreations are innocent, and all games of hazard, swearing, improper talk, and bad behaviour are strictly forbidden.

They must attend Divine service regularly, and their masters must remind them of their lowly circumstances, and inculcate humility, so that they shall not disdain the meanest work. The object of this is to mark a certain difference between these children, although innocent and forsaken by their parents, and such as are reared by their parents in virtue and humanity, although they may have been just as poor.

When any person reclaims a child, the Director has first to inquire if he has any right to the child, and is able to support it, and what security he would be able to offer ; also in what way he could refund the outlay. When all this has been settled, inquiries are made as to whether the wished-for child is still alive, so that it may be returned ;

but the Hospital clothes are retained. When the children leave, or have attained the required age of twenty-five in the case of males, and twenty-one in that of females, or when girls marry with the consent of the masters, they may be allowed the requisite clothing, etc., but this must not exceed the value of £10 sterling, nor must the allowance be made more than once, and only in cases where the necessary articles cannot be procured by the individual industry of the person leaving.

After having seen the entire management of this exceedingly useful institution, we drove to the Garden of Marylebone, a poor copy of Vauxhall Gardens.

On the evening of the 20th we went to Drury Lane and saw the comedy *Every Man in his Humour*, and, in place of the after-piece, *The Coronation*, which really forms part of Shakespeare's play of *Henry VIII*. The whole procession of the Coronation, the dinner in Westminster Hall, and the challenge of the champion, are so naturally represented, that it would be almost impossible to see anything more lifelike.

On the 21st we saw the tragedy *Richard III.* at Drury Lane, in which Garrick performed as perfectly as only such a great actor can. The after-piece, *The Intriguing Chambermaid*, is adapted from the French piece, *Le Retour Imprévu*.

On the morning of the 22nd we intended to see Westminster Abbey, which is famous for its large number of costly monuments ; we accordingly went there, but found that the scaffolding for the Coronation had not yet been removed, which prevented us from seeing most of it. We must therefore appoint another day for the purpose. We went to Westminster Hall, but found it in the same state, and both Houses of Parliament were under repair.

On the 23rd we started upon a tour, accompanied by Herr von Lenthe and Herr von Leyser. We had made an agreement with a livery stable to take us forty miles at the most every day in a landau with four horses, which we were to keep for the whole journey, as well as a riding-horse for a servant. After we had dined and had fed the horses at Great Missenden, thirty-four miles from London, we drove on the same afternoon as far as Aylesbury, where we remained the night.

On the 24th we drove through Buckingham, straight on to Stowe, the country seat of my Lord

Temple. The large and indisputably fine garden
is on the whole laid out in the usual English style,
but has many parts, decorated with statues, which
are more regular than is customary. Now, variety
in itself improves a garden, and makes it pleasanter,
but here I was not struck so much by this as by
the small and large buildings which exist in such
numbers that you come across a resting-place
every ten paces. The original object of such
buildings was naturally to supply decorated seats :
I am inclined to think that they ought not to be
so overcrowded as to destroy all inclination to
enter them.

Here we found that we could not get on as far
as Oxford, on account of the bad roads, unless our
coachman was allowed to have two more horses.
He wished really to turn back altogether, so we
sent him back with one of our servants and the
riding-horse, and took two post-chaises, with two
horses each, and made our two other servants
ride, as I had proposed from the first. This
mode of travelling is a little more expensive, but
it has the advantage, not only of enabling you to
travel as you like, but of saving the payment to
the coachman of his 27s. a day, when you stop for
that time anywhere ; on the other hand, you can

do double the distance in one day with a post-chaise, and are not forced to stop at inns on the road for feeding purposes and meals.

We reached Woodstock on the 25th, but although it was only a journey of twenty-two miles, we did not arrive until the afternoon. The drive was through heavy clay, as the road is not a high-road, and the weather of the last few days had not improved it. Woodstock is a small town, which, however, is renowned all over England for its fine workmanship in steel and gloves, as well as from the fact that it is quite close to Blenheim Palace. The Woodstock workmanship in steel is much preferred to that of Salisbury, and it is not unusual to find steel scissors, buckles, and watch-chains which cost from ten, fifteen, to thirty or more guineas. The best steel goods in London come from Woodstock, and there is hardly a steel-worker who does not employ several workmen. The wash-leather gloves are also decidedly the best to be obtained.

But what makes Woodstock more famous than anything else is the close vicinity of Blenheim, a splendid palace, which Queen Anne ordered to be built with money voted by Parliament, and which she presented to the famous Duke of

Marlborough, in the name of the entire English
nation.   Formerly, an old royal palace stood
there.

You enter the park just outside Woodstock
through a large gateway ornamented with Corinthian columns and inscriptions.   The front of the
building, from one end of the wing to the other,
is 348 feet long ; the roof is surrounded by a
stone balustrade with statues, and many small
turrets or cupolas, which do more to disfigure
than to ornament it, giving it a heavy look.   This
is perhaps the origin of the inscription on the
tombstone of the architect, John Vanbrugh—

> "Lie heavy on him, Earth, for he
> Laid many a heavy load on thee."

The south front, except for a large bust of
Louis XIV. on the top, taken from the citadel at
Tournay, is less overloaded.

The finest thing in this palace, according to my
idea, is the splendid library, which is 180 feet
long, with corresponding height and width.   The
Doric pillars, each made of one piece of marble,
support a costly and beautiful cornice, and the
walls beneath are of black marble.   The ceiling
is no less beautiful.   The famous library of the

late Lord Sunderland, which is believed to contain 24,000 volumes, is preserved in this room in gilt bookcases protected with wire doors.

In a cabinet, a collection of some very beautiful Dresden and Japanese china is kept; the first is supposed to be a present from the King ot Poland, but we were told that it is not shown.

In one of the wings of the chapel is the splendid marble monument of the Duke and Duchess of Marlborough, with their two sons who died young, also a representation below in bas-relief of the taking of Marshal de Tallard prisoner.

The garden is nothing to speak of; but the park is nearly twelve miles in circumference. Over one of the small water-courses a stone bridge has been built, which merits, more than the palace does, the remark which Voltaire applied to the whole pile : " Que c'était une grosse masse de pierre, sans agrément et sans gout." Under this bridge are some living-rooms and closed chambers, and a waterfall, which flows into a kind of basin. It is a pity that the bridge, one arch of which measures 190 feet in diameter, is so dreadfully out of proportion with the little stream.

In the park is a pool of good clear water, which flows between the rocks, and is called

"Rosamond's Well." It is said to have been the bathing-place of Fair Rosamond, the mistress of King Henry II. of England, who is supposed to have brought her here into safety ; but, as history says, the Queen discovered her, and caused her to be put to death clandestinely.

Having nothing more to see here, we drove that same afternoon on to Oxford. We employed the whole of the 26th, as well as the 27th up to noon, seeing the sights of Oxford, which I will now briefly describe in succession. The town itself, situated on high ground, is an English mile long, and just as broad, including the large pleasure-grounds, which are near the colleges and suburbs. A fine and very wide street passes through the whole length of the town, which contains few good houses, with the exception of the colleges and public buildings. The size of the town may be judged from the fact that it includes fourteen parishes. St. Mary's Church is the so-called University church, where the members attend to hear the sermon on Sundays and holy days. When viewed from outside, it is rather a fine building to look at. All Souls' Church is handsomer, and is ornamented outside with Corinthian pillars. It is said to be very fine inside, and has no pillars to support the vaulted roof, which is of considerable height. It is asserted that there existed a university in Oxford as early as 872.

The famous Bodleian Library is the principal sight to see. It is supposed to be the largest in Europe, excepting the one in the Vatican at Rome.

It takes its name from Sir Thomas Bodley, who died in 1612, and who was its principal founder. Since that time many others have enriched it, by gifts and legacies, especially of rare manuscripts, in such numbers that it would be difficult to find a finer collection. The building itself is a good-sized Gothic pile, in the form of a Latin H, but I cannot say that it is handsome inside. A valuable collection of old statues, bas-reliefs, and busts in marble and stone is exhibited in one of the schools, until a building has been erected for the purpose ; they were formerly at Euston, the country seat of the Earl of Pomfret, and have lately been presented to the University by my Lady Pomfret. Exceedingly fine pieces of their kind are to be found amongst them, but many have been damaged by the action of time ; they are partly

left as they were, and partly repaired by having
pieces stuck on, often in a very unsuccessful
manner. The largest is a very high marble
fluted column, in two pieces, which has been
brought over from Greece, from the ruins of
the temple on the island of Delos ; it supports
a statue. But the finest statues are those of
Greek women, the drapery of which is so well
chiselled that through the outer covering of thin
material you can see quite clearly the naturally
falling folds of the under-garment and the shape
of the body.

I was almost lost in admiration of the famous
statue of Cicero, who is represented holding in
one hand a roll of parchment or paper, and in the
other a cloth. The inside of the eyes is cut
hollow. It is difficult to imagine how it was
possible to express in mere stone the whole genius
of this great orator, who by the brilliancy and
force of his speeches convinced his hearers of his
views. When you gaze at the remarkable result
thus achieved, you might almost believe that the
sculptor had seized the opportunity of taking his
likeness during the delivery of his great speech
against Catiline.

Another statue, less striking, is also apparently

that of an orator, who is holding a roll of paper
in one hand, and with the other is striking
his chest.   The strong muscles, which are well
defined, make it likely that this is meant for
Demosthenes.   On the whole, there are certainly
a hundred or more statues of all kinds in the
collection.

The so-called public school forms a square,
with one wing as a library.   In the middle of
the principal façade, where the Savile Library
is placed, is a large archway with a turret over it,
which contains an observatory.

Close to this building is the theatre, which
is almost in the shape of a D.   It is ornamented
outside with sculpture, consisting of the statues
of Charles II., the old Duke of Ormond, and
Archbishop Sheldon.   Inside are portraits of the
two last-named and of the builder of this edifice,
the famous Christopher Wren.   All the other
paintings on the ceiling have been taken down
for repairs, and the whole building was filled
with scaffoldings, so I cannot say more about it
than that the public lectures are held here, and
that it is considered one of the best buildings in
Oxford, having been erected, at a cost of £15,000,
in 1669, by Archbishop Sheldon, who bequeathed

a further £2000 towards its maintenance. The ceiling is flat, and made of short beams, fitted into each other in such a way that they are supported only by the walls on the side, and by one another, although the width is seventy feet and the length eighty feet.

Close by is the Ashmolean Museum, which is a building in modern style, of freestone (a quarry stone), sixty feet long, very much ornamented, and with a splendid Corinthian portico; it was built for the University by Christopher Wren, in 1683. It contains a collection of natural history specimens, which was presented in the same year to the University by Sir Ellis Ashmole, from whom the museum derives its name. Subsequently, several others have given it rich collections of Egyptian hieroglyphics and other curious antiquities, animals and herbs collected in China, curious manuscripts, an entire mummy, and a good library; so it is quite worth while seeing. It is only a pity that so little time is allowed to strangers in such places, that they can only see everything superficially, and cannot give sufficient attention to the objects of most interest. In addition to this, it must be remarked that generally, and especially in

England, the people who show you over such places are porters, or caretakers, who seldom know much about them, merely show visitors round, and are glad when they leave. They earn their money so easily that they show you nothing at all, or only such objects as they consider worth seeing, which are usually well-known things, and to be seen every day in any collection ; so that the rarest objects often escape the eye, and remain unobserved.

We had the same experience in the Bodleian Library, which was shown us by a young student, who wasted time in pointing out beautifully illuminated missals, of which better specimens are frequently to be seen in Germany, although, I am convinced, far more valuable manuscripts and antiquities are preserved here.

In the former building the chemical and anatomical lectures and experiments are held, in special rooms.

On the other side of the theatre is the Clarendon printing-house, which was erected in the year 1711,[1] from the profits realized by the sale of Lord Clarendon's History, the manuscript of which his sons, the Lords Clarendon and

[1] It was completed and opened in the autumn of 1713.

Rochester, had given to the University. It is built of stone, is 115 feet long, and has a fine Doric portico, the columns of which reach to the height of both stories. On the roof stand figures of the nine Muses, and above the entrance a statue of Lord Clarendon. The whole building is occupied by the printing-offices of the University. In one room hangs a fine portrait of Queen Anne, by Kneller. In return for the fee you give to see the whole building, you receive a well-executed woodcut, with your name printed on it, surrounded with ornaments.

The most costly and the handsomest building is the Radcliffe Library. This new edifice stands by itself, in the middle of a large square, surrounded by small obelisks and lamps, and cost £42,000, £2000 more than the founder, Dr. John Radcliffe, a physician, had intended. He also gave £100 a year for the purchase of new books, and another £100 for keeping up the whole institution. The building is in the form of a rotunda, or, to be more correct, consists of sixteen angles. Eight of these angles are prettily decorated, and seven of them have real entrances with doors, whilst the doorway in the eighth, behind which is the stair-case, is false. The whole measures 100 feet in diameter. The upper story is ornamented outside with double Corinthian columns, and windows and niches alternating. A handsome gallery with a balustrade runs all round, and the whole is surmounted by a fine cupola.

Beautiful and splendid as it all is, and however much you may admire this gallery on entering, your admiration decreases when you see how few books there are, compared with the quantity which so extensive a building leads you to expect. The number is so small that the man who shows you over voluntarily makes an excuse for this, stating that all the volumes have not yet been put in their places ; but as the building was finished in 1749, there would have been time enough to place them there. But for this drawback, I do not believe that a similar institution could be found anywhere, for at one glance you look over an enormous library placed in a handsome building.

The large botanical garden for herbs and plants is situated in the suburbs, opposite Magdalen College, and was presented to the University by the Earl of Denbigh, in 1632. His statue, and those of Charles I. and Charles II., stand in niches over the large and fine gateway, which Inigo Jones designed. In the garden, all kinds

of native and foreign plants and herbs which can
be cultivated in the open air are to be found,
and some very rare ones in hot and cold glass-
houses. At the time of our visit one very tall
aloe, seventy-seven years old, was just flowering
in the open ground, where it had been planted
several years before, without having suffered, as
the result showed. Two enormous pedestals, with
flower-pots and flowers, each cut out of one single
stem of yew, stood on either side of a broad walk,
which, with a high avenue of the same trees, do
not produce a bad effect.

As to the colleges, there are altogether twenty
in Oxford, namely, Magdalen, Queen's, New,
University, All Souls', Brasenose, Lincoln, Jesus,
Exeter, Trinity, Balliol, St. John's, Wadham,
Corpus, Merton, Oriel, Christ Church, Pembroke,
Worcester, and Hertford ; there are also five
halls—St. Alban's, St. Edmund's, New Inn, St.
Mary's, and Magdalen. These differ from the
colleges in that each does not form so compact a
body in itself, and has also no special funds, but
is only supported by the fees of the students, who
merely swear that they will observe the rules of
the halls.

All the members wear a black gown, made in

the shape of an open domino ; in addition to this they have a peculiar head-gear, which consists of a black and tight-fitting cap, covered by a flat square lid or top, one point of which is worn in front. There are small differences in the costume, such as black silk in some of the gowns, and silver or gold tassels fastened on the hats, which mark distinctions of class, as well as the grades amongst the various members of the University.

The principal work in all of the colleges being very similar, we contented ourselves by seeing six or eight of the best. These are,—Queen's College, over the wide entrance-gate of which is a statue of Queen Caroline, surrounded by columns bearing a cupola. Through this gate you enter into two quadrangles, one behind the other, and surrounded by a piazza, or covered passage with cells which contain the offices ; over them are two stories, in which the rooms of the members of the college, as well as the hall and chapel, are situated. One side of the second quadrangle is taken up by the library. All the buildings, especially the last-named, have fine large interiors. The chapel is 100 feet long and 30 feet wide ; the ceiling is vaulted and painted by the famous Thornhill, and over the altar is a picture of the

Nativity by another good painter, named Price. All the windows are old coloured glass of the most vivid tints ; two of them represent the Last Judgment, and two others the Ascension.

The hall is 60 feet long, and half as wide, and is handsomely ornamented by columns both inside and out. From a gallery behind you can look down into it, so we took advantage of this, and saw the whole college dining together at different tables. It is the custom in this college, on Sundays and holidays, for one of the students to stand up during dinner-time and make a speech on a theological subject, and one on philosophical sciences on weekdays.

A curious custom exists here ; on New Year's Day every member receives a needle and thread from the housekeeper, with these words, "Take this and be chary of it"—in allusion to the name of the founder of the college, Robert Egglefield (*aiguille fil*). The call to table is given by a trumpet. The library is beautiful, both as regards the building and the collection of books and manuscripts.

The second college which we saw is called New College. This is larger than Queen's, and consists also of two courts. In the middle of the first stands a large statue of Minerva. The chapel is one of the largest in the University, being 180 feet long and 35 feet wide. The finest thing in it is the altar-piece, painted about sixty years ago by a clever English artist, named Coke ; it represents the perspective of half a " rotunda," in Doric style, with a cupola in mosaic, all painted, so as to appear as if the chapel ended there. As the chapel is partly panelled with wood and partly painted, the illusion is increased, especially as the sides are panelled. High over the altar is a picture of the Annunciation to the Virgin Mary by the angel Gabriel, with a number of angels in the clouds, waiting for Gabriel's return ; in between are painted columns, which appear to be real. All this produces a magnificent effect when seen from the entrance to the choir in the distance. On each of the eight windows is a life-size picture of one of the saints, painted by Price, for which he received £100 a window. In the hall, which is also very handsome, hang several good portraits of the principal founders and benefactors of the college, which contains a considerable library, arranged in two tiers, one above the other.

A hedge with a low arch adds considerably to

the charm of a large garden, which is laid out daintily. A number of students walk round the court at noon and again at six in the evening, calling everybody in French to their meals, in these words, " À manger tous seigneurs."

University is supposed to be the oldest of all the colleges, and consists of one quadrangle of old, and another of new, buildings, with nothing very remarkable in them except a fine statue of King James II. over the main entrance.

All Souls' College also is formed of two quadrangles ; in the first, called the old one, is a sundial, which shows both the hours and the minutes. One side of the fine Great Court, 170 feet long and 155 feet wide, is formed by the library, and the other by the hall and chapel. The altar in the chapel is of small-grained dark marble, and above it is a picture by Thornhill of the founder, Dr. Henry Chicheley, Archbishop of Canterbury, being taken up to heaven. A vase stands on each side of the altar, on which the two Sacraments are represented in bas-relief by the same artist. The new library is a fine gallery, 200 feet long, 30 feet wide, and 40 feet high, built of white chiselled stone. The outside is Gothic, in order to correspond with the three other

sides of the quadrangle. Inside are two large
bookcases, one above the other, the upper one
being a kind of gallery, supported by Ionic and
Doric pillars.

A successful bust of Archbishop Chicheley, by
the famous Roubillac, is placed over the door, and
in the middle of the hall, a statue of Colonel
Codrington on a marble pedestal ;[1] the inscription shows that he died in 1710, was Governor of
the Leeward Islands, a member of this college,
and presented it with £6000 for the purpose
of building the library ; that he also gave his own
library and £4000 for the purchase of new books.
All this combines to make the library, which
contains many books in foreign languages, one of
the finest and best in the colleges at Oxford.

Lincoln College also consists of two courts,
and the chapel is the principal object of interest.
The inner choir is panelled throughout, even on
the ceiling, with cedar wood, from which a lasting
and agreeable odour pervades the whole chapel.
All the windows are of stained glass. Four on
one side of the altar contain figures of the
twelve Apostles, larger than life-size, and in the
four on the other side are those of the twelve

[1] Christopher Codrington.

Prophets; but the finest window is the large one over the altar, which is divided into five parts, representing typical scenes from the Old Testament, and their fulfilment in the New.

In the garden are two large mulberry trees, which they say bear well, and which were planted in the year 1686, when the garden was laid out.

Trinity College also has two courts, but the first is small and insignificant; the second is quite new, and is bordered on three sides by buildings in freestone, built by Christopher Wren; it is with reason considered one of the ornaments of Oxford. On the fourth side are iron railings, and a gate leading into the garden, to which the railings serve as a division. The chapel and altar, panelled with cedar wood, and beautifully carved by the famous Gibbons, are very handsome. The carving is not alike on both sides, and the figures on the inside are quite different from those on the outside; but unless you examine the sides closely in succession, you do not perceive this, and remain under the impression that the carving is alike throughout.

In the library a manuscript of Euclid is preserved, which is considered to be six hundred years old, and to be a translation from the Arabic into Latin, of an older date than the Gothic translation originally used in Europe.

Corpus Christi College consists of one quadrangle only, but it is handsome, and is built in modern style. The cylinder-shaped sun-dial is fixed at right angles to the horizon, and the usual partitions of lines and numbers are all elliptic, with the exception of midday and the equinoctial circle in the middle of the axis ; it is considered a very fine specimen of gnomonics.

In the library is a manuscript which gives a full description of it. This library contains also a large collection of pamphlets, from the time of the Reformation to the Revolution, about three hundred manuscripts, an English Bible which is supposed to be older than the one by Wycliffe, besides various other curiosities ; also a large parchment—the genealogical tree of the royal family, with several collateral branches, from the time of Alfred down to Edward VI., with their arms, which are attested by the signature of officials in the College of Heralds, which deals with everything connected with the genealogy and heraldry of English families.

Christ Church consists of four quadrangles, besides smaller courts. The inner measurement

of the first, which also is the largest one, is 264
by 261 feet. On one side of the large entrance
stands a fine Gothic building, 382 feet long,
flanked on each side by a kind of round tower.
At the entrance, in the middle, is a large tower
designed by Christopher Wren, and containing a
big bell, called Tom, which is sounded every night
at nine o'clock when the students have to be at
home, each in his own college. I was told that
101 strokes were given each time, being the
number of rooms for students in this college. The
bell measures 7 feet 1 inch in diameter, is 5 feet
high, and is said to weigh 7000 lbs. In the
middle of this quadrangle is a fountain with a
statue of Mercury standing on a rock.

The hall is considered the finest in all Oxford.
The wooden ceiling is well made, and gives a
good impression. There are about three hundred
divisions, which are decorated with coloured
armorial bearings. Pictures are hung all round ;
amongst them portraits of Henry VIII. and
Cardinal Wolsey, as well as twenty-three others of
remarkable men, mostly archbishops and bishops,
who had been educated in the college.

Amongst other things of note in the chapel is a
window representing Peter being led out of prison

by an angel, in which are many other figures and
Roman soldiers asleep in different positions. A
young man named Oliver painted this scene, at
the age of eighteen, and presented it to the chapel
in 1700.

The second quadrangle bears the name of Peck-
water. Three sides are formed of buildings, which
are exactly alike, and each of which has fifteen
windows. The fourth side consists of a building
141 feet in length, which contains the library.
This building, though fine, does not correspond
with the three others in appearance. The exteriors
of the other smaller courts are not remarkable,
but inside one of the halls is a fine marble
chimney-piece by Rysbrach, with a bust of the
benefactor of the college, named Busby.

I forgot to mention that in New College you are
shown the crozier of its founder, the well-known
Wykeham, Bishop of Winchester ; it is about
seven feet long, of chased silver-gilt, and beautifully worked in Gothic style, with figures of angels
and tutelary saints ; the workmanship of which
could not be surpassed at the present day. It is
well preserved, and has lost none of its beauty and
brightness, although it is over four hundred years
old, and a slight polishing would make it look like

new. In addition, it is very heavy, and would tax the strength of the present generation.

I have mentioned the most interesting things which were shown us in these colleges. Although there are always many interesting objects to be found if you have time to go and see them all, we were unable to remain longer, as we had little time at our disposal. We had promised George Schütz to pay him a visit at his pretty country place in the neighbourhood, called Shotover, and dine with him the following day.

On the next day I went alone to the Oratorio, as my three companions did not care to accompany me ; it was *Esther*, by Handel, and the voices were rather indifferent. I had an opportunity of seeing a large number of Oxford ladies, who, with the old and young gentlemen of the colleges, represented the whole of the company present.

Shotover is a country place which was given by the King to August Schütz, father of the present owner. The house, although not one of the biggest, is certainly not one of the worst of the English country seats, and has such a look of comfort about it that I preferred it to many others. It is the same with the garden, which, without being like our artificial and symmetrical gardens, is not quite in the English style, but contains several straight avenues, rectangular ponds, and not more than three or four Gothic and other summer-houses. At this place we found the highest and finest trees in all England, and this is the case not only with one or two amongst them, but with all. As the garden was formerly too much enclosed, and consequently the view was obstructed, the present owner is altering it, and is making various improvements and enlargements, in the shape of vistas and ha-has. The vistas are made by cutting openings to extend the view, and a ha-ha serves the same purpose. As a wall, a hedge, palings, and things of that kind in every direction, prevent an open view, it is now the custom to substitute broad and deep ditches, which cannot be noticed or seen until you come close upon them ; from the exclamation uttered when this unexpected obstruction was met with, the name ha-ha has originated.[1]

In the evening we drove back to Oxford, which we left next morning (the 28th), arriving in good time in the evening at Bath, by way of Witney, Burford (well known for its yearly horse-races), Cirencester, Tetbury, and Petty France. On the

[1] Sunk fence, which is unknown in Germany.

highest peak of one of the hills which surround
Bath on all sides, called Lansdowne, stands a
monument, with an inscription on it, erected by
the late Lord Lansdowne, in honour of one of his
ancestors, named Sir Beville Granville, on the spot
where he fell, during the civil war of Charles I.'s
time, fighting for the Royalists against Sir William
Waller.

Although we might have gone to a concert on
the evening of our arrival, which did not begin
till seven o'clock, we preferred dining and resting
to the trouble of dressing, and deferred our introduction to the Master of the Ceremonies, Collet,
until the next morning, the 29th ; this the Dean
von Vincke and his travelling companion, Colonel
Campbell, kindly arranged. Collet is an old
Frenchman, who has lived here many years, and
assumed the office of director and arranger of all
entertainments, after the death of Richard Nash,[1]
who formerly held the office. The name and
remembrance of this Richard Nash are even now
held in high esteem, as though he had been a man
who had deserved well of the whole state. In

---

[1] Beau Nash, King of Bath ; leader of fashion at Bath. B. 1674,
d. 1761. Appointed Master of Ceremonies at Bath in 1704, and
filled the post more than fifty years.

reality he has earned the esteem only of the town and society of Bath. Everything here testifies to his long years of activity, and to the well-considered and excellent improvements and rules which he introduced for the benefit of the bathers and in various other directions. His picture and statue are to be seen both at the Wells and in the Saloon. His office included the introduction of all new arrivals to those who were already there, the arrangement of the minuet dancers according to their turn, and seeing that proper order was kept and that all the rules were duly observed ; in short, he was the director and head of the whole society, and was called the titular King of Bath.

The present director is nearly seventy years old, but still very active and diligent ; he dances like the youngest, and is civility itself to every one, but more especially to foreigners ; so that we and others could not find praise enough for him as he rushed about with us for hours, showing us everything which was in the slightest degree worth noticing.

Bath itself is situated in a deep valley surrounded by hills, which are all of considerable height, and this, without doubt, is the origin of the mineral springs, as is often the case with watering-places. The heat of the water is so great that the large baths and cisterns in which it is collected emit so much steam that you can hardly see the water itself. Although the water springs out of the ground only in three places, five baths have been erected, viz. the Cross, the Hot, Lepers', the King's, and the Queen's. The third and fifth have no wells of their own, but are filled by the overflow from the Hot and King's bath, which are situated close by. This is the reason why the water in the Queen's is not so hot as in the King's. The so-called Lepers' bath is close by, and is quite hidden, so that you generally only count four bathing establishments, excluding the one which is least known.

As is usual when you drink water which comes out of such springs, the taste differs little from that of bad warm water, and you do not perceive any mineral flavour. Although the water is very strong, and must not be drunk by persons who have consumption, inflammation, hæmorrhage, or diseases of the lungs, it is of great use in all diseases which originate in the stomach, such as cholera, constipation, and want of appetite (so long as there is no inflammation), also giddiness, faintings, and internal gout and stone, and all gouty

affections. A curious circumstance connected with
this water is, that the three wells spring out from
less than a third of an acre of ground, and that
in this district, at a depth of about 750 feet, no
less than five wells of cold mineral water have
been opened during the last century.

It is maintained as a fact that cold water is to
be found in the ground within fifty feet or less
from the hot water. Notwithstanding this, there
are at present no cold baths in the town itself, as
most of these wells have been closed for building
purposes or other reasons ; but I am told that,
not far from the town, there is one belonging to
a private person, who keeps it in good order
for such people as may want to use it. The
quantity of water daily springing up out of the
soil amounts to 1282 barrels (the barrel, at a
rough calculation, is counted at four hogsheads),
without reckoning what is pumped up, or runs off
through the drains. This calculation was made in
the last century, but the quantity is thought to
have been considerably diminished in consequence
of the soil having been very much disturbed in
one way or another.

The Well, or Pump House, is situated near the
Cross bath, and, though rather pretty, has been

built much too small for the yearly increasing
company, being only 34½ feet long, 26 feet wide,
and 18 feet high, from which the space occupied
by the numerous benches, which are placed one
behind the other for the convenience of the
public, must be deducted. At one end is a
gallery for the band, which plays every morning,
and at the other end is a statue of Richard
Nash, placed high up in a niche on the wall.
In the middle, against the wall, is an ordinary
pump, through which the hot water is pumped
out into the glasses.

The usual times for taking the water are spring
and autumn; but it is principally taken during
the autumn, as the company is more numerous
and of a better class before the opening of
Parliament, and before the winter gaieties of
London, both of which last far into the summer,
and prevent many people from visiting Bath
during that time. But as the baths can be taken
at all seasons, I am told Bath is never without
society, more especially as the cheap living attracts
people, who come for four or five months or
more in the winter to economize. A room costs,
as a rule, not more then ten shillings a week,
except at the inns, and provisions are much

cheaper here than in London. A large number
of sedan-chair men—at present over a hundred—
find sufficient subsistence, and charge a moderate
fare ; for a distance of 500 yards, sixpence ; for
an English mile, one shilling ; and over that
distance, one shilling and sixpence ; and so on in
proportion. Few people, or scarcely any, use
carriages in the town, except to take a drive ;
many who do not live too far off, or do not use
the waters, go on foot in fine weather. For going
to the waters there are specially made sedan chairs,
which are quite small and low, bowed out below
so as to give room, and with very short poles, for
the purpose of carrying the people straight out
of their beds, in their bathing costume, right
into their baths.

The company begin to assemble at the Pump
House in the morning from seven or eight
o'clock, in order to drink the waters. Between
the glasses, which generally number only three,
or at most four, the company take short walks,
when the weather is favourable, in the vicinity
of the Pump House, which is especially laid out
for the purpose. These walks are taken in
addition to longer ones in Orange Square or
Grove, and on the Parade. The square is laid

out with evergreens, grass-plots, and gravel walks, and in the middle Richard Nash erected, in the year 1734, a small obelisk, in honour and remembrance of the Prince of Orange, who took the waters with great benefit in that year, and at the same time gave his name to the Grove. The Parade is a broad path, paved with stone flags, in front of a long row of houses. It is made like the ancient *horti pensiles*, or "gardens suspended from a height," being eighteen feet higher than the garden, which is carried the length of the Parade.

After having spent a few hours in walking about, the people go home to breakfast, either alone or in company, if a large breakfast is given by some one, which generally occurs several times a week. It is the custom for those who take the waters or baths to go to church afterwards, but some make frequent exceptions to this rule. In fine weather, they pass the rest of the time until dinner walking, riding, driving, or in reading and paying visits.

There is a fine large bookseller's shop here, where everybody, on arrival, can subscribe five shillings for the whole season, which gives him the privilege of taking home any book he likes

to read : this is certainly a great comfort, and
brings to the bookseller, Leake, a large profit,
as he receives nearly as many five shillings as
there are visitors to Bath. But those who neither
care to read nor to take a walk, or who are
prevented by bad weather from walking, can go
at one o'clock to the Assembly Rooms, where
they will find many of the visitors, including
ladies, and where they can either play or pass
the time in conversation until three o'clock,
when everybody hurries home to dress, for
in the afternoon everybody appears in evening dress. Numerous people here give
dinner-parties, so you are rarely without good
society.

After dinner, the rest of the day is spent in
various ways, according to the day of the week.
Three times a week, that is to say, on Mondays,
Thursdays, and Saturdays, there is acting in the
pretty little theatre, and although the actors are
not as good as those in London, still they are
fair.   On Tuesdays and Fridays dances take place.
There is also an Assembly every day in one
or other of the two rooms, which exist for the
purpose, and where the company assemble after
seven o'clock, and pass the time until eleven or

twelve o'clock playing cards. Games of hazard
are entirely prohibited.

Large as these rooms are, they would not be
sufficiently so if everybody were generally to go
to them ; as it is, there are plenty who prefer a
private game in their own houses to one in the
public rooms, but some of these people are to be
met in the evenings at dances. I am sure that
there were three hundred ladies present at the
first dance to which we went, but we were told
that a large number had remained at home. This
was very likely, as we ourselves knew of several
who were not there ; amongst them, for instance,
the Duke and Duchess of Norfolk, the Duke and
Duchess of Athol, etc., etc.

The rooms in both houses are fine and lofty ;
that in Simpson's house is 61 feet long, 29 feet
wide, and 28 feet high ; the one in Wiltshire's
house being 87 by 30 feet ; both have extra rooms,
in which card-playing goes on, while dancing is
taking place in the large room. In order that the
company should not be divided, by some going
to one, and some to the other house, an old
custom prevails of keeping only one house open
at a time, that is to say, each alternately. For
instance, when the Assembly at noon, and in the

evening, has been held one day at Simpson's
house, it will take place the following day at
the other ; the same arrangement applies to the
balls, which always take place in the house where
the Assembly is held.

Everybody who intends to remain any time at
Bath, pays, on arrival, if I am not mistaken, ten
shillings at each house towards the expenses of
the assemblies, for the whole time of his stay,
also a moderate sum for the balls, for which he
receives three ladies' tickets ; finally, every man
pays an entrance fee to the coffee-house for which
he puts his name down, and of which he becomes
a member, and for the whole time he is at Bath
he can use the ink, pens, and paper, and read
all the newspapers and other publications to be
found there.

At seven o'clock the ball is opened by a couple
appointed by the Master of the Ceremonies ;
then, with his permission, all the others follow in
their turn, so that every man dances his two
minuets. The ladies who intend to dance a
minuet wear large hooped dresses, but the others
do not. When they have all had their turn, they
begin to dance " English " dances, until about
nine o'clock, when tables, chairs, and benches are

brought in which fill the whole room ; then some
of the gentlemen divide, and each treats his
invited guests to tea, bread, and butter. Herr
von Vincke and Colonel Campbell had invited a
large party, including ourselves. This interval
does not last an hour, as people try to get back
as soon as possible to the dancing, which continues until after eleven o'clock, when everybody
separates.

These are the usual entertainments of Bath, but
there are also good concerts and other amusements
from time to time. We tried to benefit by them
as much as possible during the three days we were
there, which is much easier to do at Bath than in
London, for you make acquaintances much quicker,
as it depends on yourself whether or not you are
introduced by Collet to those whom you wish to
know. The quantity of Irishmen here, of whom
the greater part are Roman Catholics, who have
been educated out of their own country, in
France and the Netherlands, without doubt con-
tributes very much to make this place especially
pleasant to foreigners. They are easy of access,
and take pleasure in showing civility to strangers ;
in this they are aided by their French, which
they speak more frequently and better than most

Englishmen. For these reasons, as well as on account of the prevalence of the social customs of Dublin, which are said to have many advantages, the place was decidedly agreeable.

The second day we dined with Colonel Schütz and his wife, and we spent two evenings at the theatre and Assembly, and one at a ball. As I neither play nor dance, I had more opportunity of noticing everything, and of making several acquaintances.

Having mentioned everything concerning the society and amusements, it only remains to notice the town itself and the quarries in the vicinity, situated on a hill, which belong to a man named Allen, who has built a costly house and laid out a garden and farm, which I went with some ladies to see on the last morning.

The town of Bath is one of the oldest in England. It is proved that the Romans settled here and kept two legions for security against the old inhabitants, and that they built several hot baths, a part of which has been found lately under the surface, close to the present ones. They cannot be called good specimens of the famous and splendid Roman architecture, but it is obvious that they were built of bricks, without any great art or science, and probably by the Roman soldiers themselves, and it was not worth our while to go and see them.

Round one part of the town there still remain portions of an old wall, which to this day is called the Saxon wall, and was without doubt built by the Saxons. In many places bricks with Roman inscriptions are to be found, which were employed in the masonry, and in several, which have been used to fill up the gaps, inscriptions have been cut through—a proof that the old Saxons were not as curious as we are nowadays about such things. In one place on the outside of this wall there is a curious thing, which is not known to many of the inhabitants themselves, and of which we should not have heard unless Collet (who did not know of it himself) had taken us to the architect Wood, in order that he might show us the plans of the beauties of the town, both those which were finished as well as those in prospect. He pointed out the curiosity, which is a stone that attaches itself to the wall, from the foundation upwards. It increases visibly and continually in height and thickness, so that, although it was entirely cut off from the wall fourteen or fifteen years ago, it has again attained more than half a man's height, and a thickness, at its base, of one to two feet. It is easy to understand, however, that this is caused by mineral exhalations from the water rising out of the soil, which settle on the wall and petrify it. Similar results are to be found frequently in caves, where the water oozes out from above and forms stalactites. In this instance, however, the curious circumstance is that the stone grows in the open air, and upwards, but I have never heard of a similar case. You can see how it runs up against the wall, and increases in size and height each year like a tree. But in contradistinction to the saltpetre which attaches itself to damp walls, it is noticeable in the case of this stone that the saltpetre exudes from the wall, on every side of the stone, and irrespectively of it, and that this stone grows out of the earth, so to say, and continues to sprout like a tree, so that the new growth can clearly be traced by its white colour.

So as to be better able to judge of the hardness of this growing stone, and on account of its apparent rarity, we each knocked off a piece with a hatchet, which gave us some trouble, as although the stone has a spongy appearance, it is very hard.

K

The town of Bath possesses a fairly good pavement (which appears to be better than it really is), compared with that of London. If the place continues to increase in beauty, as it has done for the last twenty-four to twenty-five years, it will certainly become one of the finest towns in England. The new streets, especially one long and broad thoroughfare, are lined with handsome houses, many of which have been built in the same style, in accordance with a settled plan.

An instance of this arrangement is Queen's Square, which is a large four-cornered place, in the style of a London square, with a large grassplot, gravel walks, and flowers, and a basin of water in the centre, all surrounded by a low wall and balustrade.

This is not the finest part of Bath ; another square, which is being built, will be finer than all the rest, and it will be difficult to find its equal. The new streets, Queen's Square, and many other houses, have been designed by the father of the architect, Wood, and built by others, after he had bought the ground and let it out, for a yearly rent, to the builders, on condition that they followed his designs.

His son mostly works on the same plan, and

has bought a large plot of ground for this purpose from the rich Mr. Allen, who owns the quarries. The ground-rent for a house of three windows, with courtyard and garden, is eight guineas a year. In this way, he not only gets a good return from the ground, but also makes a large profit by the quantity of buildings he erects as architect. Mr. Allen also, the seller of the land, does not make a bad bargain, as all the buildings are built with stone from his quarries, which is very cheap, the quarries being so near and numerous.

Amongst others, William Pitt, the former Secretary of State, has built a fine house of nine windows, which is just finished, and for which, consequently, he pays twenty-four guineas ground-rent. He is one of the representatives of the town in the House of Commons, and the old General Ligonier [1] is the other. The stones for these buildings come from the quarry situated on a hill close by, which keeps its old name, Camelodunum.

These quarries are quite close to the owner's fine house, the outside only of which we saw, as he was absent. I can say little about it, therefore,

[1] Field-Marshal Lord Ligonier, Commander-in-Chief from 1757 to 1766.

except that it seems very large and has a splendid
Corinthian portico, and could take its place beside
many of the best houses in England. The garden
is prettily arranged, with several summer-houses,
and its beautiful and agreeable situation on the
side of the hill, its undulating ground with artificial water-courses and splendid views, make it
all that is desirable.

The stone from the quarries is partly raised
out of pits as deep as a house. The whole hill
consists of rock and stone lying close to the
surface, but it is quarried deep in order to save
space ; the raising of the stone, in enormous
blocks, is accomplished by means of a huge crane,
like those used for unloading. The wheel is
turned by a horse, which is trained to walk round
and round, and backwards if necessary. The
stone is brought in a remarkable way down the
hill towards the town. On each side of the road,
iron, two or three inches broad, in the shape of
carriage-ruts, is laid down ; the stones are put
into low but strong trolleys, with broad iron
wheels, with an outer rim projecting in such a
way that they cannot slip out of the iron ruts ;
the horses attached to the trucks have consequently nothing more to do than to put them

into motion, as afterwards they run down by themselves with great speed, so that the horses can hardly keep their proper place in front. But the trolley can be stopped at any moment by means of a spring attached to it, which causes an iron bar to catch into the wheel. When these stones are brought out, cut, and used for building, they look very soft, and no better than sandstone, which in reality they are; but the older they get, the harder and whiter they become, so that the houses which have been built several years look handsomer than those which are quite new.

Allen is one of those men who are favoured by fortune to rise from the lowest class to great wealth. He was originally educated as a poor boy in a charity school; later on, a man who had organized a line of mail-coaches on the cross-country roads throughout England, adopted him out of charity, liking his look, and employed him, first to wait upon him, and, later on, for copying, writing, etc. When he noticed his cleverness, and that he was a good hand at accounts, he made him first clerk, and subsequently partner in the office, and left him everything at his death. Now that the Crown has taken over all these mails and amalgamated them with the others, he has been paid an indemnity of £30,000 (so I was told on good authority) ; whereby, in addition to the quarries and other sources of income, he has become one of the richest commoners in these parts. He is said to make a good use of his fortune, and I have heard nobody, in or out of Bath, speak otherwise of him than as a kind-hearted, well-disposed man, who has done much good for the town through his many charities.

There is also a useful institution in Bath, which is kept up by private subscriptions, like most institutions of the kind in England ; this is the General Hospital. It is a good building, intended for poor and indigent patients of all kinds, who have to take the waters and baths. They are not taken in, except through a written order from their doctor, describing all the particulars of their illness, and with a certificate from their parish clergyman that they are deserving and really poor. The inmates are well cared for free of charge, and enjoy every comfort, have their own doctors, surgeons, chemists, and clergymen, who have not only to attend them without any charge, but must also minister to large numbers of outdoor patients, who do not live in the Hospital, though they otherwise receive all its advantages.

As there was nothing inside worth seeing, and not wishing to be detained longer, we left Bath next morning, going by Chippenham, Marlborough, Reading, and Newbury to Maidenhead Bridge. As we had been told that the remains of a supposed antique temple had been found near Marlborough, in the shape of a quantity of stones, we hired riding-horses at Marlborough, and again at Calne (leaving our servants in the post-chaises with the luggage), so as to get a nearer view of it. We found nothing more than a high mound of earth, which did not seem to be a work of Nature, but to have been made by human hands; as we agreed it would be of little use to waste time in exploring it, we continued our journey, riding on horseback when the weather was fine. We spent the night at Maidenhead Bridge, in a good inn, near the bridge over the Thames, 26 miles from London; towards noon on the 2nd of November we arrived in London by way of Hounslow.

We took two days to make the 108 miles from Bath to London, but the journey can be accomplished in one day by starting a little sooner than we did, especially if you change horses every ten miles; or, better still, if you take four horses, by which means you may accomplish the whole journey without trouble in eleven hours. We changed horses, however, only every eighteen or nineteen miles, besides riding for an hour and a half, and making use of the post-chaises also for two hours; nine to ten miles an hour can easily be accomplished without overworking the horses, so in this way 200 miles can be covered in twenty hours without much trouble.

On the evening of our return to London, we went to Privy Councillor von Münchhausen's Assembly.

On the 3rd of November we went to the Upper House of Parliament, which was opened by the King on that day by summoning the Lower House to the bar and recommending them, through the Lord Chancellor, to elect a Speaker, and to present him on a certain day for approval; before this is done, the House cannot proceed to business.

This affords me a good opportunity to give some particulars concerning both Houses. We proceeded at once from the Upper House to the Lower, in order to witness the election of the Speaker. The earliest notice extant of a

Parliament in England dates from the year 833,[1] when the Kings of Wessex and Mercia called an Assembly together for the purpose of opposing the inroad of the Danes. The Upper House consists of all spiritual and temporal peers of the kingdom, and sixteen peers of Scotland; Ireland has its separate Parliament. The head of the family only is a peer of the realm, although his brother, or one or two of his sons, may be titular lords; for instance, the Duke of Rutland's eldest son, the Marquis of Granby, is a lord by courtesy, but, in spite of this, has no seat in the Upper House, until, upon his father's death, he becomes Duke of Rutland. The number of temporal English peers is not fixed, as the King frequently creates new ones; the number varying in consequence. From this year's Almanack, I find that the Upper House consists, when all the members are present, of twenty-five dukes, including the Dukes of York and Cumberland, one marquis, eighty-one earls, twelve viscounts, sixty-three barons, and eleven peeresses in their own right (amongst the peeresses are Lady Yarmouth, Lady Chesterfield, and Lady Northumberland),

[1] This was the Witenagemot, the mother of the first true Parliament summoned in the thirteenth century.

sixteen Scottish peers, two archbishops (Canterbury and York), and forty-two bishops. All these, except peeresses or Roman Catholics, such as the Duke of Norfolk, Premier Duke of England, the Earl of Shrewsbury, Premier Earl of England, and others, who can neither enter Parliament nor hold office, have votes in the Upper House.

The hall in which they meet is roomy, but not very large. The tapestry represents the invincible Spanish Armada in its different positions before and after its defeat by the small fleet of English ships. The throne, which stands at the top of the hall, is raised by several steps. The present King has had a new one made, cushioned with red velvet, and embroidered on the back with the royal arms. We saw it, so to say, inaugurated. The King always enters Parliament in his robes, and wearing his crown, the sword of state being carried before him. On the right of the throne is a seat for the Prince of Wales, and on the left for the princes of the royal house who are peers. Behind, and on the sides of the throne, the lords who have no votes, foreign ambassadors, and others stand. Below the throne, on the right, the archbishops, and beyond them the bishops are seated, and on the left as many peers, above the rank of baron, as there is room for. But these benches are for the most part taken up by ladies who are looking on.

The President of the Council, and the Lord Privy Seal, although they may be only barons, sit above all the dukes, as also the Earl Marshal, the Lord Steward, and Lord Chamberlain, all of whom hold equal rank. Between these benches the Lord High Chancellor, with the Great Seal and Mace, as Speaker of the Upper House, and, close by, the Lord Chief Justice and the other judges sit on great red woolsacks, just opposite the throne. The judges have no votes, but are only consulted in cases where knowledge of rights and laws are required ; principally in criminal cases and appeals, the Upper House being the highest court of appeal. Behind a table sit the Clerk of the Crown and the Clerk of Parliament, to keep the records of the proceedings, and behind these are benches for the rest of the members. The furthest end of the House is divided by a bar, where the Gentleman Usher of the Black Rod has his seat. It is his duty to summon the Lower House, and bring them to the bar ; also to take into custody any

member of Parliament or any one present whose
arrest has been ordered. He is also Usher of
the Garter.

When the King opens Parliament, the ceremony is carried out with great pomp, and he is
accompanied by the highest officers of the Court,
part of the Grenadiers on horseback, Horse
Guards, Yeomen of the Guard, gentlemen pensioners and liveried servants on foot; twenty-
one guns are fired off when the _cortége_ enters
and leaves the House. On arrival, the King
puts on the royal robes in a private room, where
he subsequently takes them off again.

The hall in which the Lower House meets is
much too small to hold its members, if they were
all present, although the space is utilized as much
as possible, and benches are placed all round, in
the form of an amphitheatre. At one end is
the seat of the Speaker, in a kind of niche, surrounded with the British arms and other decorations, and before the seat is a table, at which
his clerk also sits, and on which are placed the
mace, as the sign of his office, and books, papers,
etc. Above is a gallery for lookers-on and
listeners of both sexes, which goes all round
the chamber. If it were occupied solely by the

members of Parliament, without any strangers, there would still be insufficient room for all, unless they could find seats below, as every place in England, which has the rights of a borough, as well as the two universities of Oxford and Cambridge, sends two members to Parliament, the whole number amounting to 558.

Every parliament is elected for seven years, when it must be dissolved, and a new one must be called; but the King has the power to dismiss it whenever he likes. As soon as the King dies, the parliament and all its offices should really cease; but latterly this rule has not been adhered to, in order to avoid many inconveniences, and the parliament has continued until dissolved by the King. This practice was observed at the recent demise of the Crown, when Parliament remained sitting into the summer.

After the King had called upon the House of Commons to elect a Speaker, we followed at once into the Lower House, and heard Lord Barrington, an Irish peer, who consequently has no seat in the Upper House, propose the present Speaker, Sir James Cust, whereupon George Grenville seconded him in another speech. He is the only brother-in-law of Pitt,[1] and, as he did not lay down his office with him, he lost the expectation of £3000 a year, which his brother, my Lord Temple, had intended to leave him. As nobody in the House raised any objection, these two members led the Speaker to the chair, from the acceptance of which at first, and for form's sake, he excused himself; then he expressed his thanks, and named a day for being presented to the King.

On the meeting of a fresh Parliament, every member of both Houses must be newly sworn in, even if he has been a member of the former one.

A few days later the King came again to the Upper House, and the Speaker was presented to him and confirmed in his office, as it rests with the King to sanction his election or not, although he has not the power of appointing him. After this, the speech from the throne, which is always published in every newspaper, was read to both Houses; then each House considered its answer separately, and delivered its address of thanks in an audience at St. James's.

The Speaker cannot enter upon his official

[1] The administration of the Duke of Newcastle and Mr. Pitt was followed by the Earl of Bute's in 1762.

duties unless at least forty members are present, and the same number is necessary when the King summons him to the Upper House, or when the Speaker delivers an address in the name of the Lower House. He has no vote himself, but only manages the general direction of affairs. Each member may speak once only during the session on the same subject, unless he finds it necessary to give any explanation or elucidation of what he has said in his speech.

Each subject of debate has to be moved by one member, and seconded by another. This is called "making a motion." After every one who has asked permission to speak upon the motion has spoken, the Speaker calls first upon those who are of opinion that the subject is to pass as it has been moved and proposed to answer " Yea," then upon those who are of the opposite opinion to answer "Nay." If there is no opposition, the motion is passed ; otherwise the " Yeas " and " Nays " leave the House, and each side is counted by two members appointed by the Speaker for the purpose, so as to ascertain the majority. After this a committee is formed, who have to put the motion into the shape of a bill, which, when it has been read three times, and has been passed

after amendment, if necessary, is sent up to the
Upper House, and finally approved of by the
King with the well-known formula, *Le Roi le
veult.*

On that day we dined at Lady Yarmouth's, but
my brother was obliged to leave the table and
return home, having been taken ill with an attack
of ague.

On the 4th of November we went to stay with
my Lady Howe, and I dined in company with
some Germans at the Almack Tavern, but kept
my brother company for the rest of the day,
although he had no recurrence of the fever.
Whether it was only a slight attack, or had been
cured by my Lady Howe's remedy—a teaspoonful
of Hungarian water taken in the morning with
sugar—I cannot pretend to say.

On the 5th of November I went to Court,
and afterwards dined with the Netherlands
Minister, Borcel, and supped with Privy Secretary Meyer.

On the 6th of November we dined at my Lord
Howe's, and in the evening we went to my Lady
Northumberland's assembly. She had invited at
least six hundred people, amongst them the
Minister from Tripoli, with his son, both of whom

GRAF CARL KIELMANSEGGE, CHURFURSTLICHER CAMMER-
PRAESIDENT IN HANNOVER.

spoke a little English, especially the son, who was not bad looking.

The house is well adapted for so large a party, and is rightly considered one of the best houses in London, particularly on account of its large saloon and gallery. It is situated close to Charing Cross, and consists of a large courtyard, and a tall gateway on the side facing the street, opposite which the principal part of the building, and the large entrance hall, are situated. The hall is 82 feet long and 12 feet wide. The external as well as the internal decorations, and the furniture, are in keeping with the size and the magnificence of the whole building. There are more than 140 rooms in the house, the principal ones being hung with pictures by Titian and others.

The great gallery is situated in one of the wings, and deserves especial description. It measures 106 feet in length, a quarter of this in width, and the height is equal to the diagonal of the square of its width, which is a line drawn from one angle of such a square to the opposite one. This is considered the best proportion for a gallery. The ceiling is decorated with gilt stucco, and divided into five parts, in which are painted Fame on the wing, a Diana, a triumphal chariot

drawn by two horses, a Flora, and Victory with a
laurel wreath. Over the nine windows on the
garden side are small ones, which are hardly
noticeable, and serve only to give more light to
the ceiling. The opposite wall is divided into
three parts by two valuable marble chimney-pieces,
the corners being supported by figures of Phrygian
prisoners, which are said to have been copied
from those in the Capitol at Rome ; over them
are life-size portraits of our host and hostess in
their peers' robes. The wall-spaces between the
chimney-pieces and the two end walls are occupied by five pictures, copies of famous Roman
paintings. In the middle and largest division is
Raphael's famous " School of Athens," copied by
Raphael Mengs from the original in the Vatican.
On the two side divisions are the Meeting and
the Feast of the Gods, after the original of
Raphael in the small Farnese Palace in Rome,
by Pompeo Batoni. On one of the end walls
is Annibale Carracci's triumphal procession of
Bacchus and Ariadne, from the Farnese Palace,
by Felice Costansi, and at the other end Guido's
" Aurora," from the Villa Rospegliosi, by Masuccio,
a pupil of Carlo Maratti.

Four large crystal chandeliers, each with

twenty-five candles, light up the room even more brilliantly than is necessary, and I certainly think that it would not be easy to imagine a more splendid sight than this gallery presents when filled with people, all vieing with one another in the beauty of their dress.

But nothing is perfect, not even in this house ; the inconvenience of getting away is a very great drawback, the courtyard being too small for the quantity of carriages and sedan chairs, and everybody has to come in and go out by the one gateway, which is very narrow. The quantity of sedan chairs prevented any coach from getting into the court, consequently many people had to wait until two or three o'clock before they could get away. This inconvenience does not exist at the Duke of Bedford's house, which I saw later, as the courtyard is so big that the greater part of the coaches and sedan chairs found room to wait in it.

Northumberland House is noteworthy for the fact that General Monk was received in it by Lord Northumberland, and the first conference of royalists for the restoration of King Charles II. was held there.

In the morning of the 7th of November I went

to hear Miss Four's concert. She is a pupil of
Schumann, and has performed here for some
time on musical glasses. She plays entire concerts
with one finger, on a row of tuned wine-glasses,
and is accompanied by a violoncello; she sings
well, and has a good voice, accompanying herself on the " viola di Gamba " and guitar, and gives
her audience a varied entertainment. The rest of
the day we remained at home, keeping my Lady
Howe company, who was not well.

On the 8th of November we went from the
church to Court, and to Countess Delitz's, and
in the evening to the two usual Sunday parties
at the Dutch Minister Hop's and my Lady
Harrington's.

The 9th of November was the famous Lord
Mayor's Day, of which I am only able to give a
slight description, as I hardly managed to see
anything of it. The fact is, we neither of us felt
inclined to get far into the crowd of people, nor to
pay one to two guineas for a place on a roof, or
on an unsafe stand, where the whole procession
passes, and the less so, as we had promised Lady
Yarmouth to dine with her. We contented
ourselves, therefore, with seeing some of the
City guilds, the City Guards, the King and his

suite when he drove to the City in the morning, and the Lord Mayor as he returned by water. The return by water on this occasion was *incognito*, so to say, and without the usual splendour, as it would have lasted too long.

The Lord Mayor is the first and chief magistrate of the City of London, which has twenty-six aldermen, as heads of the twenty-six divisions of the City, and a number of lower officers. He is elected every year out of one of the twelve principal guilds of London, which are :— (1) the Mercers, (2) Grocers, (3) Drapers, (4) Fishmongers, (5) Goldsmiths, (6) Skinners, (7) Merchant Taylors (tailors are included as merchants for buying the requisite clothes), (8) Haberdashers, (9) Salters, (10) Ironmongers, (11) Vintners, (12) Clothworkers.

Although twenty-nine guilds exist in all, the Lord Mayor can only be chosen out of these twelve. On the 8th of November he is sworn into office at the Guildhall, and at Westminster on the 9th, the day on which his office begins. On this day the aldermen and sheriffs wait for him at the Guildhall, and drive with him from there to Crane's stairs, one of the stairs by the Thames, where the old and the new Lord

Mayor, with their suites, take their places in the state barge of the City, and proceed in procession with all, or with the majority of the different guilds, with bands playing and their large flags flying, to Westminster. After the new Lord Mayor has been sworn in before the Barons of the Exchequer, the procession returns, and disembarks at Blackfriars stairs, situated not far from the beginning of the City and Temple Bar. From here the whole procession proceeds by land to Guildhall, the magistrates in coaches, and the guilds on foot. Amongst the guilds I saw some with flags of such size, that four pairs of boys had to carry them in a line, at certain distances from one another. Each guild has its specially coloured cloaks and flags.

The different companies of City guards form lines on both sides of the street, and the artillery proceed in front of the Lord Mayor. As it is customary for the Sovereign, at least on the occasion of the first election after he has been crowned King, to be present, together with the entire royal family, at the great feast and ball which take place at the Guildhall on Lord Mayor's Day, at the expense of the City, the

King, with the Queen, the Duchess of Ancaster as
Mistress of the Robes, and Lady Egremont, lady-
in-waiting, drove to the City in a state coach drawn
by eight splendid cream-coloured stallions which
had come that summer from Hanover, and accompanied by the Secretaries of State and principal
officers of the Court, in seven or eight carriages,
and escorted by all the Life Guards, mounted
grenadiers, gentlemen pensioners, Yeomen of the
Guard, and liveried servants.

They proceeded from St. James's, first of all, to
the house of a Quaker merchant, called Barclay,
and from there witnessed the Lord Mayor's procession. The King had ordered the rooms which
he required in the house to be provided with new
furniture of red damask, which is supposed to
have cost him £1500. To me it seems doubtful
if it was worth more than £600 or £700, and it
afterwards became the host's property.

The King, on arriving, found the whole of the
royal family in the house, with their suites, and
all the foreign ministers with their sons, but without their wives, who had not been invited. Some
time after the Lord Mayor and his procession
had passed, the King proceeded to the Guildhall,
accompanied by all the people I have mentioned,

amongst whom also was William Pitt. Although
the King and Queen were greatly cheered by the
people as they passed, the cheering was nearly
exceeded by that raised in honour of Pitt, who
had some difficulty in moving on, as the populace
hung on to his carriage and horses in order to
see him.

As soon as the King arrived, the Lord Mayor
and aldermen received him at the door and presented him with the keys of the City, which he at
once returned ; between eight and nine o'clock
the whole company sat down at several splendidly
decorated tables, which were served regardless of
expense and in perfect order. The King and
Queen and all the members of the royal family
were at one table, the foreign ministers at another,
the Lord Mayor and his company at a third,
all the suites again separately, and so on, if I am
not mistaken, at eight tables. The Lord Mayor
served the King, and the Lady Mayoress the
Queen, handing them the first glass of wine ;
whereupon the King invited them to sit down
to dinner. The Lord Mayor is Chief Butler
of the kingdom, and presents a goblet of wine
to the King at the Coronation, for which he
receives a gold cup with cover and basin.

All who were present declared unanimously next day that it would have been impossible to find at any court more order, or a greater quantity of costly dishes and courses, better cooking or more artistic dessert, and finer illuminations (which were ignited by a single sulphur-thread, as at the Coronation in Westminster Hall).

At the foreign ministers' table, and at another, were two large pieces of roast beef, one weighing 227 lbs., and the other 230 lbs. During the dinner the Lord Mayor had it proclaimed aloud at the King's table that he was drinking their Majesties' health, and shortly after a counter messenger was sent by the King to the Lord Mayor's table to announce that he was drinking to his lordship's and the whole City's health and prosperity. The vocal and instrumental music is also said to have been very good.

After the banquet the royal family had tea in the adjoining room whilst the tables were cleared, and everything was prepared for the ball, which was opened by the Duke of York with the Lord Mayor's wife, the King not returning to St. James's until after two o'clock.

On the 10th January a Court was held by the Princess of Wales, which gave us an opportunity for the first time of being presented to the Duke of York.

In the evening we saw the Opera Comique, *Il Mercato*, which is rather pretty, and has some good airs. The Buffo and the Buffa are very well done by Signor Paganini and his wife ; she has a good voice, and both have much feeling. As the principal singers do not generally appear in comic operas, I had no chance of hearing either Elise or Signora Matthæi this evening. Signora Sartori has a clear, high, and pleasant voice, and its beauty without doubt excels that of Matthæi's, whom I heard afterwards ; but she wants a little more musical expression, as she sings without sufficient feeling. Of Zoucha, the bass, I cannot say that he is very good or that he is really bad. Signora Eberhardi and Signora Curione belong to the same class as Zoucha, but the worst of the lot is Leonardo, who represents a peasant in this comic opera ; he has only one eye, and one arm is stiff and quite short, with only two or three fingers, and in addition to all this, he has no voice or talent for music, and is not a good actor.

I am surprised that such a man is allowed to appear on the stage ; ladies in delicate health might be scared, and I gather that the rumour of the Queen being in an interesting state is false, as she has been several times to the Opera lately, and has seen him act. The report that Signora Matthæi, the manager of the Opera, had been taken in by Signora Paganini, who is said to have recommended him, seems highly probable. He was formerly prompter and ticket-seller at the Opera at Genoa, where the Genoese minister, Monsieur d'Ageno, and others, had known him ; his journey is said to have cost Matthæi £200, and I have been told she wishes to get rid of him.

The four principal dancers, Binetti and his wife, Signor Gallini, and Signora Ascellin, are remarkably good. The two last are decidedly better than the two first, and show far more agility, although I think I have never seen a dancer with such thick legs and feet as Signora Ascellin. Binetti and his wife dance with much grace and decorum, and keep good time to the music, whereas the others sometimes do not adapt their high and agile springs so well to the time of the music. All the three dances which were performed that evening were danced first by Binetti and his wife ; the second by all four ; and the

last, which was the best, by the other two. The
corps de ballet are mostly bad—worse than those
at Drury Lane and Covent Garden.

On the 11th we went to see Chiswick with
Herren von Lenthe and von Leyser. This
place is situated about eight miles from London.
Several people have country houses with gardens
about there, but the house built by the late Lord
Burlington is the most important. Before the
house is a courtyard, on both sides of which, at
the corners, are yew trees with trimmed heads,
and opposite two small thick clumps of trees and
cedars of Lebanon, between the dark evergreen of
which the white stone house is seen to great
advantage. On one side of the wall over a double
flight of steps is a representation of "Nature"
by Palladio, and on the other side a similar
representation by Inigo Jones. Over the portico
of six high and valuable Corinthian pillars is a
bust of Augustus. The entrance hall is octagonal,
and has a dome above it, by which it is lighted.
All the rooms are richly furnished, and are filled
with pictures by the best masters. The exterior
facing the gardens, as well as the wings, is more
simple, but handsome. It must be admitted that
the house is built in the best taste, but it is much

too small, and gives the impression of being a
model of a house of larger dimensions. All the
rooms naturally follow the same proportions, and
are as small as possible; the garden is pretty.
From the house you step out on to the lawn, enclosed on both sides by clumps of evergreens with
large stone vases between them. Near the house
stand a large stone wolf and a wild boar, by the
famous Schneemaker, and at the end of the garden
two stone lions. The vista ends with three fine
old statues which were disinterred in the Hadrian
Garden at Rome, and which have stone seats
between them. The greenhouse is separated
from the walk by a ditch, in order to prevent its
being damaged. Take it altogether, from the
description which had been given me I had
expected much more than I found in reality.
What I admired most was the splendid collection
of paintings which are to be found in this *palais
en miniature.*

In the evening I went to Covent Garden,
where I saw a musical piece called *Comus,* and a
second piece of the same kind called *Lethe.*

On the morning of the 12th of November we
went to Tyburn, to see a man hanged *à l'anglaise*
—a young man named Lee, who had been

employed as clerk or bookkeeper at a tradesman's, and had been tempted to issue false bills upon his former employer, in order to get sufficient money for his amusements. This was found out before much damage had been done, and as the consequences of such forgeries are very disastrous, especially in this commercial country, the penalty is death. He was not insolent, but had courage enough to read to the public, sufficiently loud, a speech in which he acknowledged the wrong he had committed, and represented himself as an example and a warning to his hearers. As he was a Methodist, one of the clergymen of that denomination got on the cart after the chaplain had left it, and prayed with him for some time.

During the whole time, whilst he stood on the cart underneath the gallows, a rope was kept round his neck. When he had finished his devotions, and had taken leave of his friends, who had come up on the cart to see him, the cart with all the people standing on it drove off, and he remained hanging. His best friends at once held him down by the feet, and kept holding him there, so that from the first moment nobody noticed the slightest movement. The corpse must remain hanging an hour, and is then dealt

with according to the crime, being either hung up
by chains at the place where the crime was committed, as is done in the case of murderers and
highwaymen, or taken to the school for anatomy.
The executions should in reality be performed
by the Sheriff, a respectable citizen appointed for
the purpose, but he generally pays somebody well
to do it for him.

Tyburn was formerly a village in the vicinity of
London, which vanished when the city extended
in that direction, so that at present the name of
Tyburn only applies to the site where the gallows
and a turnpike stand.

In the evening we were invited to the house of
Mrs. Richardson, *née* Völgern, a Hanoverian, who
was married here sixteen or seventeen years ago.
She has a daughter, whose looks have been spoilt
by small-pox, but who sings very well ; she herself has been beautiful in her youth, and is still
good looking. Her husband is head clerk in my
Lord Egremont's, formerly William Pitt's, department, and he is said to be a very able official.
We had supper there, and met a Polish count,
Grunizki, seventy years old, who had lived here
for the last twenty-one years, had lost all his
means in Poland owing to his religion, and had

experienced extraordinary adventures in consequence.

On the 13th of November we went to the Lower House of Parliament, as we had been told that important speeches would be made, especially as Pitt was going to render an account of his actions during the time he was in office as Secretary of State. The present intrigues which have been on foot in all directions have occasioned a strict regulation, since the beginning of the present war, that nobody should be admitted to the House unless introduced by a member of Parliament of his acquaintance, who has to apply to the Speaker for permission. A Marquis de St. Simon, who had served with the Prince de Condé, and had been in Hanover with him in 1759, had been accused of having availed himself of the freedom of entry into the House, when he was here a year or two ago, to take notes of the speeches and transmit them to his court, probably by order. He had been removed therefore from the House when this was discovered.

We had the greatest difficulty in getting in on this day, as so many people were trying to obtain admittance ; but at last my Lords Barrington and Howe took us in just when the speeches were beginning. I do not remember ever having been in a greater crush and heat, and I could hardly use my legs and arms the next day ; still, I should be wrong if I were to say that I had found the time tedious, although I had to stand from two till eight o'clock. The reason for this was the number of very fine speeches, which were often delivered on the spur of the moment, and which gave expression to many different opinions and ways of thinking.

The principal point at issue was the answer to the speech from the throne, in which mention is made of all the chief questions of the day ; this gave members an opportunity of speaking on the German war, the militia, the war with Spain which was about to commence, etc., etc.

Lord Middleton made the motion, and read a draft of the answer prepared by him and several others, which was seconded by Lord Strange. This method of procedure was disapproved of by a young Scotsman named Dempster, who had lately entered Parliament, and who demanded that the reply should be drawn up by a duly appointed committee, and not, as it were, be extracted casually from the pocket. His action was justified, as such a committee is usual ; but he did not know that it had been customary for a long time for some of the ministers and of the leading members to meet the day before at the Cockpit in Whitehall in order to agree upon the draft, which is then proposed to the House of Commons.

The same plan is followed in the House of Lords, a meeting for the purpose being held at the Duke of Newcastle's.

This young man spoke at the same time very strongly against the German war, and especially against the establishment of the militia, expressing a wish that it had never existed, and that, as the bill would lapse with the current year, it might never again be thought of. It would be wrong to say that he had not represented his case as well as the matter permitted.

After him a man named Beckford rose, a member for the City of London, and a brother of my Lady Effingham ; he made a vigorous speech in favour of the German war, ascribing to it all the advantages obtained by the English in the four quarters of the globe, and only decrying the bad financial management in Germany, which, he insisted, had occasioned the shameful expenditure, and not the war itself ; therefore he advocated endeavours at improvement in that direction. At

the same time, he was decidedly in favour of the
Spanish war, on which he expressed himself very
vigorously ; he declaimed so loudly and with so
many exclamations, that he confirmed the current
opinion that he was eccentric. After a few other
speeches, in strong opposition to the German
war, the Speaker's brother, Cust, made a lengthy
calculation of the cost it had hitherto entailed and
was still entailing, and demanded that a proper
account be rendered to Parliament, and he attacked
Pitt's administration generally.

At last Pitt stood up, and, in a brilliant speech,
justified the whole of his proceedings during the
time that he was Secretary of State. There can
be no denying that he is one of the most powerful speakers of our time ; he had undoubtedly
prepared his speech beforehand, but he answered
categorically, and in a very thorough manner, all
the reproaches which had been levelled against
him during the day, and the arguments brought
against his opinions. When he speaks, a look
of fixed attention is promptly visible upon the
features of all present, and absolute silence reigns
in the whole House, especially amongst strangers,
so that you do not lose a word. He refuted in
a very decided way the reproach of having tried

to bring about the Spanish war, although he did
not deny having advised that the right moment
should not be lost, convinced, as he was, that, under
the circumstances which existed, war must come.

Turning to the war in Germany, he dwelt upon
its necessity, and showed that the nation had to
attribute to it all the advantages which it had
acquired ; he expressed a hope that the young
man who had spoken so well, although against the
motion, would one day sit in the Cabinet, when he
was convinced a year would not pass before he
would hold the same views as he, Pitt, was now
uttering, for he himself also had previously not
seen the matter in the same light. He expressed
himself further to the effect that even if the whole
nation were of one mind, and thought differently
from him, rather than change his opinion, he
would hold firm to his conviction, at the price
of submitting to public scorn. As to the cost of
the German war, he would allow there was much
to be said against the financial management, but
he was of opinion that in many respects it would be
impossible to alter this, and generally he expressed
the view that it was impossible to demand from
a Ministry accounts of financial management as
accurate as those which a merchant could keep in

his shop, and that it would be unfair to call upon
them for such. He referred principally to the
remarks of the Speaker's brother, a merchant who
had called for the submission to Parliament of an
accurate account of all moneys voted towards
carrying out the German war.

After Pitt, his brother-in-law, George Grenville
(who was the only one of the family who had
remained in office), spoke at great length against
him, attacking him principally for the manner in
which he had thrown up his office as Secretary of
State, and for pretending that the fact that his
colleagues did not share his opinions was not
sufficient cause for his resignation.

Meanwhile it was getting late, and his speech
was so very inferior to the previous one, and so
very long and had so little sequence, that it was
hard to know what he was driving at beyond the
fact that everything was obviously intended to
damage his brother-in-law, without any reference
to the previous debate. Consequently, he began
to bore not only myself, but apparently all the
others, who left during the speech.

At last, towards eight o'clock, after the House
had been sitting since ten in the morning, having
previously transacted business of less importance

regarding the election of several members, the
Speaker put the question whether the answer to
the speech from the throne, as proposed by Lord
Middleton, should be passed or not. It was
agreed to without contradiction from any one,
although, as has been mentioned, one or other
had objected not so much to the contents of the
address, as to the way in which it had been
proposed.

On the morning of the 14th of November we
drove, in company with Herren von Lenthe and
von Leyser, to Vauxhall, so as to get some idea
of the place, although it was impossible to see
this famous resort illuminated, as it is only open
in summer-time. I take this opportunity of
correcting an error which I made at the beginning
of this journal, when I remarked that Ranelagh
remained open in winter. This was incorrect,
and I should have said summer only. The
quantity of people who have been drawn to
London by the King's wedding and coronation
was the reason why the proprietor had availed
himself of the opportunity of keeping Vauxhall
open to the public at the present time.

Vauxhall was originally a village close to
London, on the other side of the Thames, in the

parish of Lambeth. The garden in question is
the first which had ever been fitted up for this
kind of entertainment. In the centre is a large
orchestra with an organ, where the band and
singers perform. The boxes round are so
arranged that you can hear the music very well.
In most of them are said to be paintings by
Hayman, which are removed in winter, especially
the four large and fine pieces representing scenes
from Shakespeare's plays, which are in the large
pavilion. The avenues and trees are all planted
in good taste, with vistas of fine high trees and
hedges between them. Some of these vistas end
with representations of old ruins amidst land-
scapes, and others are decorated with triumphal
arches. Amongst the statues is an especially good
one by Roubillac, of Handel with a lyre, representing the figure of Orpheus. There are also a
large saloon and a ballroom with an orchestra, to
be used in bad weather. Here we saw several
pictures which had been taken down, but one
had been left on the wall, representing English
magnanimity, in the person of General Amherst,
raising the inhabitants of Canada, who had thrown
themselves at his feet.

The garden must be a wonderful sight when

the greater part of it is lighted up with nearly 1500 glass lamps. At one end of an avenue, when a curtain is withdrawn, a landscape is to be seen illuminated by hidden lamps, the principal feature being a miller's house, with an artificial cascade. You fancy that you see water driving the mill, and that you hear the rush of the water, though in reality there is none. It is managed just as these things are arranged in theatres and panto-mimes, but though it never lasts long, it is supposed to be far better and more cleverly done. When the garden is open to the public, tea, coffee, cold dishes, bread and butter, etc., are procurable by any one who pays for them.

We dined at Almack's Tavern, where we had been invited by the two Prussian ministers, Baron von Knyphausen and Mitchel, to form a club, and to dine together every Sunday until Christmas, in company with Herren von Lichten-stein, von Werpup, von Vincke, the English Colonel Prévôt, a Swiss by birth, Captain Campbell of the Guards, the Genoese minister, D'Ageno, the Baron von Edelsheim, from the German Empire, and several others.

In the evening I saw the opera, *Alessandro nelle Indie*. The principal performers in it, besides

those already named, and excluding the Buffo, the
Buffa, and Leonardo, are a singer named Elise
and Signora Matthæi. Elise is the better of the
two, and her voice is as fine and high in tone
and pitch as any woman's. Matthæi's voice has
to a certain extent already reached the point at
which it no longer improves, but rather declines.
She is the only one who sings with much expression—almost too much, in fact, and in con-
trast to the others, so that she almost appears
affected. But this is said to be the fashion
and taste all through Italy and France at the
present day, so that it cannot be called a fault in
her. Matthæi has undertaken the management
of this opera, with the support of several lovers
of music; amongst whom are several foreign
ministers, who help to keep up the opera, and
have supplied and advanced the money, in return
for which they take half the profits, after deducting
all the expenses, and the £800 which Matthæi
receives as principal singer.

On the 15th of November we went at noon to
Court, and afterwards dined with the Russian
Minister, Prince Gallitzin; in the evening we went
to the King's Arms Tavern in Cornhill, in the City,
in company with Herren von Münchhausen, the

Councillor of the War Department, the Herren von Lenthe and von Leyser, and our banker, Joseph Solomon, Esquire. This Jew had expressed a wish that the gentlemen who banked with him should spend an evening with him, and drink a bottle of good old Rhine wine. He is one of the richest Jews here, and has given to each of his two sons, who have already settled, £30,000 for setting up their houses; the youngest is still at home. He is sometimes to be seen at Court, as well as a very rich Portuguese Jew, Salvadore, who is to be met everywhere in society, at Münchhausen's, the foreign ministers', and elsewhere. As they do not wear beards, they cannot be distinguished at all from other people, although the former (Joseph Solomon) is a German Jew from Amsterdam, and his wife is from Frankfort-on-Main. He invited us at once to dine with him next Wednesday.

On the 16th of November we went with our two travelling companions to see the British Museum, which deserves a full description. It originated in a bequest of Sir Hans Sloane, by whom the first foundation was laid; he was a rich man, who passed his life in collecting, at great expense, everything that seemed in any way remarkable. He is said to have spent about £50,000 upon the collection, the whole of which he left, when he died in 1753, for the benefit of the public, on condition that Parliament should pay his executors £20,000.

Parliament therefore arranged a lottery of £300,000, of which two-thirds went for winnings, £20,000 for the above-named purpose, £10,000 for the purchase of Lord Oxford's manuscripts, £30,000 for a public fund for the salaries of the necessary servants, and the rest for the purchase of a suitable building. Parliament further decreed that the Cottonian Library, the Harleian Manuscripts, and Major Edwards's collection of books, should be united to it, and that the sum of £7000, bequeathed by Major Edwards, should be employed for the purchase of further objects of interest.

Later on, small libraries of deceased kings have been added by the orders of King George II., all in the name of the British Museum, and everything has been submitted to the supervision of the Academy of Science.

Montague House in Great Russell Street, near Bloomsbury Square, was purchased for the collection at a cost of £10,000, or, including all the internal fittings, for £25,000.

As it is impossible to refer to everything, I propose to mention only a few things which appeared to me especially worthy of notice.

The original Magna Carta, the basis of the English constitutional freedom given by King John, 1215, which is, however, much damaged by fire.

A Greek Bible on parchment, written fourteen hundred years ago, without any distinctive marks, and without any separation of the words one from another, so that the whole is written in one continual line.

An autograph letter of King Charles I., which is highly interesting. Amongst other things, he had been accused of having had a share in exciting the Irish disturbances of those days, and of having had secret knowledge of and of having encouraged the rebellion in Ireland. This, however, had never been proved against him. The end of this letter consists of a row of ciphers, the key to which had been found after his death and lies beside the letter ; from this the ground of the accusation becomes quite clear, as he says "that he approves of what is being done in Ireland."

Another old manuscript is worth mentioning,

principally on account of the title of some of the first kings of England. If I am not mistaken, Alfred assumes in this manuscript the title of Lord over all the British Islands and the surrounding seas. When, in the last century, two great men of science, Grotius and Selden, disputed the question whether a lordship over the sea existed, the latter referred, amongst other proofs, to this manuscript, for the purpose of showing that in the olden times kings had already arrogated to themselves the dominion over the sea, and had assumed such a title.

Everybody can obtain a ticket, and receive permission to enter the Museum daily for some time to look over the books, and no servant or warder, etc., is allowed to receive a penny under penalty of dismissal. It is said that the wages of the people employed, and the cost of the maintenance of the building and objects, and the heating of the rooms, amount to £8000 annually.

On the same day we dined at Privy Councillor von Münchhausen's with the Countess of Yarmouth, my Lady Howe, and a few foreign ministers.

On the 17th of November we dined and spent the evening with Mrs. Richardson, where we

heard a young girl of eleven years old sing, the
daughter of a German who is living here ; she had
made wonderful progress, considering the short
time she had devoted to music, much more than
could reasonably be expected from such a mere
child.

On the 18th of November Mr. Dickson, the
architect of the new bridge which is being built
over the Thames, between London Bridge and
Westminster Bridge, at a place called Blackfriars,
showed us over the works in progress. We went
with him by water. Under the contract, the
bridge is to be finished in seven years, and to
be built entirely of Portland stone ; it will be
very similar to the two older ones, excepting
that it will have more ornamentation. On the
sides of each of the large piles upon which the
arches are to rest are to be placed Corinthian
columns, between which the architect proposes to
place the statues of famous men ; for instance,
between the centre columns one of General
Wolfe, who fell before Quebec, with an inscription
beneath it.

The Lord Mayor and the Corporation of the
City have been authorized by Parliament to raise
the necessary funds, which are gradually to be

paid off by a toll to be levied on the bridge, on condition that the loan does not exceed £30,000 a year, and £160,000 in all.

How stupendous this work is may be concluded from the fact that the bridge is to be 900 feet long, over a stream of considerable force, as the tides reach higher up than London. Consequently the arches must be wide, so as not to obstruct the shipping. The large ram, for ramming down the piles, is very remarkable, and is worked by a horse, which draws the machinery and continually goes round in one direction ; thus not only is the weight raised, but a hook is made to run down and catch the weight again after it has fallen. The enormous blocks of stone are also raised by a crane, by means of a small piece of iron, which is not known with us in Germany, and it is not easy to explain how it is brought down into its proper place. But, for curiosity's sake, and perhaps to use as a model, I had an instrument of this kind made for myself ; it is called " Luis."

We dined afterwards with the architect at the house of our banker, Joseph Solomon, Esquire, and his family, who treated us very well and magnificently with three courses, one of which consisted of fish. He has a very pretty dinner-service of Japanese china with his arms on, consisting of a lion with a woman's face and three outstretched hands (*des armes parlantes*, for grasping). We played a game at whist, and the rest of the company were obliged to remain for supper, which, by giving some excuse, we got out of with great difficulty.

On the evening of the 19th of November we went to Lady Yarmouth's, who had had some company to dinner, and then on to the house of the Dutch Ambassador, Borcel, where there is an Assembly every Thursday.

On the 20th I remained at home, on account of a bad cold, but my brother went to an Assembly at the Duchess of Bedford's.

On the 21st we went on foot to see some of the remarkable buildings and sights of London, which we had postponed doing until the winter. The first was the Guildhall, which was built as early as 1411, but was thoroughly repaired and renovated, as it now is, after the great fire in 1666. Over the Gothic frontispiece at the entrance are the King's arms, and over the door is a balcony with a niche on each side containing figures of Moses and Aaron, and below, the four principal virtues, as well as the arms of the twelve guilds. The grand hall is 153 feet long, 48 feet wide, and 55 feet high. In it is the Lord Mayor's Court, which is raised by nine or ten steps, and above it is a balcony supported by four iron pillars, in the shape of palm trees. Opposite to this is a clock, on which are representations of the four principal virtues with a figure of Time, and over these on each side is a carved cock. The most remarkable objects here are two horrible-looking giants with enormous heads, standing close to the wall, one holding a halberd, and the other a large ball with huge iron spikes which hangs to a chain as a kind of weapon. They are believed to represent an ancient Briton and a Saxon. Round the Hall hang the French standards taken at the battle of Ramillies, and on the wall are the King's arms, between the portraits of George I. and William and Mary, as well as twenty-three life-size portraits of judges in their red robes, whose memory the City wished to preserve. In the other rooms the different City courts are held, with their various departments.

From there we went to the Royal Excise, a large brick building, in which there is nothing particular to see ; then to St. Stephen's Church,

Walbrook. Externally, it has nothing remarkable to note, but the inside is supposed to be a masterpiece of the architect, Christopher Wren.

Close to this church is situated the Mansion House, or the house inhabited by the Lord Mayor for the time being, the inside of which we did not see, as it is not yet in order, the new Lord Mayor being busy refurnishing it. It was finished in 1743, and is built entirely of Portland stone, with a fine Corinthian portico, over which is a large emblematic piece in *basso-relievo*. The principal figure, in *alto-relievo*, is a woman wearing a crown of turrets, representing the City; with her left foot she is treading down Envy, who is trying to rise; with her left arm she rests on a shield, and in her right hand she holds a staff. Near her, on the same side, stand Cupid, holding the cap of Liberty on a short wand over his shoulder like a club, and a river-god with his urn and an anchor who represents the Thames. On the left side is Plenty, in a kneeling posture, offering the City fruit, and behind are two little boys with large bales of goods, representing trade.

The South Sea Company's House is a fine large building, inside a well-paved piazza, surrounded by a covered passage with Doric pillars.

The House of the East India Company does not contain anything worth noticing. It is large, without much ornament, and was built in 1726 in Doric style.

The frontage of the Bank of England towards the street is eighty feet long, and of the Ionic order. The building itself consists of several squares ; round the roof is a balustrade with fine vases. The hall is situated in the first court, which is in the Corinthian style, and there you see the arms of the founders, viz. Britannia sitting with her shield and spear, and a cornucopia at her feet shedding fruit. The hall is 79 feet long and 40 feet wide. At its upper end is a statue of King William III., with an appropriate inscription. The other rooms and buildings are used as apartments for the officials and for the money vaults. It is easy for any one who understands the importance of the Bank of England to conceive what a quantity of money, or rather of paper representing its value, daily changes hands in this hall. Its original fund was very large, and it has to answer for a large portion of the National Debt, having from time to time advanced enormous sums to Government, which it had raised on its own credit.

The Royal Exchange dates its origin from a famous merchant named Sir Thomas Gresham,[1] who built it in 1567 at his own expense. Having been consumed by the great fire of London in 1666, it was rebuilt by King Charles II. in a grander style for £80,000. The space over the arches is divided by pillars into twenty-four niches, nineteen of which are filled with statues of English kings, beginning with Edward I. and concluding with George II. Edward V. has the crown suspended only over his head, as, although king, he was never crowned, having been murdered in the Tower by his uncle, Richard III. The kings Edward II., Richard II., Henry IV., and Richard III., have been left out entirely, the last two probably because they were considered usurpers, although the son and the grandson of the first of these two, Henry V. and Henry VI., have found a place. The reason why Edward II. and Richard II. have been left out must be that they had withdrawn from the City their letters of freedom (Charter of Exemption), which were subsequently returned. Under the archways themselves are twenty-eight niches, but in two only have

---

[1] Sir Thomas Gresham, b. 1519, d. 1579, acquired the title of the Royal Merchant.

statues been placed ; one is of Sir Thomas Gresham,
and the other of Sir John Barnard, another famous
citizen, who was thus immortalized in his lifetime.

In the middle of the piazza is a fine statue of
Charles II. in Roman costume, on a marble
pedestal, with an iron railing round it, sculptured
by the famous Gibbons.   The pedestal is adorned
with the English arms, different emblematical
figures, and appropriate inscriptions.   The whole
of this square and the colonnade form the
Exchange proper, where the merchants daily
assemble from twelve to two, and after four,
and where each company has its fixed place with
its name attached, so that any person you wish
to speak to is easily found.

An incredible tradition maintains that the
Tower of London was first begun by Julius
Cæsar; on the other hand, it is as good as
proved that William the Conqueror was the
builder of part of it, in 1076, probably in order
to secure a stronghold in case the English should
try to recover their lost liberty.   It lies close
to the Thames, and forms a special citadel,
or keep, protecting the City against hostile
attempts by water.   It always has a garrison,

both of the Guards and the Yeomanry. The gates are closed and the drawbridge raised every night, when all communication with the inside ceases. A staircase also leads from the Thames into the Tower, and the small door at the head of it is called the Traitors' Gate, because the prisoners were brought to the Tower by water, in order to avoid the crowd in the City, and were taken in by this little door. A broad ditch surrounds the Tower, and the batteries are supplied with sufficient guns, especially the whole side which commands the river.

The Constable of the Tower is always a person of distinction ; he has to attend at coronations and other important functions, and the Regalia are intrusted to his keeping. The present constable is my Lord Cornwallis. He has a lieutenant and a deputy-lieutenant under him. The latter is generally called the Governor of the Tower. He has, further, a great many people under him, and about forty Yeomanry who live there. The first things you see on entering are the wild animals, amongst which are several lions, so tame that you can touch them with perfect safety. Their number has been increased by presents from the Algerian ambassador.

Amongst them is one particularly fine lion. There are also tigers, leopards, hyenas, large eagles, a horned owl, different kinds of monkeys, a tiger-cat, and other outlandish animals. After having seen this, we were taken to the Mint. All English money is coined here, and nowhere else, either in England or in Scotland. The stamping only is shown, as the system of edging is kept secret. The coining is done exactly in the same way as in the Harz Mountains, by means of a press, which is worked by four men, whilst a fifth moves the sheet in and out.

The "White Tower" is really the building erected by William the Conqueror, and consists of three stories, with roomy vaults underneath which are used principally for the storing of saltpetre, etc. All these three stories are filled with war materials for service by sea and land. On the top of one of the four towers of this building is a cistern, or reservoir, to supply the garrison with water; it is sixty feet long, and is filled by means of artificial pipes from the Thames. Not far from the White Tower is the so-called Spanish Armoury, in which everything is preserved that was taken from the Invincible

Armada, in lasting memory of that splendid victory. Here all kinds of curious implements and arms are to be seen.

After this we were shown the large building used as an armoury, which is 240 feet long and 60 feet wide, is built of stone, and has a fine entrance with Doric columns, decorated with the royal arms and trophies. It was begun by James II. and finished by William III. Several rooms in it are used as workshops for repairing and cleaning muskets. We were first shown up a staircase into the hall, where you can see at a glance muskets for eighty thousand men, in such a perfect state of order that they are all ready to be served out for immediate use. This is called the "Arms Wilderness;" all the muskets have been arranged by an armourer called Harris, in such a curious and clever way that you can take out any piece without touching the others. The vast numbers of these different kinds of old muskets, pikes, bayonets, swords, etc., are hung up in every possible kind of figure, such as columns, pyramids, rising and setting suns, serpents, moons, shells, and large organs (one of which consists of two thousand pairs of pistols), garters, stars, and armorial bearings, Jupiter with a thunderbolt in a chariot drawn by eagles with a rainbow over him, a large gate of double doors made entirely of halberds, Medusa's heads, etc. A large part of these weapons has been taken at different times from rebels ; amongst others are the sword of mercy and the sword of justice, which the Pretender had carried before him in 1714.

Beneath this large hall, on the ground floor, and in another hall of the same size, all the ordnance requirements are kept.

From the Tower we went to the Custom House. The building is situated by the Thames, and all incoming and outgoing goods must be unloaded and loaded here and the duty on them paid. It is 189 feet long, built in 1718 of brick and quarry stone, with two wings, below which is a good Tuscan colonnade, although the columns on the upper story are all Ionic. A hall runs through the whole length of the building, in which the custom-house officers are on duty.

From here it was not far to the Monument. This is a very large fluted Doric pillar, which Parliament erected in commemoration of the Great Fire, close to the site where this awful fire began in 1666. The famous architect,

Christopher Wren, took six years to build it.
It is said to exceed in height the famous
columns of Trajan and Antony in Rome, and
that of Theodosius in Constantinople. That of
Antony is said to measure to the highest point
only 172½ feet, and to be 12 feet 3 inches in
diameter, whereas the column of the Monument
is 15 feet in diameter, and 120 feet high, the
height of the pedestal and the top being respectively 40 and 42 feet, that is to say, 202 feet
high in all.

As the Monument is situated near London
Bridge, we passed over the bridge, partly in order
to see it, and partly to take a new way home
through the City. The first bridge on record over
the Thames must have been built between the years
993 and 1016, but, according to old documents
of 1209, a stone bridge had been finished previously to that date, after having taken thirty-three
years to build. It had been damaged subsequently by fire, water, war, etc., and the houses
built on both sides of it were destroyed by fire
in 1666. In 1746 the City magistrates decreed
the abolition of all the houses, and ten years
later applied to Parliament for powers to raise,
by means of a toll on the bridge, the requisite

funds for repairing it and for furnishing it with a parapet. The estimate amounted to £95,000. With this in view, a temporary wooden bridge was speedily erected in 1751, at the side of the old one, in order to keep up the communication between the City and the suburb of Southwark, but in 1758 this caught fire, and was entirely consumed, so that all intercourse by land between the two sides of the Thames ceased, part of the stone bridge having meanwhile been taken away. Yet it was only a fortnight before everything was replaced in its former state, and Parliament gave the City £15,000 towards the work. At present, the stone bridge, including the greater part of the parapet, is finished, so that the passage over it is open, and the temporary bridge has been taken away. The Thames being 915 feet wide at this part, this is the length of the bridge, and the width is 31 feet for carriage traffic, with 7 feet on each side for foot-passengers. The heavy parapet is like that of Westminster Bridge, to which, when everything is finished and the lamps are fixed, it will not be inferior. Under the middle arch is a water-shoot, over which the boats continually pass. Having crossed the bridge, you are

in Southwark, which is regarded as a suburb
of London, but is by no means a small place in
itself, as it consists of four parishes. The Lord
Mayor has jurisdiction over it, as it belongs to
London, and has formed one of its parishes since
the time when Edward VI. sold it to the City.

On our road through Southwark we went to
see St. Thomas's Hospital for invalids and
wounded, but we only saw the outside. In front
it has a large iron gateway, which forms the
street side of a square, the other sides of which
are taken up by the main building and two
wings, in front of which a covered stone colonnade runs, with benches under it. On each
side of the entrance gate is a stone statue representing an invalid. There is a clock over the
main building, and under it, in a niche, a statue
of King Edward VI., with a gilt sceptre in one
hand, and the charter of foundation in the other.
This hospital, the yearly expenses of which
amount to £8000, consists of nineteen wards,
containing in all 474 beds, which, it is said,
are always occupied. Whoever pays a yearly
subscription of £20 to £40 becomes one of the
life-governors, as in most other benevolent institutions, this arrangement being common to

public institutions of the kind in England. The governors meet at stated times, elect a president and secretary, and appoint the necessary servants, pass the requisite rules of the house, control the accounts, etc., and usually appoint a committee to meet weekly, without whose consent no patient is taken in, or discharged when he is cured.

This hospital alone has eighty-six servants, including the president, the chaplain, physicians, surgeons, etc.

We went right through Southwark and St. George's Fields, an open field between Southwark and Westminster Bridge, where the Thames makes a large curve. On the way to the bridge we went to see an enormous pig, which could not move for fat, and was also of an exceptional size, as big as a small horse, and had therefore been brought to London to be shown.

Not far from this spot we found a quantity of outlandish animals, such as a large, white-haired, four-footed water animal, which we took for a sea-bear from Greenland, a camel, a quantity of monkeys, eagles, civet-cats, etc.

Westminster Bridge is 1223 feet long, consequently 200 feet longer than London Bridge. Its width of 44 feet includes a 7-foot pathway

on each side for foot-passengers, and a 30-foot
roadway for carriages, so that three carriages and
two persons on horseback can pass each other.
The bridge rises a good deal from the bank
towards the centre. On the day of the Coronation, the bridge, which opens on to a wide
street, was filled with people, and presented an
incomparable sight, creating the impression of
an amphitheatre, seen from a distance, with
thousands of heads ending the *point de vue*, as
if by art. The arches under the bridge, for
the shipping traffic, are nearly four times the
width of those of London Bridge, without any
water-shoot, and are consequently free from the
slightest danger to boats. In former times,
instead of a bridge there was a ferry here, but
this, owing to the quantity of traffic going backwards and forwards, occasioned so much trouble
and danger, that, as early as 1730, a proposal was
made to Parliament by the Archbishop of Canterbury, who has his seat in Lambeth, as well as
by several other people, to build a bridge. So
much time, however, was lost in procuring and
preparing the material, in making plans and
removing impediments which were raised by
the ferrymen, who saw the prospect of losing

their living, that the foundation was not laid until the year 1738. At the end of 1747 the bridge was completely finished, so that nearly twelve years were spent on the work from its beginning. The cost, which was raised by different lotteries, amounted to £389,500.

We finished our wanderings by going home through St. James's Park. This park is situated behind the palace, and has in its length of half an English mile three broad walks, besides the drive, close to each other, of which the middle one was formerly the Mall. The walks are lined with very high trees, and consequently form three fine avenues. One of the walks goes round the park, skirting an island with a shrubbery on it, a duck-pond, and a small narrow field with a canal in it. The whole park is surrounded by houses, excepting near St. James's Palace, where the green park branches off, and is only separated by a railing.

At one end of the park is Buckingham House, exactly facing the avenue; it is a fine building with two wings and a large courtyard, separated from the park by a high iron railing and gate. At the other end of the park is the Horse Guards at Whitehall.

Between this park and Piccadilly lies the Green Park, separated from the street by a wall ; it consists of grass, with gravel walks, except in one place, where there is a small wilderness of trees, which is rather pretty, and in front of this is a canal, which is bordered by a walk, yet it can hardly be called a canal, as it is really only an oblong fish-pond.

Opposite, on the other side of Piccadilly, begins Hyde Park, which, if it were not separated by a wall and the street from the Green Park, would form, with it and St. James's, one single park. Hyde Park is the largest of the three, as it reaches as far as Kensington. It is principally used for driving and riding, and one of the drives leads all round, and is called the Ring. There is a great deal of game in this, as well as in the Green Park, but there is none in St. James's.

We dined on this day at our Saturday's club, and in the evening saw Shakespeare's play, *King Henry VIII.*, at Covent Garden, and " The Coronation" as an after-piece. This we had already seen some time ago at Drury Lane, but that was nothing compared with the representation at Covent Garden. The quantity of people forming the procession, the richness and splendour of the

costumes, the accurate copy of the festivities, so
far as this can be accomplished on the stage, and
the inclusion of the principal features of the
Abbey, combined to make the whole a wonderful
sight. The scene during the procession, representing stands before the houses, which were
crowded, stands and houses alike, with numerous
lookers-on, was excessively pretty and picturesque.
The whole of the Westminster choir sang all
the time that the procession was passing across
the stage, in exact imitation of the real procession.
The same number of cymbals and trumpets were
there ; the bells were rung ; and the guns and regi-
mental bands in lines, through which the procession
continually passed, were painted on the scenery.
When the Queen came on the stage, followed by
the King, cheers were given behind the scenes so
realistically, that those who had not seen the actual
coronation procession and the dinner at Westminster Hall could undoubtedly form a pretty
accurate idea of them.

During the dinner, when the scene representing
the galleries in the Hall was filled with people, the
coronation anthem, which had been performed in
the Abbey, was sung to the accompaniment of a
full band.

o

The dresses, all of which are of velvet, gold, and silver, the decorations, and other expenses, are said to have cost the owner of Covent Garden theatre £3000. This is the famous old Rich, formerly the best harlequin who ever appeared on the stage, and whose last act was the arrangement at this theatre of the coronation of the King and Queen. He has since died, leaving to his heirs the profit, so long as the performance runs. The interest on the capital invested is very good, as the crush is always very great, and the return during the run of three or four months must have been very good, although it is now decreasing. But I can say without exaggeration that there can hardly be any one in London, of high or low degree, unless his conscience prevents him from going to the theatres, who will not have seen the play at least once. The daily expenses, which have been considerable, have to be deducted, as there are decidedly over a hundred people in the procession alone—who certainly do not appear for nothing—besides the actual actors, who have been engaged especially for the purpose. Each of the theatres employs altogether about sixty to seventy or more people, some of whom are yearly servants, while others are only paid for each piece in which they act. I certainly believe that there is no stage in the world which equals the English in its choice of actors; at Drury Lane, for example, you have an impression that every actor has been expressly made for his part. Garrick is, however, the only one who can delineate every character with equal skill, from the philosopher down to the fool, from the king to the peasant, and who appears to put on a different face with each character.

On the 23rd we accompanied my Lady Howe and her daughters to the Opera Buffa *Il Mercato*, which the King and Queen and the whole of the royal family also went to see. Afterwards, we went to a party at Privy Councillor von Münchhausen's.

On the 24th a court was held for the first time by the Duke of Cumberland in his new house in Grosvenor Street, at which we, as well as our other compatriots, were presented to him. In the evening my brother went to the play, whilst I remained at home, except during half an hour which I spent with Lady Yarmouth.

On the 25th we remained at home during the whole of the day, excepting the morning, when we went out on foot to different shops.

On the 26th we went to Court, and in the evening to an assembly at Soho. This consists of a concert and a ball, which take place every fortnight in a fine room, which has been much improved this year. Several ladies have a book, in one of which every one signs his name, paying five guineas for twelve nights. In order that only those people may be subscribers who are known to one of the ladies, the subscription books are kept by the ladies only, and the power to admit or to exclude whom they like is confined to them, and is not given to the owner of the rooms, who is an Italian of the name of Cornelia.

The rooms in which they play, as well as the large ballroom, are very fine and beautifully lighted, and exceedingly well furnished. The vocal and instrumental music, by an orchestra at the end of the room, begins at seven o'clock and lasts until nine ; dancing afterwards goes on until one or two. Tea, lemonade, and cake are served in two rooms. As at first we did not know how long we should be able to remain in England, and as we did not feel inclined to spend ten guineas perhaps for nothing, and also as my deep mourning [1] did not allow me

---

[1] He had recently lost his first wife, Countess Dernath.

to dance, we did not subscribe. But as every subscriber who is prevented from attending may give his ticket away, we got tickets from friends and went with my Lady Howe's youngest son.

On the 27th 'of November we drove in the morning to the Duke of Newcastle's, who holds a kind of *levée* every Friday in winter. In the evening we first went to a small party at the house of Mrs. Haywood, sister of the young Lady Howe, and from there we went on to an assembly at the Duchess of Bedford's, which also takes place every Friday. Her house is in Bloomsbury Square, and is one of the best in London. The hall, or gallery, on the ground floor, is a fine room, although it does not equal that of Northumberland House. In the place of tapestry there are fine copies of the nine large cartoons by Raphael in the gallery at Hampton Court. The courtyard in front of the house, which is so large that a great many carriages have room to stand there, is separated by a wall from the street, and, as there are two large gateways, this house has the great convenience, which is wanting at Northumberland House, viz. of enabling you to get away whenever you like without having to wait from two to three hours for your carriage.

On the 30th the birthday of the Princess of Wales was celebrated, although she had begged, as she generally does, that no notice should be taken of it. She did not hold a court herself, but, notwithstanding this, the King and Queen drove incognito to see her in the morning. The Court at noon was remarkably crowded, and the crush, as usual on such occasions, very great. In the evening we went to look on at the ball from the benches prepared for the foreign ambassadors, placed below and on the right hand of the King. The room is poor, and looks more like the refectory of an old convent than the principal room of the palace of the King of England; but it is in entire keeping with the rest of the building.[1] In former times there was a convent on the site where the palace now stands, which was built by Henry VIII. You cannot easily imagine a worse building than this, especially when seen from the outside.

Amongst the rooms there are several which are rather large, but they are spoilt by the bad and old furniture, and are altogether too small for

[1] St. James's Palace.

England, where you meet, especially on State
days at Court, several thousand people, amongst
whom are hundreds of ladies in large hoops.
The front faces towards Pall Mall and St. James's
Street, and the back looks over the park ; the
whole consists of three little courtyards, and is
built of brick. The entrance faces St. James's
Street exactly, and resembles an old gate between
two towers which have been left deserted. In
spite of all this, the kings of England have resided
here during the winter ever since 1697, when the
palace at Whitehall was burnt down. There is
a rumour, however, that the present King has
repeatedly expressed his intention of building a
new palace in peaceful times, but not in the same
position.

But to return to the ball. The place for
dancing is divided from the rest of the room by
a railing ; inside this space nobody is admitted
except the royal family and suite and those who
dance minuets. All the rest of the room is
occupied by benches, and a gallery runs all round
for lookers-on and the band. Only one couple
dances the minuet at a time, and as there are
usually more ladies than gentlemen, each lady
dances only one minuet, and every man two.

The Duke of Devonshire, as the King's Chamberlain, calls up every one in turn, and, in order that he may know how many people wish to dance, each person must send in his name on the previous day to be put down on the list. Rank in England is decided exclusively according to class, and not according to service; consequently, the duchesses dance first, then marchionesses, then dukes' daughters, then countesses. Foreigners have no rank at all in England, so they may not dance before the lords and barons; after them, all the rest who have no rank and happen to be near, are called up by the Chamberlain. For this reason, foreigners seldom dance at Court; exceptions to this are Herr von Edelsheim, amongst the gentlemen, and amongst the ladies, Privy Councillor von Münchhausen's daughter and granddaughter, who have received permission from their mother; much to the astonishment, however, of foreigners and natives, as it frequently happens that they only dance quite at the last, and after people who rank much below them.

Towards twelve o'clock, as soon as the second English dance has taken place, the King and Queen retire, as English etiquette does not allow

them to dance at public parties. We also followed
their example, and went home.

On the 2nd of December we dined with
Countess Delitz, and in the evening we went to
Drury Lane to see *Cymbeline*, and a second
piece, *The Old Maid*. In the first, a new
actress, Miss Bride, took the principal part, and
scored a great success, being received with an
applause which she fully merited, particularly as
on this second representation of the play she began
to shake off the shyness shown by an actress who
makes her first appearance in public. It seems
remarkable that she should make her first appearance on the stage in a most important and difficult
part, without having previously essayed smaller
ones ; but this may be explained by the fact that
she has acted before, not on the London stage,
but in a small summer theatre in Richmond.

On the morning of the 4th I saw the King
driving through the park on his road to Parliament. He goes with the lord-in-waiting in a state
coach drawn by eight horses ; the other principal
court officials and the rest of the suite drive in
two or three coaches drawn by six horses. Part
of the Yeomanry and liveried servants, as well as
a detachment of Horse Guards, walk in front of

the King's coach, and another detachment closes
up the procession.

In the evening we were going at eight o'clock
to a party at Bedford House, but on account of a
fearfully thick fog, which prevented us from seeing
the lamps and the burning torches in the streets,
and from finding our direction by them, we were
obliged to wait until after nine o'clock, when the
fog cleared, although not much.

On the morning of the 5th of December we
went to see the famous church of St. Paul's.
The English consider it the finest church in the
world, and if they were to add " Protestant," I
should say they were decidedly right.   It is said
that a church stood there in olden times, which,
though destroyed at the time of the Emperor
Diocletian's persecution of the Christians, was
immediately afterwards rebuilt.

In later times the church has always remained
on the same site, having been either rebuilt or
repaired, so that, as early as the year 1240, the
church, which was then new, was considered one
of the finest buildings extant, being 690 feet in
length, 130 feet wide, and 150 feet high in the
middle, whilst the tower was 534 feet high from
the ground.   Accurate accounts are preserved of

the splendour and beauty of the inside of this church. But in the length of time even this work has perished. As early as 1444 the wooden tower was burnt down ; in 1462 it was rebuilt ; one hundred years later it experienced the same fate, and not only the tower, but also part of the church was consumed by fire. The latter, but not the tower, was restored some time after.

In the year 1632 the famous architect, Inigo Jones, spent nine years in repairing the whole of the old building, which was in ruins with the exception of the tower, at a cost of nearly £36,000. Throughout the Revolution, which took place in England soon after, this church suffered so much, that soon after King Charles II. came to the throne, preparations were made, not for impossible repairs, but for building quite a new church, and the second English "Vitruvius," the architect Christopher Wren, received orders to prepare the plans.

In the church is still preserved the artistic and complete wooden model of his first plan, which was rejected, as the bishops did not think it adapted to a bishop's cathedral, although the architect had designed it with great beauty and splendour. After this, a second plan of the church (as it now is) was approved of, and the work was begun in the year 1665.

When you read how difficult it was to pull down the old building, you cannot help admiring the way in which it was accomplished ; in my opinion, this is so remarkable that I cannot resist mentioning it here. At first they began to pull down the old walls, but as this cost the lives of so many workmen, in consequence of the height (eighty feet) and great danger, Wren was obliged to try something else, viz. powder. He had a pit dug, about four feet wide, under one of the foundation pillars, and thence a hole of about two feet square drilled by a special tool right in the centre of the pillar, in which he placed a box containing powder. This hole was then closed up again as tightly as possible, leaving only a narrow tube to light the powder by.

This small quantity of powder lifted not only the whole pillar with the two arches resting on it, but also both the adjoining ones, with everything above them. All this it appeared to do quite gently, as the walls broke right to the top and fell in one heap in the middle after the centre weight had been lifted about nine inches, and without the least scattering of any part. This lasted about half a minute, when the dreadful heap of rubbish opened in two or three places and the smoke issued out.

All this was not accomplished without so much shaking that the neighbours took it for an earthquake. A second similar experiment was made by another person appointed by the architect. Thinking himself very wise, he did not conform strictly to the instructions received, but used a larger amount of powder, and failed to stop up the hole well, or to dig right down to the foundation. This caused a stone to fly, as if it had been shot out of a gun, through the window of a house in the vicinity, which frightened some women sitting there at work, but luckily did not cause any further damage ; whereupon the use of powder in this work was entirely prohibited.

The architect had consequently to think of some other invention, which he finally adopted from the battering-rams which the ancients used in war. He prepared a mast forty feet long, stoutly encased with iron in front, and with cords and straps nailed on to it ; he then put thirty men to move it, and to hit it against the wall all day long ; but without any effect. In spite of this, he was not discouraged, and he resumed operations

next day, when he found after a short while that
the wall began to move ; at last it suddenly fell
right over.

The church, which is built on the site where
the former building stood, is in the form of a
cross ; the thick walls are supported and adorned
by two rows of double columns, one above the
other, the lower ones Corinthian and the upper ones
composite. The spaces between the windows and
the architrave of the columns are filled with many
beautiful decorations. The west facade has a
handsome portico, with twelve double Corinthian
columns below, and eight composite ones above,
all fluted, with a fine little turret at each corner, so
that on approaching the church from Temple Bar,
this entrance, with the two turrets and the huge
dome in the middle at the back, strikes the eye
by its splendour.

The whole church has been built of white
Portland stone. In front of the entire length of
the façade are steps of a kind of black marble.
In the pediment over the portico is a representation of the Conversion of St. Paul, by an artist
called Bird who was immortalized by this work.
The most difficult problem in this bas-relief was
to express the light descending on St. Paul, which

he succeeded in doing with the same success as he showed in the rest of the work.

The huge dome over the centre of the building has a very striking appearance ; twenty-four feet above the moulding of the church is a circle of thirty-two columns with niches between them, and over the moulding is a fine gallery and balustrade. Over this again are pillars, with windows between, shaped into the dome, which here begins to decrease in width gradually, until it ends in a vault thirty-two feet high. A balcony leads all round this, and in the centre above rises the lantern, which is adorned with Corinthian columns and ends at the point with a huge gilt ball and cross. Around this entire building, measuring 2292 feet in circumference and 340 feet in its full height, a low stone wall is built, with a balustrade of cast iron, $5\frac{1}{2}$ feet high, with seven wide gateways, which is considered by the English to be the finest in the world. The cost of this alone amounted to £11,202 0s. 6d.

On going up the steps on this side, you come to three doors, close to one another. The middle one, and the largest, is encased in marble, and above is a fine bas-relief representing Paul preaching to the Athenians. On entering by this door,

near which hang the standards taken from the
French at the capture of Louisburg in the year
1758, you are struck by the magnificent sight of
the high and thick pillars which divide the church
into the principal nave and two side aisles, and
of the large choir at the end, the whole being
covered with many decorations, quite in keeping
with the splendour of the building. According
to the architect's intention, the entire vaulted
ceiling was to have been inlaid with mosaic, but
this was not approved, and good paintings by
Thornhill were substituted, eight of which represent scenes from the life of St. Paul.

The last or highest stone in the tower was
laid by the architect's son, also named Christopher
Wren, in the year 1710; so that the building
was erected within thirty-five years by the same
architect and the same principal master mason,
and during the lifetime of one Bishop of London,
named Dr. Henry Compton.[1] The only building
which could be compared with this would be St.
Peter's at Rome, which took 150 years to build,
under twelve architects, one following the other.

From St. Paul's we made a tour through the
City, to look at several of the so-called Inns or

[1] Dr. Compton was translated from Oxford in 1675.

Colleges; amongst them Gray's Inn and New Inn. But we found nothing in their exterior worthy of remark.

On the 8th there was a great court at the Princess of Wales's, and after dinner we went to introduce Herr von Lichtenstein to Countess Delitz, and subsequently returned home.

On the 9th, although we went to the Lower House of Parliament, we had to turn back, being unable to reach the Gallery, after having been pushed about for hours, on account of the crowds of people, who were principally women. This obstruction had been so great that even many of the members could not get in; the consequence was that on the following day a law was passed to the effect that, as a rule, members only were to be admitted during debates.

In the evening we saw the comedy *Rule a Wife and have a Wife* at Drury Lane, and the second piece, *The Old Maid*, in two acts; both are rather good.

On the 10th of December we remained at home until the time for the theatre, when I saw *Cymbeline* performed at Drury Lane for the second time, and a pantomime, *Fortunatus*, but my brother went to Covent Garden, where he saw *The Miser*, by Molière, and a musical after-piece, *Thomas and Sally*, or *The Sailor's Return*.

On the 11th we went to the King's *levée*, and in the evening to the Countess of Yarmouth's.

On the 12th we dined at the Club, and spent the evening at Privy Secretary Meyer's house, where we remained to supper.

On the 13th we went to Court, and after dinner to Lady Yarmouth's, and to the Sunday assembly at my Lady Harrington's, also to Princess St. Severino's, who has taken this Sunday for her assemblies, as the parties at Madame Hop's have ceased since the death of her husband.

On the morning of the 14th we drove to Rotherhithe, a district on the other side of the Thames, close to Deptford and nearly opposite to the end of the City ; as it adjoins Southwark, it is considered to belong to it, and consequently also to London, although in former times it had been a village by itself. We saw there a new East Indiaman launched, which received the name of *Britannia*, and was built as usual to carry thirty guns.

Before she was launched, Mr. Thomas Howe, who himself commands an East Indiaman, showed us the whole internal and external arrangements.

All ships of the East India Company are built
alike, and although they are pierced for thirty
guns, they invariably carry no more than twenty-
six ; notwithstanding this, they look, owing to
their size, like men-of-war of forty guns. On
account of the cargo which they carry, they are
built larger than ships of thirty guns generally
are. With a full cargo, they draw nineteen feet
of water. Owing to their size and apparent
strength, they are rarely attacked by privateers,
who generally fear that they are men-of-war of
forty guns. Furthermore, it would take a good-
sized privateer to tackle an East Indiaman, which
carries twenty-six guns and is otherwise fully
manned. Thus they have nothing to fear unless
they meet a man-of-war or several privateers in
company.

Before the *Britannia* was launched, her new
captain, the son of an East India Company's
director from the City, drank a glass of wine
with his father and others of the Company, and
broke the bottle against the keel of the ship—a
custom which is always followed—the band on
the ship striking up and continuing to play
during the ship's progress into the water. The
dock was not at all steep, and the high water

came up close to the ship when on the stocks ; she did not move at all fast, on the contrary quite slowly. The captain had prepared a grand repast in the shipbuilder's house for those of both sexes who had been invited, and in the evening he gave a ball in the City, to which he asked us ; but we excused ourselves and drove straight home, in order to enable my brother to go after dinner to Privy Councillor von Münchhausen's, and I remained at home.

On the 17th of December we went to Court, and in the evening to Drury Lane, where a good comedy, *The Way to Keep Him*, was performed. As we had seen the second piece, *Polly Honeycomb*, several times before, we left after the hornpipe, which Miss Dawson danced very nicely, and went to Countess Yarmouth's.

On the morning of the 19th we went to Madame v. Münchhausen's, who receives every Saturday, and dined at the Club. In the evening my brother went to Drury Lane, and I to Mrs. Richardson's, where we had supper, my brother coming on there after the play.

On the 20th my brother went to Court, and we dined with Lady Yarmouth, and in the evening went to the Princess St. Severino's.

On the 21st we went to the King's *levée*; we dined with Mistress Fettyplace, my Lady Howe's second daughter, and the rest of the day we spent at Privy Councillor Münchhausen's Monday assembly.

On the 22nd we dined with Stanhope, one of the three Gentlemen Ushers of the Privy Chamber to the Queen, who had made my mother and sister's acquaintance at Stade,[1] where he had been one of the suite who had received the Queen on her way to England : for this reason he showed us much civility. He was married to the granddaughter of the late Duke of Chandos, and daughter of his eldest son, the Marquess of Carnarvon, who never became Duke, having died before his father. She had first been married to a Captain in the Life Guards, and brought him a fortune of £70,000, so that he is pretty well off. She is now Lady Catherine Stanhope, as she keeps her title by courtesy as an earl's daughter, according to the English custom, with "my Lady" prefixed to her Christian name and her husband's surname, although he is not a lord.

In the evening I went to Lady Sharp's, where

[1] Where his father was Commander-in-Chief.

we had been invited, and afterwards to Lady
Yarmouth's, who had also invited us to an
assembly.

On the 23rd we dined at my Lord Howe's,
and in the evening saw Shakespeare's tragedy,
King Lear, played at Drury Lane. This play is
very much in the style of the old English plays
in fashion when the author wrote it, in which
most of the characters go mad, or get blind, or
die ; but as English taste has changed latterly,
many alterations have been made in this tragedy ;
amongst others the omission of the court jester,
who in the original brings his tomfooleries in
everywhere, even in the most tragic scenes ; but
he is the only servant who remains faithful to
his old king and master. The second piece,
Polly Honeycomb, we had to put up with
again.

On the morning of the 24th we drove in
company with the Commander-in-Chief, Count
von der Schulenburg, Herr Dean von Vinke,
and Herr von Arnheim, to Greenwich, five
English miles from London Bridge, close to
the Thames, and consequently just opposite the
last houses of London. We went first to the
Park, in which stands the Royal Observatory ;

in the hall of this building are telescopes and
spy-glasses, which are used for astronomical and
land observations. In two rooms over this hall
are large tubes fixed to stands with a quadrant
for the purpose of taking daily observations of
the sky. Several fine lines in front of the
objective glass represent the meridian, the first
line of noon cutting through them at right
angles. A lamp cleverly placed above throws
sufficient light into the tubes on dark nights to
show the fine threads. By a long hair fastened to
it you can see at once whether the tube has been
displaced or not, as absolute accuracy is of the
utmost importance. The largest quadrant in
existence is to be seen here ; it measures seventeen feet. In the east room are also several
barometers, and a pendulum clock, made by
Graham of London, which is so correct that
we were assured that it had not altered a second
during the year. This shows how accurate the
workmanship must be. On the roof, in a small
receptacle, a camera obscura has also been
provided. A special person, paid by the King,
lives here in order to keep the instruments in
order, and to make the daily astronomical
observations, and to enter them in a book for

the benefit of the public, and principally for the
Academy of Science and for the Admiralty.

From here we went to the large Hospital for
indigent veterans and such sailors as have become
unfit for the King's service; without doubt one
of the grandest buildings in all England. It
stands on the site where there was formerly a
royal palace, and in fact Charles II. had erected
one wing of the present building for a palace, so
I was told, for the sum of £36,000. King
William III. dedicated it to the present purpose,
with a further sum of £19,500, and when a
private person had endowed it with £20,000
more, these sums were supplemented by further
voluntary contributions, which raised the available
fund altogether to £58,000. This sum covered
the expenses of building and fittings, so that as
early as 1705 a hundred old sailors were taken
in. Subsequently Parliament gave to the Hospital
the entire property of the Earl of Derwentwater,
as well as that of the principal leaders of the
rebellion of 1715, amounting to £60,000 a year.

All these buildings stand on a large square,
so constructed that the side facing the Thames
remains open, and the buildings on each flank
are set back. The size of all these buildings can

be gathered from the fact that, besides the houses
for the Governor, the other officers, and all kinds
of servants, there is room for 2000 sailors, and
for several hundred boys who are educated here
and turned out as sailors.

The numerous columns, decorations, splendid
porticos, and colonnades are all of Portland stone,
the best freestone in England.   There are many
points of beauty, such as the side which faces the
Thames, King George II.'s statue placed in the
middle of the square, the park adjoining the building at the back, which give to the whole the
appearance of a royal palace rather than that of a
hospital.   The chapel equals the rest in beauty
both inside and out.   The finest part is the Hall,
where dinners take place on special occasions only ;
it is very large, and painted with remarkable art
and skill by Sir James Thornhill.   The whole
ceiling and the upper end of the Hall, which is
cut off by a low balustrade, are filled with very
successful emblematical decorations.   Especially
worthy of notice amongst other pictures on the
wall at the end are the Electress Sophia, King
George I., King George II., Queen Caroline, the
Dowager Queen of Prussia, the late Prince of
Wales, the Duke of Cumberland, and their sisters,

all in different attitudes in one picture. The
curious fact is that, however keen your eyesight,
you would suppose, unless you touched them,
that all the artificial frames, which enclose the
pictures, as well as the fluted Corinthian columns
between the windows, a false door, a similar large
window opposite a real one, were really of carved
workmanship ; they are painted so transparently
that the cleverest are deceived, and suppose that
they see real objects through the glass. The
painter accomplished this optical illusion by his
cleverness in mixing his colours and in applying
them with the right amount of light and shade.
This illusion is considerably increased by the fact,
that all the windows throughout the length of
one side have been closed and painted as niches,
with large statues in each representing the Sciences.
All these niches being hollowed out, you naturally
trust your eyes readily with regard to the columns
and the rest of the decorations. Had the windows
been left open, the light in the hall would have
been strong and false, more like that of a glass
house, whilst if there were no windows the
symmetry outside would be spoilt. It cannot be
denied that the deception almost surpasses those
at Windsor and in the chapel at Oxford, and I

take this to be one of the best signs of a painter's skill.

As regards the interior arrangements of the large rooms in which the men live, there are partitions contrived like small wooden cabins and shaped like church pews or ships' cabins, sufficiently large to contain a bed, a table, and a chest for clothes, so that all the men sleep separately, though during the day they are together. Very few sailors, I believe, have been so well housed before, for every man is allowed per week 7 lbs. of bread, 3 lbs. of beef, 2 lbs. of mutton, a pint of peas, 1¼ lbs. of cheese, 2 ounces of butter, 14 quarts of beer, and 1s. for tobacco. Those who have been boatswains, mates, or other petty officers, are allowed in proportion 1s. 6d. to 2s. 6d. for tobacco. They receive also, every other year, a complete blue suit, a hat, three pairs of socks, two pairs of shoes, five neckties, three shirts, and two nightcaps. In addition to what the Hospital fund returns, and to what is added by voluntary contributions, every sailor, both in the King's service and in the Merchant Navy, has 6d. a month deducted from his pay for the benefit of the Hospital. Each sailor is taken in on showing a certificate that he is unfit for further

employment in the service of his country. At
present there are about fourteen to fifteen hundred
pensioners in the Hospital.

We went from here by water to Deptford,
which is on the London side of Greenwich and
adjoins it, in order to see the yacht *Charlotte*
in which the Queen came over to England, as
well as the royal dockyard and the storehouses.
The yacht is very luxurious, having gilt carving,
cut glass, red velvet, damask, mahogany, etc.,
everywhere. The royal cabins and sleeping
apartments are all panelled with this wood. We
also saw three men-of-war of 74 guns in process
of building ; this gave us a good opportunity to
judge of the manner of construction, as they were
all in different stages of progress.

From here some of the officers, who were
superintending the whole, took us about and
showed us the ships and stores. In a large square
building of several stories everything required
for the building and fitting out of ships (except
armament) is kept in great quantities, and in
such a state of readiness that it can be used at
any moment without any further preparation.
For instance, the sails are ready fitted with rings,
ropes, and blocks, so that they can be brought

out at once, according to their sizes, be placed on board the ship, and be fitted to the yards.

Besides the smithies for working the requisite iron, there is an especially large smithy provided for the manufacture of anchors. Each ship of 90 guns carries six anchors at least, of which the best or largest weigh 80 hundredweight, the price of each amounting to about £160. The sail-cloth costs generally 30s. for 40 yards. I asked if they did not receive a great part of the linen from Germany, but the officer said they did not, and that it all came from English manufactories; he was also of opinion that the German cloth was too broad, and chiefly $1\frac{1}{4}$ yards wide, whilst this is about three quarters of a yard in width. After having seen all this, we drove home for dinner, and remained at home the rest of the day, as well as the following, Christmas Day, the 25th, more particularly as my brother had another attack of fever that night.

On the 26th I dined at our Saturday club, and in the evening went to see *Romeo and Juliet,* and an after-piece in two acts with several songs and dances, called *Harlequin's Invasion.* In the play an entire funeral is represented, with bells tolling, and a choir singing. Juliet, feigning death, lies on a state bed with a splendid canopy over her, guarded by girls who strew flowers, and by torch-bearers with flaming torches. The choristers and clergy in their vestments walk in front, and the father and mother with their friends follow. The scene represents the interior of a church. To my feeling this appears rather profane, but putting this aside, nothing of the kind could be represented more beautifully or naturally. The funeral dirges and the choirs made the whole ceremony too solemn for theatrical representation, especially on the English stage, which has no superior in the world, and on which everything is produced with the highest degree of truth. This effect can be attained more easily here than upon any other stage, owing to the quantity of actors, including dancers and singers, of whom fifty are sometimes to be seen on one night, whilst there are probably as many absent, and the quantity of different decorations, machinery, and dresses, which are provided regardless of cost and with thorough completeness.

On the 27th I went at noon to Court, where everybody was in the greatest excitement about the Spanish war. In the evening we went to

Prince St. Severino's, and there met, amongst others, the Spanish minister, Marquis de Fuentes, with his wife, son, and daughter-in-law, who took leave of the company. I saw, for the first time, the daughter-in-law, Marquesa del Mora, who had hardly been out before, as she was just recovering from her confinement; she is said to have been twelve years old, and her husband thirteen, when they were married only a few years ago, so that even now they are mere children.

On the 29th we were invited to a ball at Lady Catherine Stanhope's, whom I have previously mentioned, to which we went at seven o'clock. The company consisted of about fourteen to fifteen couples, in addition to the few who did not dance. As I was now in quite slight mourning, I thought there could be no objection to my dancing, for some people dance here even when they are in deep mourning. I danced the first and second dance with Lady Harriet Bentinck, to whom I had been introduced for this purpose by the host, and afterwards with several others. She is an unmarried daughter of the Duke of Portland, and sister to my Lady Weymouth, one of the Queen's ladies of the bedchamber. Before one o'clock the company sat down to supper, and afterwards dancing went on again till four o'clock, when the ball was wound up with several minuets. Amongst the company was a certain Miss Pitt,[1] a very pleasant young lady, who possesses at least £100,000, and dances remarkably well into the bargain, not only English dances, but more particularly minuets ; she has also a very fine voice, combined with much talent and musical feeling. To please the company, she sang without accompaniment some airs from the Italian operas, which were not at all easy. The hostess, Lady Catherine Stanhope, likes dancing herself very much, and it was, in fact, her birthday, which her husband celebrated by this well-arranged entertainment.

On the 30th of December I had supper and played cards at Privy Secretary Best's, whose wife is a daughter of Privy Secretary Meyer's.

On the 31st of December I went to Drury Lane to see the comedy *All in the Wrong*, which is quite like a French play, and which was followed by a remarkably pretty pantomime, *The Genii*,

---

[1] Harriet, daughter and heiress of George Norton Pitt. Married, 1762, fifth Duke of Ancaster ; d. 1763.

the setting of which was handsome, whilst the dancers were good. The principal interest of the piece centres round a married couple (the lover and the sweetheart are jealous of each other), and is very well sustained until the unravelling of the plot. Yates, his wife, O'Brien, and Mistress Palmer, a daughter of the celebrated actress Pritchard, acted very well. In the pantomime a small boy danced a hornpipe very prettily, and two other children a ballet, amidst much applause. Between the first and second piece the gallery and pit made a great noise, calling out to the orchestra to play "God save great George, the King," and they would not desist until Garrick ordered it to be played, when everybody joined in and sang this well-known anthem in loud voices, which amused the King and Queen not a little.

As we had received tickets through Miss Howe from the Duke and Duchess of Richmond for the ball this evening in Soho Square, we went there after the play.

On the 1st of January, 1762, the Court at noon was very full, on account of its being New Year's Day. On these occasions an English ode, set to music, is played by the

Court band ; it did not last half an hour, and was not badly done. On this day Lady Stormont[1] was presented. She had only just arrived from Germany ; she is *née* Countess von Bernau from Dresden, and a relation of Baron von Münchhausen's, and had been married before to the Danish minister at the Saxon court of Berregard. She is handsome, has a miniature face, and is not tall. In the evening we went to the Münchhausens' and to Countess Yarmouth's, and played a game of cards at Privy Secretary von Hinüber's. The King gave a private ball again this evening.

On the morning of the 2nd we paid a number of visits, amongst others to my Lord and my Lady Chesterfield.[2] We dined at the Club, and afterwards went to see the new opera *Tolomeo*. This opera has met with more success than the former one, although I must confess that the first time I saw it I was not so much pleased with it as I was later on. There are several good airs in it, but some I had heard before

[1] Wife of the second Earl of Mansfield, seventh Viscount Stormont.

[2] Philip Dormer, fourth Earl, mar. 1722, Melusina of Schulenberg, natural daughter of George I., created in 1722 Countess of Walsingham and Baroness of Aldborough ; died without issue.

and knew well. The dances, especially the first and third, are very good, and well danced by the four principal performers.

On the 3rd my brother went to Court, and in the evening we went to my Lady Harrington's [1] and to Prince St. Severino's.

On the 4th we witnessed from Herr von Vinke's house the proclamation of the declaration of war against Spain, which took place in front of St. James's Palace. The Horse Guards, with their standard, band, and trumpeters, opened the march; four court trumpeters and one kettledrum followed; after these came the officials from Westminster, viz. the High Constable and High Sheriff on horseback, with their beadles, constables, and others; next followed six Heralds-at-Arms in full dress, each accompanied by his two assistants with their chains and two of the Horse Guards as escort, all on horseback; after these again four trumpeters with their kettledrum. All the Life Guards, with their standards and band, closed the procession.

The Queen, *en négligé*, leaned on the window-sill, which greatly increased the cheers of the

[1] William, second Earl, mar. Caroline, eldest daughter of Charles, second Duke of Grafton.

people. After the declaration of war had been
read in front of the palace, and then at Charing
Cross, the procession went on to Temple Bar,
the beginning of the City. Here the law officials
from Westminster retired, and in their stead the
Lord Mayor, Aldermen and Corporation joined
the procession, which they accompanied on its
further progress, reading the proclamation at
several places in the City, viz. Temple Bar,
Chancery Lane, and the Royal Exchange. The
evening we spent at Privy Councillor Baron
von Münchhausen's.

On the 5th of January we were presented
to Princess Amelia, the King's aunt, who held
a court for the first time during our stay in
England. We passed the time until dinner at
my Lady Yarmouth's, and we remained at home
in the evening.

On the 6th we dined at Colonel Schütz's
and spent the rest of the day with him. A few
letters, received the night before, caused us to
put off our journey to Battlestone, which had
been fixed for that day, until after the next
mail-day, although my Lady Howe started.

On the morning of the 7th I walked to the
City to see our banker, who lived close to

Tower Hill, as I intended to go to Court at noon. I did the distance, which is said to be four English miles, in an hour. I had another hour in which to transact my business with him and his clerk, who lives in another place, and an hour more to do the four miles home again, arriving in good time for luncheon. At noon we went to Court, and in the evening we had a game at cards with several foreign ministers and Germans at Baron von Münchhausen's.

On the 8th of January we remained at home until eight in the evening, on account of the post, except for our usual walk in the morning, when the weather is fine, in St. James's Park, and we spent the evening with Mrs. Richardson.

On the morning of the 9th we drove from London by High Barnet, St. Alban's and Dunstable to Battlestone, forty miles, where we arrived towards two o'clock. This property really belongs to Sir Gregory Page, who has lent it for his lifetime to his younger brother, Mr. Page, whose wife is a sister of the late Lord Howe. It lies in a remarkably pleasant situation, with a continual variation of small hills and valleys, which form the principal feature of

the place, and provide pleasant walks, especially
as some pretty wooded hills belong to it, which
are well stocked with high trees and underwood,
through which the well-kept gravel walks wind
along ; it is thus decidedly preferable to a
garden, and differs from a park only in not being
enclosed.   Below and all along the road runs a
pretty serpentine river.

The house is old and not magnificent, but
rather large and comfortable.   The dining-room
is especially well proportioned, according to my
idea, as it is 41 feet long, the width and height
being 25 feet each ; it is panelled throughout
with oak, and has a good chimney-piece of
white marble with black columns of the same
material.   The kitchen-garden is well laid out,
though not over large.

On the 13th, our host and hostess having
gone to London on business for two days, we
remained on with my Lady Howe, and drove
to Woburn Abbey, the seat of the Duke of
Bedford.[1]   The house is well built, though old,
but its situation is a great drawback, being on
low ground, which makes it so damp that fires

---

[1] John, fourth Duke of Bedford ; the Duchess, his second wife,
was Gertrude, daughter of John, first Earl Gower.

have to be kept up in all the rooms throughout the winter to preserve the valuable furniture and good pictures, which occasions no small cost, especially in England, when the coal has to be brought from a distance of nine to twelve miles. A chaldron of coal costs in London £2, and in these parts ten to twelve shillings more. If you consider how much each fireplace requires per day, and reckon the cost per year, you find that firing, however expensive it may be with us, is nothing compared with its cost in England. In a small household like my Lady Howe's it costs her yearly £70, and from this you may judge how much Woburn Abbey, in its damp situation, must cost in superfluous firing alone. The housekeeper assured us that owing to the quantity and size of the rooms, she had to keep fires for a week before they were thoroughly heated through.

The Duke, however, can easily meet this expense, as he has an income of £40,000 a year. The keeping up of all these continuous fires is all the more necessary as there are several fine pictures by old and living artists, amongst them a large piece representing David and Abigail, which I admired very much, but

I could not ascertain the name of the painter. In the long gallery are hung a quantity of large and small pictures, mostly of members of the Russell family, to which the Duke of Bedford belongs.

The house itself forms a large square ; the façade, with the entrance through it, is part of the old abbey, from which it derives its name, and serves now for the stables. Opposite, on the height, the Duke has built two wings, for stables, riding-schools and offices, each forming a square in itself with a court in the middle. The Duke is reported to have contemplated building a new mansion between these two wings, which would have had many advantages over the old one, if only from being placed on a height ; but it is said that want of water prevented him from carrrying out the idea. Probably there were other reasons, as it would have been barely a hundred yards from the old house, where there is actually a well in the offices ; consequently want of water was probably only an excuse.

Close to the house is a rather pretty garden, not over large ; but the park surrounding the house (which does not stand in the centre) is very extensive and fine, both as regards the landscape and the quantity of timber. It certainly measures from ten to twelve miles in circumference, and has varied scenery, including a stretch of about two miles planted only with pines and evergreen trees, through which broad gravel and grass walks lead. At the end is a large sheet of water with an island in the middle, on which is a Chinese pavilion. On another pretty little lake close to the house is a fine yacht of thirty to forty tons, carrying ten guns, with other smaller boats.

On the 14th fine weather permitted us to go about all the morning, but on the 15th we had to remain at home, as it rained the whole day long, and as our host and hostess came home at noon, we were able to return to town on the 16th. We were the more glad to do so, because both we and my Lady Howe wished to see her second son, Lieutenant-Colonel Howe,[1] who had returned from Belle Isle, and we had received news that he had been appointed general aide-de-camp to Lieutenant-General my

[1] Sir William Howe, seventh Baronet, succeeded his brother, fifth Viscount, general officer in the army, and colonel 19th Dragoons. B. 1729; he left no issue. He was employed in America during the War of Independence, and had chief command 1776-1778.

Lord Albemarle,[1] who had been ordered on an expedition with a corps of 16,000. In the expedition to Belle Isle he had held an appointment as Brigadier-General. He is considered by all to be a very able officer who has made a name for himself both at Belle Isle and in America.

A few weeks ago, the King gave him an appointment as Governor of Belle Isle, but he asked through his brother, Lord Howe, to be relieved of this, as he preferred to serve in the field as long as the war lasted. He is the tallest of his family, and really belongs to General Anstruther's regiment, which is at present in America, and which he himself raised as Major at the beginning of the war, as one of the ten new regiments.

On our arrival in London we found the whole family assembled (Mr. and Mrs. Howe having also arrived a few days before); a very rare occurrence, which is not likely to last long, as all three sons will soon be dispersed in different parts of the world. My Lord Howe

---

[1] Lieut.-General George, third Earl of Albemarle, Commander-in-Chief at the reduction of the Havannah in 1762, aide-de-camp to the Duke of Cumberland at the battle of Fontenoy, 1745. B. 1724, d. 1772.

will shortly take command of the fleet on the
French coast ; the second son will probably go
with the expedition to the West Indies ; and the
youngest will sail in February with his ship to
East India.

In the evening we went to the opera *Tolomeo*;
the presence of the Queen and Princess of
Wales made the singers and dancers surpass
themselves, and we were therefore much better
pleased than when we first saw it.

On the morning of the 17th we went to
Court ; and in the evening to Countess Delitz's
and to Prince St. Severino's. On the 18th the
Queen's birthday was celebrated. It is really
in the summer, but as the King's birthday also
falls at that time of year, the celebration of the
Queen's has been fixed for the winter ; otherwise everybody would have to get two new
summer costumes, besides having to get one
for winter. As matters are arranged, you can
now do with one new suit for each season. The
crush on this day was very great, especially
in the evening, when it took us a long time to
get into the ballroom. I am certain it would
not be possible to find so many beauties together
in one place as here. Amongst the sixty-two

who danced the minuet there were very few who could be called plain, and most of them deserved to be called good-looking, if not real beauties. The King and Queen left towards twelve o'clock, and we followed soon after, immediately we could get through the crowd.

On the 19th we went to see the Opera Buffo, *Bertoldo;* it is poor and has met with so little success that it has only been performed twice, and in its place the old opera *Il Mercato* will be reproduced till a new one is ready.

On the 20th Lady Northumberland gave a large assembly (I have already given a description of the house during the beginning of my stay here); this party was again very numerously attended, and the hostess herself said that she had sent out 636 invitations, not counting the people whom she had asked by word of mouth, and as there were hardly any refusals, it is certain that 700 people were present. Amongst them the minister from Tripoli and his son were present. To the father the time must have appeared very tedious, as he cannot converse with any one; but the son, who speaks English, associates with everybody. At last, about half-past twelve, we got our carriage, although we had intended leaving much sooner.

On the 21st we passed the afternoon and evening at Mrs. Oliver's, whose acquaintance, and that of her two daughters, we had made at Bath.

On the morning of the 22nd we went to a *levée* at Court, and were present at the ceremony of the presentation by the Lower House of the address to the King, in answer to his speech in Parliament of three days previously. In it he had given them the reasons which induced him to declare war with Spain. On such occasions the King sits on his throne, with his hat on his head, and in this position he awaits the Speaker, who approaches him accompanied by many of the members. After making three bows, the Speaker reads the address. After the King has given a short answer, which he invariably does offhand and with much charm, the Speaker retires backwards, again making three bows.

In the evening we went to the usual Friday assembly at the Duchess of Bedford's; this was the first party she had had since Christmas.

On the 23rd we drove to Drury Lane to see the comedy, *The Alchemist*, and the pretty pantomime, *The Genii*, in which the dances and decorations are so beautiful. The weather was so fine all the week that we were able to take a walk every day for a few hours about noon. When it does not rain, you see everybody on the promenade in St. James's and the Green Parks. I just remember that I have not yet given a description of St. James's Palace itself; but, to confess the truth, it is not worth while, as there is absolutely nothing inside or out worth describing.

At noon on the 24th we went to Court, and in the evening to the Countess of Yarmouth's, and to the usual assembly at Prince St. Severino's. The Court was so full that we had trouble to get through the quantity of coaches and sedan chairs, so much so that I could not at first understand the reason, but the fact was, a false rumour had been spread that the Queen's brother had arrived, and this had attracted a quantity of people to Court, especially from the City.

On the 25th we attended the Monday party at Privy Councillor Baron von Münchhausen's.

On the 26th we dined with Mr. and Mrs. Heywood, sister and brother-in-law to the young Lady Howe, and we spent the evening at

Herr v. Fincke's, in company with Herren v. Vinke, Lichtenstein, v. Werpup, and v. Reden.

On the 27th we wrote our names down at Prince Charles of Mecklenburg's, the Queen's brother, who had arrived on Monday night; from there we went to the King's *levée*, and dined at noon with Prince Charles. In the evening we first went to Madame Hinüber's and played a game at cards, and from there by invitation to a party at my Lady Holdernesse's. My Lord Holdernesse's house is, to my idea, one of the prettiest I have seen, the furniture, and particularly the pictures harmonize with the whole. The first room which you enter is situated between the two other rooms where the company was assembled, and is vaulted, so that the light falls from above.

The Court was numerously attended on the morning of the 28th, especially by ladies (the Queen's brother being the principal attraction), who came partly out of civility to the Queen, who was surrounded by all her ladies-in-waiting, some of whom were on duty, others not, and partly out of curiosity to see the Prince. The Queen, who is always remarkably gracious, was especially so to-day towards us, and assured us that she was glad her brother had arrived at a time when he would see so many good friends and acquaintances, and also that she was pleased to hear from him that he had left the whole of our family in good health.

In the evening we saw the comedy *Florizel and Perdita* at Drury Lane and *Catherine and Petruchio* as the second piece; afterwards I went to the ball, which takes place every fortnight in a house in Soho Square, my brother being prevented from going by a bad cold.

On the 29th I went to Covent Garden to see *The Beggars' Opera* and a fine pantomime, *Apollo and Daphne*, or *The Burgomaster's Tricks*, and my brother went to Countess Yarmouth's.

On the 30th we played cards at Lady Diana Clavering's,[1] a daughter of my Lord De La Warr, and wife of the English minister to the Landgraf of Hesse Cassel.

On the 31st, at noon, we went to Court, where there was again a great crowd of people, and in the evening we went to Prince St. Severino's, and from there to the party at the Duchess of Hamilton's,[2] whose present husband

---

[1] Daughter of John, seventh Lord and first Earl of De La Warr.

[2] Duchess of Hamilton, eldest daughter of John Gunning; she married, secondly, Lord Lorne, Duke of Argyll.

is my Lord Lorne, who will become Duke of
Argyll after the present Duke's death, so that she
will become a Duchess for the second time. She
is the elder of the two Miss Gunnings from
Ireland, whose beauty created a great sensation,
and procured for both of them most advantageous
marriages, although they did not come of a great
or rich family. Her sister, who became Lady
Coventry, is said to have been even handsomer,
as you can gather from her portrait.

On the 1st of February we went to see a cock-
fight, which lasted the whole of this week, where
heavy bets, made by the Duke of Ancaster and
others for more than 100 guineas, were at stake.
The fight takes place at the Cock-pit, close to St.
James's Park, in the vicinity of Westminster. In
the middle of a circle and a gallery surrounded by
benches, a slightly raised theatre is erected, upon
which the cocks fight ; they are a small kind
of cock, to the legs of which a long spur, like
a long needle, is fixed, with which they know
how to inflict damage on their adversaries very
cleverly during the fight, but on which also they
are frequently caught themselves, so breaking
their legs. One bird of each of the couples
which we saw fighting met with this misfortune,

so that he was down in a moment and unable to rise or to help himself, consequently his adversary at once had an enormous advantage. Notwithstanding this he fought him with his beak for half an hour, but the other bird had the best of it, and both were carried off with bleeding heads. No one who has not seen such a sight can conceive the uproar by which it is accompanied, as everybody at the same time offers and accepts bets. You cannot hear yourself speak, and it is impossible for those who are betting to understand one another, therefore the men who take the bets, which are seldom even, but odds, such as 5 to 4, or 21 to 20, make themselves understood to the layers of the bets by signs. There is not the slightest doubt that the bets are duly paid, although frequently the parties do not know one another, or have never even seen one another. We were satisfied with seeing two fights, although we might have remained to see still more for the 2s. 6d. which we paid on entering.

In the evening we drove with Lady Diana Clavering, her unmarried sister Lady Cecilia West,[1] my Lord De La Warr's daughters, Miss

---

[1] Daughter of first Earl of De La Warr, mar. 1763 to General James Johnston.

Speed and the gentleman she was engaged to, Baron de la Perrière, a son of the Scandinavian minister, Count de Very, to a ball given by a certain old bachelor called Räper in his house close to Gray's Inn. We took the road round the town, which was more convenient than through the City, although several miles longer, but we provided ourselves with an armed servant on horseback, because my Lady Huntingdon had been robbed a few days previously of her watch and money by a highwayman in those parts. We remained close together in our three carriages, and divided our party so that we drove in pairs, Lady Cecilia West with my brother in front, Miss Speed, who had most jewellery and was most frightened, with Baron de la Perrière, in the middle, whilst Lady Diana Clavering and myself closed the procession as rear-guard. We found only a small party, about forty ladies and as many men, all of whom, with few exceptions, consisted of City people. We danced until twelve, then had supper and dancing again afterwards, and drove home together at half-past two, but this time through the town, after having spent a very pleasant evening. I danced, amongst others, with a very pleasant and rich merchant's wife,

named Nesbit, who at once asked our entire party
to dinner on the 18th, and to go with her afterwards to the great subscription ball in the City,
to which guests are invited.

We spent the evening of the 2nd of February
with Countess Yarmouth, after having paid a few
visits in the morning. On the 3rd we went
to my Lady Holdernesse's Wednesday party, to
which the ladies, whom the hostess desires to
see, receive an invitation on each occasion, but
gentlemen, and especially foreigners, may always
come to it uninvited. We spent the evening
of the 4th at the house of Mrs. Bladon, who
lives opposite us, and on the 5th we went to the
Duchess of Bedford's.

The weather, which had become colder during
the last few days, did not prevent us from taking
our usual walk in the Park or from paying visits
on foot, and going about to the shops, all of which
form a part of the necessary exercise which you
must take on account of the substantial food you
get here. On the 6th we dined with Prince
Charles of Mecklenburg, and in the evening went
with him to the opera *Tolomeo*.

On the 7th we went to Court, and in the evening first to Lady Diana Clavering's and afterwards

to my Lady Barrington's. At the first of these
places we found the two Misses Bladon, who vie
with each other in perfection of beauty, amiability,
and accomplishments. Perhaps the younger surpasses her sister in skill on the piano and also
sings better, but nothing can equal the voice of
the elder, the clearness, technique and power of
which cannot be surpassed. Lady Diana Clavering herself sings very nicely, and the daughter of
old General Rich, sister of the younger General
Rich, is supposed to be one of the best musicians
among the ladies ; she also sings with much taste,
although the strength of her voice has been
impaired in consequence of a constitutional weakness of chest from which this humpbacked lady
suffers.

These four ladies gave us a most pleasant
musical entertainment until ten o'clock. The
two Misses Bladon are also rich "parties," for
they are said to have £20,000 to £30,000 each,
a sum which will be doubled after the death of
an uncle.

On the morning of the 8th we drove into the
City in order to pay visits ; to Mr. Räper, at
whose house we had danced, and to our host and
hostess with whom we are to dine on the 18th.

In the evening we saw the opéra comique, *Le Nozze de Dorina,* which does not meet with much success. After the opera we went to Baron von Münchhausen's party.

On the 9th we went first of all to the studio of an artist, Miss Reed, in order to see her portrait in pastille of a lady of our acquaintance, Lady Diana Clavering, whose picture we took home with us. From the various good portraits which I have seen by her, I gather that her work is very successful; some of her portraits of the beauties of society were very good likenesses. After this we drove to the court at the Princess of Wales's, where the crush was again so great that we did not get our carriage before a quarter-past five o'clock. We spent the evening at Lady Egremont's party, to which we had been invited. On the 10th we dined with Privy Secretary von Reiche in Almack's tavern, and in the evening went to my Lord De La Warr's.

On the 11th we dined with a large party at the house of the Dutch ambassador, Borcel; whence we went to Privy Councillor Baron von Münchhausen's for half an hour, and then on to the usual ball at Soho.

On the afternoon of the 12th we joined a party at Lady Diana Clavering's, where we found the two Misses Bladon. On the 13th we went to the opera *Tolomeo*.

On the evening of the 14th we called on the Countess von Delitz, and afterwards went to the Neapolitan minister's, Prince St. Severino.

On the 15th we dined with my Lady Yarmouth, and afterwards went to the Opera to see the fine Burletta, *Il Philosopho di Campagna*, and from there to a special subscription ball at Soho, and on the 16th to a party to which we had been invited by Lady Northumberland.

On the 17th we went at one o'clock to the large saloon in Spring Gardens, where four Germans gave a concert with the clarionet and French horn. We dined at noon, and spent the evening at Privy Secretary von Hinüber's, but we went between whiles at two o'clock for half an hour to Lady Holdernesse's Wednesday party.

On the morning of the 18th we went to Court, and drove from there at three to the City so as to reach Mrs. Nesbit's in time for dinner; she is a pleasant, lady-like woman, one of the Cobham family. Her husband is a member of Parliament, and still a young man, who is interested in a great many businesses together with his brothers.

We had a very good dinner with a small but select company. After seven o'clock we all drove to the subscription ball, which took place in the Haberdashers' Hall in the City, where we found a very large party of 250 ladies and a larger number of men. Besides the subscribers, all of whom must be City men, as nobody from the Westminster side is admitted, foreigners were the only people in this instance, according to the usual custom, who were honoured with an invitation. The Genoese minister, D'Ageno, opened the ball before our arrival. As soon as we entered, we were asked to dance the minuet, and one of the stewards of the ball immediately proceeded to find us partners for the English dances. As usual, cards were being played in the other rooms, and tea, hot wine, bread and butter, were served round. As we and several others intended to go on that same night to the dance in the opera-house at the Haymarket, which does not open until eleven, we tried to get to our carriage before the end of the ball. We arrived after midnight at our second ball, where we found them still busy dancing minuets, so that we also began again, and went on dancing till four o'clock. The opera-house was arranged as a ballroom by means of tapestry, red damask, etc., and well lit. As everybody at both these balls was in mourning, with black buckles and no jewels, for the late Empress of Russia (here in England every one goes into Court mourning for a week), the sight was not so brilliant as it would have been ordinarily when everybody appears either in colours or in slight mourning, and with jewels, which are worn in profusion on such occasions. We did not reach home until half-past four.

On the 19th I dined with the Commander-in-Chief, Count von der Schulenburg, and Herr von Arnheim ; in the evening we played cards and had supper at Mrs. Stanley's, the mother of one of the Lords of the Admiralty, who was in Paris last summer when the treaty of peace was signed ; she lives with her two unmarried daughters in a very well furnished house in which are several fine pictures, amongst others an especially good landscape with figures of men and animals in it, by Elsheimer, which is said to be priceless. Two others, one representing a battle-piece and the other the Tower of Babel, cannot be seen satisfactorily except through a magnifying-glass, on account of the enormous number of small figures. It is well known that the Tower of Babel is generally painted with a road which winds round and gradually ascends like a covered staircase. It is so represented here, but with the addition of booths and shops all the way up, and although this can hardly be noticed with the naked eye, you discover, by means of the magnifying-glass, that there are numerous shops, in some of which meat, in others bread, etc., are sold, to suit the different requirements of mankind. Three other very fine pieces represent a true story of travellers, who fell into the hands of robbers and were murdered by them. As the hostess in her youth had painted wonderfully well in water-colours, all her own works are hung round amongst the others, and do not suffer by comparison with this collection, which, though not large, is well assorted.

To the ceilings of the rooms, which are papered, and which have been evenly painted, decorations of *papier maché* have been added, which look like stucco. This material is said to be in general use in London, and I must confess I should never have taken it for what it really is. I must mention that Mrs. Stanley is a daughter of the famous Sir Hans Sloane, who endowed the British Museum.

On the 20th of February the Prince of Mecklenburg lunched with us at my Lady Howe's. Afterwards we dined at my Lady Yarmouth's, a party of Germans, viz.: Privy Secretary von Reiche, Privy Secretary von Meyer with his wife, Privy Secretary von Hinüber and his wife, Privy Secretary Best and his wife, and my Lady Howe. We spent the evening playing cards.

On the 21st we went to Court; the Queen did not appear, as she had been taken ill in chapel. We spent the evening with my Lord De La Warr, at whose house we had supper.

On the 24th we first went to the house of Miss Speed, who had asked us to a party, and from there we went to General and Mrs. Barrington's,[1] where we had supper in very pleasant company. This is the same Barrington who took Guadelupe in 1758; he had just

---

[1] Hon. John Barrington, Major-General and Colonel of the 8th regiment, father of the third Viscount Barrington.

received orders to go to Ireland in order to take command of the troops, as he is Major-General on the Irish Establishment.

At three o'clock in the morning, immediately after returning from supper, we started off on our journey to Portsmouth in company with Prince Charles of Mecklenburg to see the embarkation of the troops and the accompanying fleet under the command of my Lord Albemarle,[1] which were leaving on an expedition to the West Indies. We had been waiting several days for orders from my Lord Anson[2] to start, and Lord Anson had been waiting for a favourable wind to bring the transport vessels from the Downs to Portsmouth. At last, on this very day, the desired wind was blowing. Thereupon the Prince left at three o'clock in the afternoon, with the two brothers Delitz and Herr von Reden, in company with my Lord Anson and two other Lords of the Admiralty, Lord Villiers and Mr. Pelham, with the intention of driving thirty-four miles as far as Godalming and remaining there for the night. As we felt convinced we should be able to catch

[1] George, third Earl of Albemarle, aide-de-camp to the Duke of Cumberland at the battle of Fontenoy, Commander-in-Chief at the reduction of the Havannah, 1762.

[2] Lord Anson, Vice-Admiral, First Lord of the Admiralty; d. 1762.

them up, provided we could only find horses on
the road, we determined to enjoy part of the
night and not to give up the anticipated pleasure
of our evening party. We did not start, therefore, until the party was over, and we arrived at
Godalming on the 25th of February at half-past
eight o'clock, barely half an hour after the Prince
and his party had left. Here we found it impossible to get on, as the others had taken twenty
horses, and those which were to be had in this
small place and in the neighbourhood were being
kept in readiness for the Duke of York, who also
required twelve to fourteen horses.

After having thought in vain for some time of
means of getting off, the hostess at last proposed
a plan, which at first we did not like at all,
but which was our only alternative, viz. to take
seats in the so-called flying machine. This was a
kind of post-coach, which travels with remarkable
speed from one place to another, as, for instance,
between London and Portsmouth. Eight of these
are on the road daily, four passing each way.
Each of the four starts in the morning from its
appointed house in London, has its own change
of horses and stopping-places for breakfast, dinner,
and tea, and arrives between 6 and 7 p.m. in

Portsmouth, a distance of seventy-two miles from London.

In such a carriage there is room for six persons ; one can sit on the box, three or four behind, on the great back seat, and, in cases of necessity, two more can sit on the top. The passengers whom I found in the coach, and with whom I made the whole journey to Portsmouth, thirty-eight miles, consisted of a captain in the service of the East India Company, called Campbell, with his young and handsome wife (they were going to the East Indies), whom he had married only four months previously in Scotland, and who was related to the Duke of Argyll's family through her mother ; also a young man whom they take with them ; a skipper's wife, and another very pleasant man. The first-mentioned couple had met with a similar misfortune to ours, and had been waiting since one o'clock at night at Godalming for want of horses, so they also were forced to take this coach as a makeshift.

My brother was less fortunate, as all the way he had the company of a fat English innkeeper's wife, who kept her brandy-bottle handy, two sailors' wives, and one other man, who was the only one of the party with whom he could converse, and who left the coach after the first four miles. As each coach has its own special stopping-places, my brother and I did not see each other again until we arrived at our destination. The moment I entered this machine I called to mind the stories in *Joseph Andrews*, *Tom Jones*, and other similar novels, in which the most ridiculous, but life-like descriptions are given of such journeys, and of the company, conversations, and adventures.

The first sight of people of different classes and sexes who are perfectly unknown to each other occasions at the outset deep silence, as nobody knows what to make of his neighbour or how to begin a conversation. At last some one begins to talk of the road and the weather; this gradually brings up other subjects, such as how long one is on the road, etc. A political discussion is sure to follow, especially with English people, so that gradually you get better acquainted, and time passes until you arrive at your destination, where, on alighting, you find dinner ready on the table.

All this happened with us, and it was not long before I became acquainted with the handsome officer's wife, who sat just opposite to me, and thus I passed the day without being bored.

Meanwhile an adventure was not wanting, as there was a quarrel between our coachman and a cart-driver, who had to make room for us. This occasioned a fight, which was settled by three of the men passengers in the coach and my servant, who was sitting behind, coming to the aid of their coachman and making the carter get out of the way by using force and administering a good licking, thus gaining the victory. Meanwhile I, as a careful strategist, guarded the baggage and coach with the lady inside, and formed the *corps de reserve*, so as to cover the retreat in case of necessity.

We had intended on the evening of our arrival at Portsmouth to go to the Prince's quarters, and we sent our servant for this purpose to the dockyard to inquire for him. But the distance by road being more than an English mile, although the yard adjoined the town, the dark night and other obstacles prevented our getting an answer before ten o'clock. We remained at home, therefore, until the following morning, when we went at once to breakfast with the Prince and my Lord Anson, whence we went on together to the Duke of York's. There we found the entire General Staff of

the expedition, viz. my Lord Albemarle, com-
manding the troops as Lieutenant-General ; the
Major-Generals Elliot and la Fausille ; Colonel
Keppel, brother of Lord Albemarle, who was
serving on this occasion as Major-General ;
Colonels Carlton, as Quartermaster-General, and
Howe, as Adjutant-General, with six aides-de-
camp of the General's ; Admiral Pocock, com-
manding the entire fleet of the expedition ;
Commander Keppel,[1] second brother to Lord
Albemarle, who will command the landing of the
troops ; and others.

An instance will rarely be found where three
brothers together form the principal persons in
one expedition, and, though jealousies between
officers in the army and navy which mar the
success of the most carefully arranged under-
takings are no rare occurrence, especially amongst
Englishmen, on this occasion there was no
ground for the slightest apprehension, but rather
reason to expect a successful issue, as every care
seems to have been taken to select the best men
whose ability can be depended upon. We drove,
towards eleven o'clock, with the whole of this
company to the other side of the town to the

[1] Commander Keppel, eminent Admiral ; d., unmarried, 1786.

S

flat shore, and saw Lord Frederick Cavendish's[1] 34th regiment of Infantry embark, after the regiment had marched past the Prince in splendid style. The 72nd regiment, the Duke of Richmond's, had already gone on board the day before.

Since the beginning of this war the English have very much accelerated the embarkation and disembarkation of troops by inventing for the purpose a kind of flat boat; in which invention my Lord Howe has taken a considerable part. These boats are arranged for fifty to sixty men; their shape is somewhat similar to that of the long boats which men-of-war generally carry, but they are much larger, and have flat bottoms for the purpose of getting closer into shore. As the arrangements for the embarkation of this regiment were the same as those adopted in the case of expeditions, we were enabled to get an accurate idea of the particular usefulness of these boats.

All these flat boats, each of which has twenty to twenty-four oars, were lying in one row along the shore, and as soon as the regiment had marched

---

[1] Lord F. Cavendish, son of third Duke of Devonshire, Field-Marshal, Col. 34th foot; b. 1729, d. 1803.

past, it formed up again close to the shore, and awaited the signal for entering the boats. Immediately on this being given, each officer marched with his men to the boat, of which he had previously received the number ;   then he and his drummer entered first and passed right through from the bows on shore to the stern, the whole division following him without breaking their ranks ; so that in two minutes everybody was in the boat.

The officers and drummers, with their corporals, sit aft near the rudder, the privates in two or three rows behind one another on the thwarts, holding their muskets before them, and two petty officers sit in the bows, but the oarsmen occupy especial rows between the soldiers, and a little in front of them, so as not to be hampered in the use of their oars.   As soon as everything has been arranged in this way, the naval officer commanding the embarkation gives a signal, when all the boats start off at the same time and row to their respective vessels.

In order to have a better view of this manœuvre, our whole company took seats in barges, in which we went amongst the boats and ships, and from which we afterwards landed at the house of the Governor.   He is really my Lord

Throwley, who was absent at the time; hence my Lord Albemarle had taken up his head-quarters there, and had invited the princes, with their whole suites of officers, and the visitors to dinner.

After having passed the rest of the time before dinner in seeing the fortifications and in playing chess, in which my brother won two games from the Prince of Mecklenburg and one from the Duke of York, we were very well entertained at a dinner of twenty-four courses.

In the evening everybody went to the Assembly Room at the Town Hall, where society had assembled for a ball which lasted until one o'clock at night, and was only interrupted for half an hour to drink tea and eat bread and butter. On the previous evening dancing had also been going on, in the presence of the Duke of York, but none of the princes took part in it.

On the 27th of February we saw two regiments embark, after having marched past as the others did on the previous day, but with greater speed, viz. the 22nd, Major-General Whitmore's, and that of Colonel Keppel, one of the ten regiments newly raised at the outbreak of the war.

After this was over the whole party went out

in several twelve-oared boats, in a kind of procession, to Spithead, the large roads of Portsmouth, where the men-of-war lie when ready for sea. An extensive sandbank projects here, which is called the Spit, and the end of it therefore Spithead. A certain captain in the navy, called Amherst, led the procession in his gig ; after him came the two princes with Sir George Pocock, my Lord Albemarle, and my Lord Anson. This barge carried the large British standard, with the white beam over the arms, as the emblem of the Duke of York, who is heir presumptive to the throne. In the third barge, which carried the Admiralty flag—a gold anchor in a red field—were seated the Gentlemen of the Admiralty and several others, as far as the space would allow ; in the fourth, which carried Rear-Admiral Geary's flag, were, besides the Admiral himself, General Elliot, ourselves, and several others. The emblem of a Rear-Admiral consists of two large balls on the English flag, and as this Admiral is of the blue, these balls were blue.

The fifth barge carried Commodore Keppel's broad pennant ; the rest, including the eleventh and last, were captains' barges.

In this order we proceeded, and for nearly an

hour passed round and between all the ships, which were manned. This means that every officer and sailor stands at his post, all sailors stand on the yards, and the Marines, with their bands, are drawn up on the upper deck. It is certainly a wonderful sight to see several hundred sailors at the same time standing upon the yards, especially from a slight distance, where it looks as if a swarm of bees had settled upon the ship. On passing any vessel near or at a distance, three cheers are given, with a general waving of hats round the sailors' heads.

At last we came alongside of a ship of ninety guns, the *Namur*, being Admiral Pocock's, upon which he entertained the whole company to dinner. As soon as the princes and ourselves had come on board, the Admiral saluted them with twenty-one guns, and had his flag at once lowered and that of the Duke of York hoisted instead ; at the same moment all ships in the roads saluted, with many guns, which was a splendid sight, as the ships were lying all around us, and gave us some idea of a naval action. We passed the time until dinner in viewing the whole ship, and afterwards dined at a long table for twenty-five persons, which, however, barely took up the whole

length of the fore cabin. The *Namur* is considered
one of the finest vessels of this size. Towards
evening we were taken back in the same order as
we had come, and were again saluted by all the
ships with manned yards and as many guns as
before ; this gave us a different view, as we were
at sea between the ships in our small boats. We
came on shore in the town, close to a coffee-house,
in which the Duke of York gave coffee to every
one ; whilst Prince Charles of Mecklenburg, my
Lord Anson, and their suite took the road back
to London, intending to reach Petersfield before
night, so as not to travel at the same time as,
or to interfere with, the Duke of York, who
wished to take the same road on the following
day, and to avoid a possible want of horses at the
stations.

The Duke, with the rest of the party, again
went to the Assembly Room, where dancing took
place as on the previous day. I danced with the
young lady whom I had met on the journey,
and as she had the honour both of starting the
minuets and the English dances, she opened the
ball with me.

On both these days, in addition to all this, we
happened to get a view of two large men-of-war

leaving the harbour (where the ships are lying under repair or fitting out) under full sail, and proceeding to the roads ready for sea ; on both occasions they passed close to our boat. On the first day it was the *Union* of ninety guns, which is bound for a fresh destination ; she is the ship which my brother had seen launched at Chatham in 1756, and she represents the union of England and Hanover, bearing the arms of both countries. On the next day we saw the *Valiant* of seventy-four guns, Commodore Keppel's ship, which came out in order to take in her guns again. She had received great damage in the heavy storm which had caught Keppel on the French coast before he gave over the command of the fleet, and the repairs in Portsmouth had been made with great expedition.

The strength of the fleet for this expedition consists only of five ships of the line from Portsmouth, the *Namur* of ninety guns, Admiral Pocock ; the *Valiant* of seventy-four, Commodore Keppel ; the *Hampton Court* of sixty-four, the *Belle Isle* of sixty-four, the *Ripon* of sixty guns. Several ships will join them at sea ; for instance, some days later I saw it mentioned in the papers that in Pylmouth two ships were added, the *Barford* of

seventy and the *Florentine* of sixty guns. Probably
it will be the same with regard to the troops,
and more will join the four regiments mentioned
and the marines of the war vessels, before they
arrive at their destination.

Of the town of Portsmouth it may be said,
without doing it any injustice, that it is one of the
worst towns in England ; the houses are bad,
the streets narrow, and the inns especially, which
are not by any means equal to those usually
to be found in England, are dirty and bad. The
only good things we found in ours were clean
and good beds in a bad bedroom. This is
the reason why hardly any strangers, who have
friends here, lodge in the town ; they prefer the
dockyard, especially as, apart from strangers
who merely come to see the place, most of the
visitors are naval men, and people who have
to do with naval matters, and there is no beauty
or society in the place to attract anybody.

The town itself, as well as the dockyard, is
provided with fortifications, which are kept in
perfect order, and this is the first place in
England which I have seen surrounded by a
rampart or other fortifications, with the exception
of those round the Tower. The ground on

which all these stand is really the end of an
island called Portsea, which is connected with the
mainland at a point where it approaches it by
a bridge. Adjoining this bridge, which is well
guarded, and a few miles from Portsmouth, a
fine fort is placed, so that nobody can get to
Portsmouth from the mainland without passing
through this fort.

The dockyard joins the town, and the gates
are closed every night. Within it everybody
resides who has anything to do with shipbuilding,
store-houses, and naval affairs in general, as well
as many artisans and servants, so that it forms
a fairly large community in itself.

The stores kept there are excessively large
and important, as a quantity of people, amounting to nearly a thousand in number, are
continually kept employed there, just as at
Deptford, Chatham, Plymouth, etc., so that the
stores, however large the consumption may be,
shall not run short. The extent of the stores
in England of material likely to be required can
be gathered from the following fact. Although
on the 1st of July, 1760, the large store-houses
filled with pitch, hemp, tar, ropes, cables, oil,
turpentine, sails, etc., were burnt down quite

unexpectedly, by a fire supposed to have been occasioned by lightning, not the slightest delay or hindrance was caused in fitting out the ships, and within a few weeks everything was replaced with incredible rapidity.

Over 1050 tons of hemp, 500 tons of ropes, and 700 suits of sails, besides a corresponding quantity of tar, pitch, etc., were destroyed. The size and violence of the fire may be imagined from the nature of the material it found to consume and to spread through, and it is certainly marvellous that the damage was not greater, and that everything in the dockyard, lying in such close compass, was not completely destroyed. Of the hemp, a large part could be used again, as it had been so tightly packed that the fire, not being able to get into it, only consumed the surface, and even more than was found fit for use might have been preserved if the rain, which was pouring down the whole time, and the water from the fire-engines had not penetrated deeper than the fire.

It is supposed that as many as a thousand vessels can lie in this harbour at the same time, and it is held to be the safest harbour, for it is provided with all necessary conveniences and good qualities, having (1) the requisite protection from most winds ; (2) sufficient depth ; (3) good anchorage without any rocks, stony bottoms, etc.; (4) perfect size without obstruction ; (5) sufficient safety and protection by forts and other fortifications at the entrance ; (6) a good watch-tower ; (7) good sites for shipbuilding, where five large vessels can lie for repairs at the same time ; (8) ample provision for all the requirements of ships ; (9) great convenience in closing the harbour at night, or in time of danger ; (10) a sufficient garrison for protection against surprise.

The Isle of Wight is just opposite Portsmouth and Spithead, so that we were very close to it, but we did not visit it, as we did not care to be kept for another day. The town of Newport on it is said to be rather. pretty, but the soil is not considered to be of the best. We went, therefore, on the morning of the 28th of February, between six and seven, in Admiral Geary's small gig to Gosport, which is a fairly sized country town opposite Portsmouth, and to which you cross in less than five minutes. There we found posthorses, ordered the night before through the kindness of the Admiral, which took us the whole twenty-four miles to Southampton.

As our journey was by unrepaired and deep by-roads, the high-road round by Winchester being too far, we did not arrive at Southampton as early as we had hoped, and were in fear every moment of being upset.

Two reasons made us take our return journey to London by way of this place : first, and principally, we wished to see the son of Privy Councillor von dem Bussche of Hanover, in accordance with our promise to his parents not to leave England without seeing him ; he is here with his tutor *en pension* at a clergyman's called Boischunes : secondly, to avoid the difficulty of finding post-horses on the road which the princes had taken.

Southampton is supposed to be one of the prettiest and healthiest country towns in England ; it is rather extensive and well populated, and possesses several fine houses. The situation close to the sea, which runs far into the land here, and the surrounding country, make it an exceedingly pleasant place. The town has its own harbour, of no great importance, however, and the trade of the place is not extensive, being less so than it might and ought to be. The slight trade which is carried on by the inhabitants is done with the islands of Jersey and Guernsey, except at rare intervals when some ships arrive with wines from Portugal, one of which had just been unloaded when we were there.

Many people come here every year, partly for sea-bathing, partly by order of their physicians, who consider the air of Southampton to be the healthiest in all England.

You can get to Portsmouth in two hours by sea from here ; but this is rarely done, least of all in winter, when the journey is not advisable, as not only the sea is not to be trusted, but you frequently get contrary winds, and may have to spend a day or two at sea.

The short time at our disposal prevented us from seeing several fine country places in the vicinity, only a mile or two distant—as, for instance, that of General Sir John Mordaunt. We continued our journey therefore in the evening, after having paid our proposed visit, and reached Farnham, a small town forty miles from Southampton, and the same distance from London.

On the 1st of March, at half-past eleven, we arrived in London again, having done the forty miles in 4½ hours in a post-chaise with two horses, which were not ordered by our servant on horseback until the moment before we arrived.

We went on the same night to the opera
Ariadne and Tesio. It was given for the benefit of
the principal singer, Elise, but the best airs were
chosen from other operas in order to improve the
entertainment. Each of the first singers and
dancers has one evening every year when the
whole of the profits, deducting the usual expenses,
are made over to him, and the same custom is
maintained in both theatres.

On the 2nd of March we went by invitation to
my Lady Barrington's party, and dined in the
evening with my Lord De La Warr.

On the afternoon of the 3rd we dined with
Countess von Delitz ; we first spent some time
with Privy Secretary Hinüber's wife, and afterwards went for cards and supper to my Lady
Edgecumbe's.[1]

On the 4th of March we went to Court, and in
the evening I myself drove to the Countess of
Yarmouth's ; afterwards we both went to my
Lady Northumberland's large party, and wound
up the evening by going to the dance at the
opera-house.

On the 5th we and the Gentleman Usher von
Reden were presented at the King's *levée* on

[1] Widow of first Baron Edgecumbe.

taking leave ; we afterwards heard, for the first time, at Covent Garden, the oratorio *Judas Maccabeus*. These oratorios are by Handel, and are composed in the style of church music. The instrumental music is very complete and perfect. The famous Gardini played a violin concerto between the second and third acts, which, according to my ideas, he performed very well indeed. Between the first and second acts the organist played a piece which was certainly not easy. The remarkable feature in it was that this man, named Stanley, has been absolutely blind since his fourth year, and, notwithstanding this, owing to his good memory, he plays all operas and oratorios by heart. In addition to several good airs and choruses in this oratorio, a chant of victory is especially beautiful. It ends with a splendid march, with kettledrums and trumpets ; the time is beaten on a stretched parchment in perfect imitation of the sound of guns, not too powerfully, but in keeping with the loud music. The voices might have been better ; one singer, by name Fraser, who had been famous, is beginning to lose her voice, but she is better than Mrs. Scott, formerly Miss Young, who takes her present name from her husband, a brother to my Lord

Deloraine. The two men's parts are taken by Bard and Quilici; the former sings and acts at Covent Garden when there are any singing parts. His first wife was a sister of my Lord Waldegrave; she was a widow, and fell in love with him when she heard him sing. His second wife is a daughter of Rich, the old proprietor of Covent Garden theatre, after whose death recently it passed to his wife and her sister, who is also married. He belongs to the King's choir, but sings no airs better than sailors' songs, which are really his forte. The second singer, Quilici, can only be ranked amongst indifferent vocalists.

On the stage an amphitheatre is erected with a platform, on which all the musicians and singers have their seats, whilst the public sit in the same places as during the plays. Every Wednesday and Friday during Lent, one of these oratorios is played; it certainly seems rather strange to hear on one day a comedy, which is often very worldly, and on the following day, in the same place, sacred music, which always ends with an Alleluia, when everybody in the theatre quietly and devoutly rises.

At the end of the oratorio we had supper at my Lord De La Warr's.

T

At eight o'clock in the morning of March 6th we went to Chelsea, which we had not yet seen, about two miles from London. We went first to Salter's coffee-house, where we breakfasted in company with Miller, the gardener of the famous Botanical Garden at Chelsea, in a room filled with a quantity of all kinds of rare and curious objects, as detailed in a small printed catalogue of the collection. In reality there are many objects which have nothing more remarkable about them than the names given to or invented for them ; and some are erroneously mentioned as rarities. Amongst other curious things are 104 silver spoons which go into a cherry-stone, and many other small things of fine workmanship.

This gardener, Miller, is the man who edited the large Garden Dictionary, which has since been translated into German, and is a very useful book, besides several other smaller works.

After this, we went with him to see the garden, which is called the Apothecaries' Garden ; it has been given to the Apothecaries' Company by Sir Hans Sloane, on condition that they pay £5 ground-rent, and show every year fifty new kinds of plants, until the number has reached two thousand. In consequence, nearly every possible plant and tree is to be seen in it, and for the preservation of these a fine large conservatory has been built, in addition to the requisite glass-houses.

From this garden we went to Chelsea Hospital, a foundation for invalid soldiers, arranged like the one at Greenwich for invalid sailors. King Charles II. began to build it, James II. continued, and William and Mary finished it, but Christopher Wren erected the whole extensive buildings. In front, on the north side, is a large green square for the invalids, and on the south side, leading down to the Thames, is a well-kept garden.

In the centre of the building is a pediment of fourteen columns, with a small turret above the house. This is the principal entrance and passage through. On one side is the chapel, with some good carvings, and over the altar is a good picture by Sebastiano Ricci, representing the Resurrection of the dead. On the other side is the large hall, in which all the pensioners dine together; the officers are at a special table at the upper end. We entered it when the covers were laid; at each place was a tin plate, with a loaf of white bread, and a mug of beer. Every private receives daily 1 lb. meat, 1 lb. bread, $\frac{1}{4}$ lb. cheese, 2 pints of beer, and a penny for tobacco ; but in the case of the officers everything is better in proportion, and they have sixpence a day in ready money. They also receive roast meat twice a week, whereas the privates have their meat roasted (or usually boiled) only once in sixteen weeks.

A good painting by Verrio is to be seen in this hall : a life-size picture of Charles II.

The Governor, who is at present General Rich, receives £500 a year, the Lieutenant-Governor half this sum, and the Major £150 ; 36 officers, as mentioned above, receive 6d. a day ; 30 non-commissioned officers and 34 cavalry ditto 2s. a week ; 48 corporals and drummers 10d. ; and 336 privates 7d. to 8d. a week.

They have to do duty and mount guard ; prayers are said twice daily. The two chaplains, the doctor, the secretary, the clerk, the deputy treasurer, the steward, etc., each have £100 a year, and in addition to all this, 8000 to 9000 invalids, who do not live in the hospital, receive £7 12s. 6d. each a year.

All these heavy expenses are raised by a deduction of 1s. per pound sterling, and one day's pay yearly, from the pay of all the officers and privates respectively, and the whole institution is under the supervision of a committee, the members of which are, the President of the Council, the First Lord of the Treasury, the chief Secretary of State, the Paymaster General, the Secretary for War, the Controllers, the Governor, and the Lieutenant-Governor of the Hospital.

After having seen the whole of this institution, and everything of note which was to be seen in Chelsea, we returned home towards noon. In the evening we went to the opera *Ariadne and Tesio*, and afterwards had supper at Mrs. Ellis's. On the 7th of March we were presented to the Queen, in order to take leave. After dinner we first paid a visit to Mrs. Richardson, and then spent the evening at Princess St. Severino's.

On the 8th we went to Baron von Münch-hausen's party, and then had supper with Lady Diana Clavering.

On the 9th we began to pay farewell visits, and took leave of the Princess of Wales and Princess Augusta ; in the evening we went by invitation to a large assembly at my Lady Yarmouth's, and supped afterwards with my Lord De La Warr.

On the 10th I drove for the second time to the British Museum, but, as before, there were so many people there, and the time was so restricted, that I was not able to look at any of the things more closely, but had to be satisfied with what was shown to the party in general, and what I had for the most part seen before. The most recent acquisition at present is the first volume of a new work printed in Copenhagen, and presented to this museum by the King of Denmark. It is called " Choix des Coquillages," and the title is very neatly engraved on copper and beautifully illuminated in the finest and brightest colours.

We went to dinner at my Lord Dartmouth's,[1] and in the afternoon by invitation to a small party at Colonel and Mrs. Erwin's ; he has served in Germany, but was obliged to return home on account of bad health ; she is a very amiable young lady, who sings very well, and is a good musician, as ladies in England mostly are. After having passed another half-hour at my Lady Holdernesse's, we supped once more with my Lord De La Warr.

The morning of the 11th of March we spent in paying a quantity of farewell visits ; we dined with Privy Councillor von Münchhausen, and in the evening went by invitation to Mrs. Whitworth's and my Lady Strafford's parties. The

---

[1] William, second Earl of Dartmouth ; b. 1731, d. 1801.

house of the latter is remarkably handsome, and is rightly considered the best appointed in London.

The 12th was the appointed day of fasting, penance, and prayer for the favourable progress of the war and for a speedy and advantageous peace. We remained at home until the evening, which we spent at the house of Mrs. Bladon and her two handsome daughters, where we had a very pleasant little concert, and afterwards supper in a small and agreeable company. An Italian who had just arrived, and who is staying with the Genoese minister, D'Ageno, accompanied the singing on his violin and played a few nice solos very well, which, together with some of the songs, Lady Diana Clavering accompanied equally well on the piano.

On the morning of the 13th we drove after ten o'clock with Stanhope, who has an appointment to the Queen, and is a son of the late Charles Stanhope, and with young Herr von Münchhausen, to Stanhope's property, Stanwell, sixteen miles from London, and beyond Hounslow. The house and garden are not large, but are very well arranged, and the former is remarkably well furnished. Though the garden is small, there are plenty of serpentine streams and winding gravel walks. The weather was particularly favourable; we had not had such a fine day for some time. After having dined there, we drove home towards the evening, so as to be in time to go to Lady Cecilia West's, and afterwards to supper with the usual party at my Lord De La Warr's.

On the 14th, after paying several farewell visits, we drove to my Lady Harrington's and Princess St. Severino's.

On the morning of the 15th we were invited by Miss Chudleigh to a concert; she does not live really in town, but opposite Hyde Park in a row of houses called Knightsbridge. Her house can justly be called a gem; it contains a quantity of handsome and costly furniture and other curiosities and objects of value, chosen and arranged with the greatest taste, so that you cannot fail to admire it greatly. There is hardly a place in the whole house left bare or without decoration, like a doll's house. Everything is in perfect harmony. The view, in front over Hyde Park, and at the back over Chelsea, is considered with truth one of the finest that could be pictured.

At noon, a rather good concert began. Miss Brandt, who generally sings, and an Italian called

Tenducci, were the performers. The Prince of Mecklenburg and a large and select company were present. About half-past two, when the concert was over, we were invited to lunch in the dining-room downstairs, where music was going on with two good French horns; a so-called "ambigue" was served at a very long table, on which there was everything which could be brought together—cakes, sandwiches, cold and smoked meat, ham, jelly, fruit, etc. Small side-tables were arranged for coffee, tea, chocolate, etc., so that I must say it was the most perfect feast of its kind.

Miss Chudleigh is Maid of Honour to the Princess of Wales, but her fitness for the post may be gathered from the following facts. She has been married for many years to a captain in the Navy, called Hervey, a brother of my Lord Bristol;[1] she has been separated from him for some time, and although every one knows that she has a husband, she has kept on her appointment as Maid of Honour, and has never announced

[1] Augustus John, third Earl of Bristol; b. 1724; Vice-Admiral of the Blue; married privately to Elizabeth, daughter of Colonel Thomas Chudleigh, and twenty-five years afterwards, 1769, that lady publicly married Evelyn Pierrepont, Duke of Kingston, for which offence she was impeached before the House of Peers, and the marriage declared illegal. She retired subsequently to the Continent, where she died, 1788.

her marriage. That she has been kept during all this time by the Duke of Kingston, from whom she receives all her riches, house, and garden, is just as well known.

After dinner we paid many visits, and in the evening we went to a party at Privy Councillor von Münchhausen's, and afterwards to supper with my Lord De La Warr.

On the 16th of March we lunched with my Lady Diana Clavering, and went afterwards with her and her sister, Lady Cecilia West, to the house of the singer Matthei, where a rehearsal of a new opera, called *La Défaite de Darie*, was held. We dined at home. In the evening we went first by invitation to Mrs. Oliver's party, and from there, towards nine o'clock, to the house of the Duke of Ancaster,[1] who gave a splendid ball in honour of the Prince of Mecklenburg. The company consisted of a large number of London's best and most distinguished society, amongst them the Dukes of York and Cumberland. The latter again played a game of quinze for just as high stakes as he had played some time before at my

---

[1] Brownlow, fifth Duke; b. 1729; married first (1762) Harriet, daughter and heiress of George Norton Pitt; she died 1763. He died without male issue, 1809, when dukedom and marquessate became extinct.

Lord Waldegrave's ; but what he won or lost this time I cannot say. On a previous occasion he had lost 1000 guineas by twelve o'clock.

Minuets were danced, and, contrary to the usual custom in England, I was paid marked distinction by our host. A foreigner has no rank at all in England, therefore at Court and other festive occasions, where they dance according to rank, those gentlemen who are not lords or baronets, and who wish to dance, are not called up until after all the lords, and just as the leader of the dance pleases. But the Duke of Ancaster paid me the compliment of asking me to dance with two daughters of earls, Lady Caroline Stanhope,[1] daughter of Lord Harrington, and Lady Warwick, Lord Cardigan's daughter,[2] immediately after the peers, and before their eldest sons, who are also lords by courtesy, although not peers.

At one o'clock a very sumptuous supper was served at three tables, two of which were provided with splendid dessert, and were lit up with a quantity of small glass-lamps and candles. At one of these tables sat the Duke of Cumberland,

---

[1] Lady Caroline Stanhope, eldest daughter of second Earl of Harrington ; married (1767) Kenneth Mackenzie, Earl of Seaforth.
[2] A mistake of Count Frederick's.—P. K.

and at the other the Prince of Mecklenburg, but the rest of the company sat down wherever they pleased. The third table was in the shape of a large horseshoe, and all three were so large that the whole company had room. Two hot courses were served, and the third consisted of fruit and dessert. Afterwards dancing went on again until half-past four, when the company began to disperse.

As soon as we got home we changed our clothes in the greatest haste, got into our post-chaise, and left London on the morning of the 17th of March at half-past five. We hastened without stopping to Harwich, where our servants and luggage had preceded us the day before, and where we arrived at five o'clock that evening; as the wind was exactly contrary, we could not go on board that day, but had to remain waiting all through the 18th, 19th, and 20th.

As there was nothing remarkable to see either in the place itself or the surrounding country, we passed our time with great tedium, having no society whatever but our two selves and Gentleman Usher von Reden, who was going to cross with us.

At noon on the 20th Prince Galitzin arrived from London to cross with us, thus increasing our party. At nine o'clock in the morning of the 21st we, that is—my brother and myself, at last went on board the *Prince of Orange*, Captain Hund; but Prince Galitzin went on board the *Dolphin*, Captain Cochrane, according to the agent's advice, as it would be more comfortable than if we all went on the same vessel.

We sailed all day in company, which, owing to the very light, but favourable wind, was very easy. The thick fog which set in during the night separated the two vessels, so that we arrived a few hours earlier, our ship being a better sailer than the other, and we reached Helvoetsluys safely on the second day (the 22nd of March) at twelve o'clock, after having been at sea 27 hours over a journey of 36 leagues, or 180 English miles.

In Helvoetsluys we did not stop any longer than was necessary to pack our luggage on waggons, and we went on foot to Briel, a good German mile distant. Briel is rather a pretty place, and very well built for a small country town. Here we got something to eat, and then hired a barge for our three selves and the three others who had crossed with us, to take us up the Meuse to Rotterdam.

As wind and water were against us, we did not arrive until midnight, and we put up at the best inn, the Schwinshoeft, or the Pig's Head.

On the 23rd we passed the morning seeing Rotterdam, and after dinner drove through Delft to the Hague, where we remained during the 24th, 25th, 26th, and 27th. On the 28th of March we drove to Amsterdam and spent our time there in seeing sights, until the afternoon of the 30th. Then we went by Treckschuyt to Utrecht, and leaving that place again on the same day, we continued our journey by the usual route. About twelve o'clock on the 4th of April we reached Hanover safely, after having been exactly seven months on our journey, from the 4th of September, 1761, till the 4th of April, 1762.

"TWENTY YEARS AFTER."

GRAF FRIEDRICH VON KIELMANSEGGE AND HIS FAMILY, ABOUT 1785.

PRINTED BY
WILLIAM CLOWES AND SONS, LIMITED,
LONDON AND BECCLES.

A Classified Catalogue
OF WORKS IN
GENERAL LITERATURE
PUBLISHED BY
LONGMANS, GREEN, & CO.,
39 PATERNOSTER ROW, LONDON, E.C.
91 AND 93 FIFTH AVENUE, NEW YORK, AND 32 HORNBY ROAD, BOMBAY.

CONTENTS.

History, Politics, Polity, Political Memoirs, etc.

Abbott.—A HISTORY OF GREECE. By EVELYN ABBOTT, M.A., LL.D.
Part I.—From the Earliest Times to the Ionian Revolt. Crown 8vo, 10s. 6d.
Part II.—500-445 B.C. Crown 8vo, 10s. 6d.
Part III.—From the Peace of 445 B.C. to the Fall of the Thirty at Athens in 403 B.C. Crown 8vo, 10s. 6d.

Abbott. — TOMMY CORNSTALK: being Some Account of the Less Notable Features of the South African War from the Point of View of the Australian Ranks. By J. H. M. ABBOTT. Crown 8vo, 5s. net.

Acland and Ransome.—A HANDBOOK IN OUTLINE OF THE POLITICAL HISTORY OF ENGLAND TO 1896. Chronologically arranged. By the Right Hon. A. H. DYKE ACLAND and CYRIL RANSOME, M.A. Crown 8vo, 6s.

Allgood. — CHINA WAR, 1860: LETTERS AND JOURNALS. By Major - General G. ALLGOOD, C.B., formerly Lieut. G. ALLGOOD, 1st Division China Field Force. With Maps, Plans, and Illustrations. Demy 4to, 12s. 6d. net.

History, Politics, Polity, Political Memoirs, etc.—*continued*.

ANNUAL REGISTER (THE). A Review of Public Events at Home and Abroad, for the year 1900. 8vo, 18s.

Volumes of THE ANNUAL REGISTER for the years 1863-1899 can still be had. 18s. each.

Arnold.—INTRODUCTORY LECTURES ON MODERN HISTORY. By THOMAS ARNOLD, D.D., formerly Head Master of Rugby School. 8vo, 7s. 6d.

Ashbourne.—PITT : SOME CHAPTERS ON HIS LIFE AND TIMES. By the Right Hon. EDWARD GIBSON, Lord ASHBOURNE, Lord Chancellor of Ireland. With 11 Portraits. 8vo, gilt top, 21s.

Ashley.—SURVEYS, HISTORIC AND ECONOMIC : a Volume of Essays. By W. J. ASHLEY, M.A. 8vo, 9s. net.

Bagwell.—IRELAND UNDER THE TUDORS. By RICHARD BAGWELL, LL.D. (3 vols.) Vols. I. and II. From the First Invasion of the Northmen to the year 1578. 8vo, 32s. Vol. III. 1578-1603. 8vo, 18s.

Baillie. — THE ORIENTAL CLUB, AND HANOVER SQUARE. By ALEXANDER F. BAILLIE. With 6 Photogravure Portraits and 8 Full-page Illustrations. Crown 4to, 25s. net.

Besant.—THE HISTORY OF LONDON. By Sir WALTER BESANT. With 74 Illustrations. Crown 8vo, 1s. 9d. Or bound as a School Prize Book, gilt edges, 2s. 6d.

Bright.—A HISTORY OF ENGLAND. By the Rev. J. FRANCK BRIGHT, D.D.

Period I. MEDIÆVAL MONARCHY : A.D. 449-1485. Crown 8vo, 4s. 6d.

Period II. PERSONAL MONARCHY. 1485-1688. Crown 8vo, 5s.

Period III. CONSTITUTIONAL MONARCHY. 1689-1837. Crown 8vo, 7s. 6d.

Period IV. THE GROWTH OF DEMOCRACY. 1837-1880. Crown 8vo, 6s.

Bruce.—THE FORWARD POLICY AND ITS RESULTS ; or, Thirty-five Years' Work amongst the Tribes on our North-Western Frontier of India. By RICHARD ISAAC BRUCE, C.I.E. With 28 Illustrations and a Map. 8vo, 15s. net.

Buckle.—HISTORY OF CIVILISATION IN ENGLAND, FRANCE. SPAIN AND SCOTLAND. By HENRY THOMAS BUCKLE. 3 vols. Crown 8vo, 24s.

Burke.—A HISTORY OF SPAIN from the Earliest Times to the Death of Ferdinand the Catholic. By ULICK RALPH BURKE, M.A. Edited by MARTIN A. S. HUME. With 6 Maps. 2 vols. Crown 8vo, 16s. net.

Caroline, Queen.—CAROLINE THE ILLUSTRIOUS, QUEEN - CONSORT OF GEORGE II. AND SOMETIME QUEEN REGENT : a Study of Her Life and Time. By W. H. WILKINS, M.A., F.S.A., Author of 'The Love of an Uncrowned Queen'. 2 vols. 8vo, 36s.

Chesney.—INDIAN POLITY : a View of the System of Administration in India. By General Sir GEORGE CHESNEY, K.C.B. With Map showing all the Administrative Divisions of British India. 8vo, 21s.

Churchill (WINSTON SPENCER, M.P.).

THE RIVER WAR : an Historical Account of the Reconquest of the Soudan. Edited by Colonel F. RHODES, D.S.O. With 34 Maps and Plans, and 51 Illustrations from Drawings by ANGUS McNEILL. Also with 7 Photogravure Portraits of Generals, etc. 2 vols. Medium 8vo, 36s.

THE STORY OF THE MALAKAND FIELD FORCE, 1897. With 6 Maps and Plans. Crown 8vo, 3s. 6d.

LONDON TO LADYSMITH VIÂ PRETORIA. Crown 8vo, 6s.

IAN HAMILTON'S MARCH. With Portrait of Lieut.-General Ian Hamilton, and 10 Maps and Plans. Crown 8vo, 6s.

History, Politics, Polity, Political Memoirs, etc.—*continued.*

Corbett (JULIAN S.).

DRAKE AND THE TUDOR NAVY; with a History of the Rise of England as a Maritime Power. With Portraits, Illustrations and Maps. 2 vols. Cr. 8vo, 16s.

THE SUCCESSORS OF DRAKE. With 4 Portraits (2 Photogravures) and 12 Maps and Plans. 8vo, 21s.

Creighton (M., D.D., late Lord Bishop of London).

A HISTORY OF THE PAPACY FROM THE GREAT SCHISM TO THE SACK OF ROME, 1378-1527. 6 vols. Crown 8vo, 5s. net each.

QUEEN ELIZABETH. With Portrait. Crown 8vo, 5s. net.

HISTORICAL ESSAYS AND REVIEWS. Edited by LOUISE CREIGHTON.

De Tocqueville.—DEMOCRACY IN AMERICA. By ALEXIS DE TOCQUE-VILLE. Translated by HENRY REEVE, C.B., D.C.L. 2 vols. Crown 8vo, 16s.

Dickinson.—THE DEVELOPMENT OF PARLIAMENT DURING THE NINETEENTH CENTURY. By G. LOWES DICKINSON, M.A. 8vo, 7s. 6d.

Falkiner.—STUDIES IN IRISH HISTORY AND BIOGRAPHY. Mainly of the Eighteenth Century. By C. LITTON FALKINER. 8vo, 12s. 6d. net.

Fitzgibbon.—ARTS UNDER ARMS: an University Man in Khaki. By MAURICE FITZGIBBON, B.A., Trinity College, Dublin University, late Trooper and Sergeant-Major 45th Company (Irish Hunt Contingent) Imperial Yeomanry. With 6 Illustrations. Crown 8vo, gilt top, 5s. net.

Fitzmaurice.—CHARLES WILLIAM FERDINAND, Duke of Brunswick; an Historical Study. By Lord EDMOND FITZMAURICE. With Map and 2 Portraits. 8vo, 6s. net.

Froude (JAMES A.).

THE HISTORY OF ENGLAND, from the Fall of Wolsey to the Defeat of the Spanish Armada. 12 vols. Cr. 8vo, 3s. 6d. each.

THE DIVORCE OF CATHERINE OF ARAGON. Crown 8vo, 3s. 6d.

Froude (JAMES A.—*continued.*

THE SPANISH STORY OF THE ARMADA, and other Essays. Crown 8vo, 3s. 6d.

THE ENGLISH IN IRELAND IN THE EIGHTEENTH CENTURY. 3 vols. Crown 8vo, 10s. 6d.

ENGLISH SEAMEN IN THE SIXTEENTH CENTURY.

Cabinet Edition. Crown 8vo, 6s.

Illustrated Edition. With 5 Photogravure Plates and 16 other Illustrations. Large Crown 8vo, gilt top, 6s. net.

'*Silver Library*' *Edition.* Crown 8vo, 3s. 6d.

THE COUNCIL OF TRENT. Crown 8vo, 3s. 6d.

SHORT STUDIES ON GREAT SUBJECTS. 4 vols. Cr. 8vo, 3s. 6d. each.

CÆSAR: a Sketch. Cr. 8vo, 3s. 6d.

SELECTIONS FROM THE WRITINGS OF JAMES ANTHONY FROUDE. Edited by P. S. ALLEN, M.A. Crown 8vo, 3s. 6d.

Fuller.—EGYPT AND THE HINTERLAND. By FREDERIC W. FULLER. With Frontispiece and Map of Egypt and the Sudan. 8vo, 10s. 6d. net.

Gardiner (SAMUEL RAWSON, D.C.L., LL.D.).

HISTORY OF ENGLAND, from the Accession of James I. to the Outbreak of the Civil War, 1603-1642. 10 vols. Crown 8vo, 5s. net each.

A HISTORY OF THE GREAT CIVIL WAR, 1642-1649. 4 vols. Crown 8vo, 5s. net each.

A HISTORY OF THE COMMONWEALTH AND THE PROTECTORATE. 1649-1660. Vol. I. 1649-1651. With 14 Maps. 8vo, 21s. Vol. II. 1651-1654. With 7 Maps. 8vo, 21s. Vol. III. 1654-1656. With 6 Maps. 8vo, 21s.

THE STUDENT'S HISTORY OF ENGLAND. With 378 Illustrations. Cr. 8vo, gilt top, 12s.

Also in Three Volumes, price 4s. each.

History, Politics, Polity, Political Memoirs, etc.—*continued.*

Gardiner (SAMUEL RAWSON, D.C .L
LL.D.)—*continued.*
WHAT GUNPOWDER PLOT WAS.
With 8 Illustrations. Cr. 8vo, 5s.
CROMWELL'S PLACE IN HISTORY.
Founded on Six Lectures delivered in
the University of Oxford. Crown
8vo, 3s. 6d.
OLIVER CROMWELL. With Frontis-
piece. Crown 8vo, 5s. net.

**German Empire (The) of To-
day:** Outlines of its Formation and
Development. By 'VERITAS'. Crown
8vo, 6s. net.

Graham.—ROMAN AFRICA : an Outline of the History of the Roman Occupa-
tion of North Africa, based chiefly upon
Inscriptions and Monumental Remains
in that country. By ALEXANDER
GRAHAM, F.S.A., F.R.I.B.A. With
30 reproductions of Original Drawings
by the Author, and 2 Maps. 8vo, 16s.
net.

Greville.—A JOURNAL OF THE
REIGNS OF KING GEORGE IV.,
KING WILLIAM IV., AND QUEEN
VICTORIA. By CHARLES C. F. GRE-
VILLE, formerly Clerk of the Council.
8 vols. Crown 8vo, 3s. 6d. each.

Gross.—THE SOURCES AND LITERA-
TURE OF ENGLISH HISTORY, from
the Earliest Times to about 1485. By
CHARLES GROSS, Ph.D. 8vo, 18s. net.

Hamilton.—HISTORICAL RECORD
OF THE 14TH (KING'S) HUSSARS,
from A.D. 1715 to A.D. 1900. By Col-
onel HENRY BLACKBURNE HAMILTON,
M.A., Christ Church, Oxford ; late com-
manding the Regiment. With 15
Coloured Plates, 35 Portraits, etc., in
Photogravure, and 10 Maps and Plans.
Crown 4to, gilt edges, 42s. net.

Hill.—LIBERTY DOCUMENTS. With
Contemporary Exposition and Critical
Comments drawn from various Writers.
Selected and Prepared by MABEL HILL.
Edited with an Introduction by ALBERT
BUSHNELL HART, Ph.D. Large Crown
8vo, 7s. 6d.

HARVARD HISTORICAL STUDIES.

THE SUPPRESSION OF THE AFRICAN
SLAVE TRADE TO THE UNITED
STATES OF AMERICA, 1638-1870.
By W. E. B. DU BOIS, Ph.D. 8vo,
7s. 6d.

THE CONTEST OVER THE RATIFICA-
TION OF THE FEDERAL CONSTITU-
TION IN MASSACHUSETTS. By S.
B. HARDING, A.M. 8vo, 6s.

A CRITICAL STUDY OF NULLIFICA-
TION IN SOUTH CAROLINA. By
D. F. HOUSTON, A.M. 8vo, 6s.

NOMINATIONS FOR ELECTIVE OF-
FICE IN THE UNITED STATES.
By FREDERICK W. DALLINGER, A.M.
8vo, 7s. 6d.

A BIBLIOGRAPHY OF BRITISH
MUNICIPAL HISTORY, including
Gilds and Parliamentary Representation. By CHARLES GROSS, Ph.D. 8vo,
12s.

THE LIBERTY AND FREE-SOIL
PARTIES IN THE NORTH-WEST.
By THEODORE C. SMITH, Ph.D. 8vo,
7s. 6d.

THE PROVINCIAL GOVERNOR IN
THE ENGLISH COLONIES OF
NORTH AMERICA. By EVARTS
BOUTELL GREENE. 8vo, 7s. 6d.

THE COUNTY PALATINE OF DUR-
HAM : a Study in Constitutional
History. By GAILLARD THOMAS LAPS-
LEY, Ph.D. 8vo 10s. 6d.

Historic Towns.—Edited by E. A.
FREEMAN, D.C.L., and Rev. WILLIAM
HUNT, M.A. With Maps and Plans.
Crown 8vo, 3s. 6d. each.

Bristol. By Rev. W. Hunt.

Carlisle. By Mandell Creighton, D.D.

Cinque Ports. By Montagu Burrows.

Colchester. By Rev. E. L. Cutts.

Exeter. By E. A. Freeman.

London. By Rev. W. J. Loftie.

Oxford. By Rev. C. W. Boase.

Winchester. By G. W. Kitchin, D.D.

York. By Rev. James Raine.

New York. By Theo-dore Roosevelt.

Boston (U.S.). By Henry Cabot Lodge.

History, Politics, Polity, Political Memoirs, etc.—*continued.*

Hunter.—A HISTORY OF BRITISH INDIA. By Sir WILLIAM WILSON HUNTER, K.C.S.I., M.A., LL.D.
Vol. I.—Introductory to the Overthrow of the English in the Spice Archipelago, 1623. With 4 Maps. 8vo, 18s.
Vol. II.—To the Union of the Old and New Companies under the Earl of Godolphin's Award. 1708. 8vo, 16s.

Ingram.—A CRITICAL EXAMINATION OF IRISH HISTORY. From the Elizabethan Conquest to the Legislative Union of 1800. By T. DUNBAR INGRAM, LL.D. 2 vols. 8vo, 24s.

Joyce. — A SHORT HISTORY OF IRELAND, from the Earliest Times to 1603. By P. W. JOYCE, LL.D. Crown 8vo, 10s. 6d.

Kaye and Malleson.—HISTORY OF THE INDIAN MUTINY, 1857-1858. By Sir JOHN W. KAYE and Colonel G. B. MALLESON. With Analytical Index and Maps and Plans. 6 vols. Crown 8vo, 3s. 6d. each.

Kent.—THE ENGLISH RADICALS: an Historical Sketch. By C. B. ROYLANCE KENT. Crown 8vo, 7s. 6d.

Lang.—THE MYSTERY OF MARY STUART. By ANDREW LANG. With 6 Photogravure Plates (4 Portraits) and 15 other Illustrations. 8vo, 18s. net.

Laurie.—HISTORICAL SURVEY OF PRE-CHRISTIAN EDUCATION. By S. S. LAURIE, A.M., LL.D. Crown 8vo, 7s. 6d.

Lecky.—(The Rt. Hon. WILLIAM E. H.).
HISTORY OF ENGLAND IN THE EIGHTEENTH CENTURY.
Library Edition. 8 vols. 8vo. Vols. I. and II., 1700-1760, 36s. Vols. III. and IV., 1760-1784, 36s. Vols. V. and VI., 1784-1793, 36s. Vols. VII. and VIII., 1793-1800, 36s.
Cabinet Edition. ENGLAND. 7 vols. Crown 8vo, 5s. net each. IRELAND. 5 vols. Crown 8vo, 5s. net each.
HISTORY OF EUROPEAN MORALS FROM AUGUSTUS TO CHARLEMAGNE. 2 vols. Crown 8vo, 10s. net.

Lecky.—(The Rt. Hon. WILLIAM E. H.)—*continued.*
HISTORY OF THE RISE AND INFLUENCE OF THE SPIRIT OF RATIONALISM IN EUROPE. 2 vols. Crown 8vo, 10s. net.
DEMOCRACY AND LIBERTY.
Library Edition. 2 vols. 8vo, 36s.
Cabinet Edition. 2 vols. Cr. 8vo, 10s. net.

Lowell.—GOVERNMENTS AND PARTIES IN CONTINENTAL EUROPE. By A. LAWRENCE LOWELL. 2 vols. 8vo, 21s.

Lynch.—THE WAR OF THE CIVILISATIONS: BEING A RECORD OF 'A FOREIGN DEVIL'S' EXPERIENCES WITH THE ALLIES IN CHINA. By GEORGE LYNCH, Special Correspondent of the *Sphere*, etc. With Portrait and 21 Illustrations. Crown 8vo, 6s. net.

Lytton.—THE HISTORY OF LORD LYTTON'S INDIAN ADMINISTRATION, FROM 1876-1880. Compiled from Letters and Official Papers. Edited by Lady BETTY BALFOUR. With Portrait and Map. 8vo, 18s.

Macaulay (LORD).
THE LIFE AND WORKS OF LORD MACAULAY.
'*Edinburgh*' *Edition.* 10 vols. 8vo, 6s. each.
Vols. I.-IV. HISTORY OF ENGLAND.
Vols. V.-VII. ESSAYS, BIOGRAPHIES, INDIAN PENAL CODE, CONTRIBUTIONS TO KNIGHT'S 'QUARTERLY MAGAZINE'.
Vol. VIII. SPEECHES, LAYS OF ANCIENT ROME, MISCELLANEOUS POEMS.
Vols. IX. and X. THE LIFE AND LETTERS OF LORD MACAULAY. By Sir G. O. TREVELYAN, Bart.

History, Politics, Polity, Political Memoirs, etc.—*continued.*

Macaulay (LORD)—*continued.*

THE WORKS.

'*Albany*' *Edition.* With 12 Portraits. 12 vols. Large Crown 8vo, 3s. 6d. each.

Vols. I.-VI. HISTORY OF ENG-LAND. FROM THE ACCESSION OF JAMES THE SECOND.

Vols. VII.-X. ESSAYS AND BIO-GRAPHIES.

Vols. XI.-XII. SPEECHES. LAYS OF ANCIENT ROME, ETC., AND INDEX.

Cabinet Edition. 16 vols. Post 8vo, £4 16s.

HISTORY OF ENGLAND FROM THE ACCESSION OF JAMES THE SECOND.

Popular Edition. 2 vols. Cr. 8vo, 5s.

Student's Edition. 2 vols. Cr. 8vo, 12s.

People's Edition. 4 vols. Cr. 8vo. 16s.

'*Albany*' *Edition.* With 6 Portraits. 6 vols. Large Crown 8vo, 3s. 6d. each.

Cabinet Edition. 8 vols. Post 8vo, 48s.

'*Edinburgh*' *Edition.* 4 vols. 8vo, 6s. each.

CRITICAL AND HISTORICAL ESSAYS, WITH LAYS OF ANCIENT ROME, ETC., in 1 volume.

Popular Edition. Crown 8vo, 2s. 6d.

Authorised Edition. Cr. 8vo, 2s. 6d.

'*Silver Library*' *Edition.* With Portrait and 4 Illustrations to the '*Lays*'. Crown 8vo, 3s. 6d.

CRITICAL AND HISTORICAL ESSAYS.

Student's Edition. 1 vol. Cr. 8vo, 6s.

People's Edition. 2 vols. Crown 8vo, 8s.

'*Trevelyan*' *Edition.* 2 vols. Crown 8vo, 9s.

Cabinet Edition. 4 vols. Post 8vo, 24s.

'*Edinburgh*' *Edition.* 3 vols. 8vo, 6s. each.

Macaulay (LORD)—*continued.*

ESSAYS, which may be had separately, sewed, 6d. each; cloth, 1s. each.

Addison and Walpole.	Frederic the Great.
Croker's Boswell's Johnson.	Ranke and Gladstone. Lord Bacon.
Hallam's Constitutional History.	Lord Clive. Lord Byron, and The
Warren Hastings.	Comic Dramatists
The Earl of Chatham (Two Essays).	of the Restoration.

MISCELLANEOUS WRITINGS.

People's Edition. 1 vol. Crown 8vo, 4s. 6d.

MISCELLANEOUS WRITINGS, SPEECHES, AND POEMS.

Popular Edition. Crown 8vo, 2s. 6d.

Cabinet Edition. 4 vols. Post 8vo, 24s.

SELECTIONS FROM THE WRITINGS OF LORD MACAULAY. Edited, with Occasional Notes, by the Right Hon. Sir G. O. TREVELYAN, Bart. Crown 8vo, 6s.

Mackinnon (JAMES, Ph.D.).

THE HISTORY OF EDWARD THE THIRD. 8vo, 18s.

THE GROWTH AND DECLINE OF THE FRENCH MONARCHY. 8vo, 21s. net.

May.—THE CONSTITUTIONAL HISTORY OF ENGLAND since the Accession of George III. 1760-1870. By Sir THOMAS ERSKINE MAY, K.C.B. (Lord Farnborough). 3 vols. Cr. 8vo, 18s.

Merivale (CHARLES, D.D.).

HISTORY OF THE ROMANS UNDER THE EMPIRE. 8 vols. Crown 8vo, 3s. 6d. each.

THE FALL OF THE ROMAN REPUBLIC: a Short History of the Last Century of the Commonwealth. 12mo, 7s. 6d.

GENERAL HISTORY OF ROME, from the Foundation of the City to the Fall of Augustulus, B.C. 753-A.D. 476. With 5 Maps. Cr. 8vo, 7s. 6d.

Montague.—THE ELEMENTS OF ENGLISH CONSTITUTIONAL HISTORY. By F. C. MONTAGUE, M.A. Crown 8vo, 3s. 6d.

Nash.—THE GREAT FAMINE AND ITS CAUSES. By VAUGHAN NASH. With 8 Illustrations from Photographs by the Author, and a Map of India showing the Famine Area. Cr. 8vo, 6s.

History, Politics, Polity, Political Memoirs, etc.—*continued*.

Owens College Essays.—Edited by T. F. TOUT, M.A., Professor of History in the Owens College, Victoria University, and JAMES TAIT, M.A., Assistant Lecturer in History. With 4 Maps. 8vo, 12s. 6d. net.

Powell and Trevelyan. — THE PEASANTS' RISING AND THE LOLLARDS : a Collection of Unpublished Documents. Edited by EDGAR POWELL and G. M. TREVELYAN. 8vo, 6s. net.

Randolph.—THE LAW AND POLICY OF ANNEXATION, with Special Reference to the Philippines ; together with Observations on the Status of Cuba. By CARMAN F. RANDOLPH. 8vo, 9s. net.

Rankin (REGINALD).
THE MARQUIS D'ARGENSON AND RICHARD THE SECOND. 8vo, 10s. 6d. net.
A SUBALTERN'S LETTERS TO HIS WIFE. (The Boer War.) Cr. 8vo, 3s. 6d.

Ransome.—THE RISE OF CONSTITUTIONAL GOVERNMENT IN ENGLAND. By CYRIL RANSOME, M.A. Crown 8vo, 6s.

Seebohm (FREDERIC, LL.D., F.S.A.).
THE ENGLISH VILLAGE COMMUNITY. With 13 Maps and Plates. 8vo, 16s.
TRIBAL CUSTOM IN ANGLO-SAXON LAW : being an Essay supplemental to (1) ' The English Village Community,' (2) ' The Tribal System in Wales '. 8vo, 16s.

Seton-Karr.—THE CALL TO ARMS, 1900-1901 ; or a Review of the Imperial Yeomanry Movement, and some subjects connected therewith. By H. SETON-KARR, M.P. With a Frontispiece by R. CATON WOODVILLE. Crown 8vo.

Shaw.—A HISTORY OF THE ENGLISH CHURCH DURING THE CIVIL WARS AND UNDER THE COMMONWEALTH, 1640-1660. By WM. A. SHAW, Litt.D. 2 vols. 8vo, 36s.

Sheppard. — THE OLD ROYAL PALACE OF WHITEHALL. By EDGAR SHEPPARD, D.D., Sub-Dean of H.M. Chapels Royal, Sub-Almoner to the King. With 6 Photogravure Plates and 33 other Illustrations. Medium 8vo, 21s. net.

Smith. — CARTHAGE AND THE CARTHAGINIANS. By R. BOSWORTH SMITH, M.A. With Maps, Plans, etc. Crown 8vo, 3s. 6d.

Stephens.—A HISTORY OF THE FRENCH REVOLUTION. By H. MORSE STEPHENS. 8vo. Vols. I. and II. 18s. each.

Sternberg.—MY EXPERIENCES OF THE BOER WAR. By ADALBERT COUNT STERNBERG. With Preface by Lieut.-Col. G. F. R. HENDERSON. Cr. 8vo, 5s. net.

Stubbs.—HISTORY OF THE UNIVERSITY OF DUBLIN. By J. W. STUBBS. 8vo, 12s. 6d.

Sutherland.—THE HISTORY OF AUSTRALIA AND NEW ZEALAND, from 1606 - 1900. By ALEXANDER SUTHERLAND, M.A., and GEORGE SUTHERLAND, M.A. Crown 8vo, 2s. 6d.

Taylor.—A STUDENT'S MANUAL OF THE HISTORY OF INDIA. By Colonel MEADOWS TAYLOR, C.S.I., etc. Crown 8vo, 7s. 6d.

Thomson. — CHINA AND THE POWERS : a Narrative of the Outbreak of 1900. By H. C. THOMSON. With 2 Maps and 29 Illustrations. 8vo, 10s. 6d. net.

Todd.—PARLIAMENTARY GOVERNMENT IN THE BRITISH COLONIES. By ALPHEUS TODD, LL.D. 8vo, 30s. net.

Trevelyan.—THE AMERICAN REVOLUTION. Part I. 1766-1776. By Sir G. O. TREVELYAN, Bart. 8vo, 16s.

Trevelyan.—ENGLAND IN THE AGE OF WYCLIFFE. By GEORGE MACAULAY TREVELYAN. 8vo, 15s.

Wakeman and Hassall.—ESSAYS INTRODUCTORY TO THE STUDY OF ENGLISH CONSTITUTIONAL HISTORY. Edited by HENRY OFFLEY WAKEMAN, M.A., and ARTHUR HASSALL, M.A. Crown 8vo, 6s.

Walpole.—HISTORY OF ENGLAND FROM THE CONCLUSION OF THE GREAT WAR IN 1815 TO 1858. By Sir SPENCER WALPOLE, K.C.B. 6 vols. Crown 8vo, 6s. each.

Wylie (JAMES HAMILTON, M.A.).
HISTORY OF ENGLAND UNDER HENRY IV. 4 vols. Crown 8vo. Vol. I., 1399-1404, 10s. 6d. Vol. II., 1405-1406, 15s. (*out of print*). Vol. III., 1407-1411, 15s. Vol. IV., 1411-1413, 21s.
THE COUNCIL OF CONSTANCE TO THE DEATH OF JOHN HUS. Cr. 8vo, 6s. net.

Biography, Personal Memoirs, etc.

Bacon.—THE LETTERS AND LIFE OF FRANCIS BACON, INCLUDING ALL HIS OCCASIONAL WORKS. Edited by JAMES SPEDDING. 7 vols. 8vo, £4 4s.

Bagehot. — BIOGRAPHICAL STUDIES. By WALTER BAGEHOT. Crown 8vo. 3s. 6d.

Carlyle.—THOMAS CARLYLE : A History of his Life. By JAMES ANTHONY FROUDE. Crown 8vo. 1795-1835. 2 vols. 7s. 1834-1881. 2 vols. 7s.

Crozier.—MY INNER LIFE : being a Chapter in Personal Evolution and Autobiography. By JOHN BEATTIE CROZIER, LL.D. 8vo, 14s.

Dante.—THE LIFE AND WORKS OF DANTE ALLIGHIERI : being an Introduction to the Study of the 'Divina Commedia'. By the Rev. J. F. HOGAN, D.D. With Portrait. 8vo, 12s. 6d.

Danton.—LIFE OF DANTON. By A. H. BEESLY. With Portraits. Cr. 8vo, 6s.

De Bode.— THE BARONESS DE BODE, 1775-1803. By WILLIAM S. CHILDE-PEMBERTON. With 4 Photogravure Portraits and other Illustrations. 8vo, gilt top, 12s. 6d. net.

Duncan.—ADMIRAL DUNCAN. By THE EARL OF CAMPERDOWN. With 3 Portraits. 8vo, 16s.

Erasmus.

LIFE AND LETTERS OF ERASMUS. By JAMES ANTHONY FROUDE. Crown 8vo, 3s. 6d.

THE EPISTLES OF ERASMUS, from his earliest Letters to his Fifty-first Year, arranged in Order of Time. English Translations, with a Commentary. By FRANCIS MORGAN NICHOLS. 8vo, 18s. net.

Faraday.—FARADAY AS A DISCOVERER. By JOHN TYNDALL. Crown 8vo, 3s. 6d.

Fénelon: his Friends and his Enemies, 1651-1715. By E. K. SANDERS. With Portrait. 8vo, 10s. 6d.

Foreign Courts AND FOREIGN HOMES. By A. M. F. Crown 8vo, 6s.

Fox.—THE EARLY HISTORY OF CHARLES JAMES FOX. By the Right Hon. Sir G. O. TREVELYAN, Bart. *Library Edition.* 8vo, 18s. *Cheap Edition.* Crown 8vo, 3s. 6d.

Granville. — SOME RECORDS OF THE LATER LIFE OF HARRIET, COUNTESS GRANVILLE. By her Grand-daughter, the Hon. MRS. OLDFIELD. With 17 Portraits. 8vo, gilt top, 16s. net.

Grey.—MEMOIR OF SIR GEORGE GREY, BART., G.C.B., 1799-1882. By MANDELL CREIGHTON, D.D., late Lord Bishop of London. With 3 Portraits. Crown 8vo, 6s. net.

Hamilton.—LIFE OF SIR WILLIAM HAMILTON. By R. P. GRAVES. 8vo, 3 vols. 15s. each. ADDENDUM. 8vo, 6d. sewed.

Harrow School Register (The), 1801 - 1900. Second Edition, 1901. Edited by M. G. DAUGLISH, Barristerat-Law. 8vo, 15s. net.

Havelock. -- MEMOIRS OF SIR HENRY HAVELOCK, K.C.B. By JOHN CLARK MARSHMAN. Cr. 8vo, 3s. 6d.

Haweis.—MY MUSICAL LIFE. By the Rev. H. R. HAWEIS. With Portrait of Richard Wagner and 3 Illustrations. Crown 8vo, 6s. net.

Hiley.—MEMORIES OF HALF A CENTURY. By the Rev. R. W. HILEY, D.D. With Portrait. 8vo, 15s.

Holroyd (MARIA JOSEPHA).

THE GIRLHOOD OF MARIA JOSEPHA HOLROYD (Lady Stanley of Alderley). Recorded in Letters of a Hundred Years Ago, from 1776-1796. Edited by J. H. ADEANE. With 6 Portraits. 8vo, 18s.

THE EARLY MARRIED LIFE OF MARIA JOSEPHA, LADY STANLEY OF ALDERLEY, FROM 1796. Edited by J. H. ADEANE. With 10 Portraits, etc. 8vo, 18s.

Biography, Personal Memoirs, etc.—continued.

Hunter.—THE LIFE OF SIR WILLIAM WILSON HUNTER, K.C.S.I., M.A., LL.D. Author of 'A History of British India,' etc. By FRANCIS HENRY SKRINE, F.S.S. With 6 Portraits (2 Photogravures) and 4 other Illustrations. 8vo, 16s. net.

Jackson.—STONEWALL JACKSON AND THE AMERICAN CIVIL WAR. By Lieut.-Col. G. F. R. HENDERSON. With 2 Portraits and 33 Maps and Plans. 2 vols. Crown 8vo, 16s. net.

Leslie.—THE LIFE AND CAMPAIGNS OF ALEXANDER LESLIE, FIRST EARL OF LEVEN. By CHARLES SANFORD TERRY, M.A. With Maps and Plans. 8vo, 16s.

Luther.—LIFE OF LUTHER. By JULIUS KÖSTLIN. With 62 Illustrations and 4 Facsimiles of MSS. Crown 8vo, 3s. 6d.

Macaulay.—THE LIFE AND LETTERS OF LORD MACAULAY. By the Right Hon. Sir G. O. TREVELYAN, Bart.
Popular Edition. 1 vol. Cr. 8vo, 2s. 6d.
Student's Edition. 1 vol. Cr. 8vo, 6s.
Cabinet Edition. 2 vols. Post 8vo, 12s.
'Edinburgh' Edition. 2 vols. 8vo, 6s. each.
Library Edition. 2 vols. 8vo, 36s.

Martineau.—JAMES MARTINEAU. A Biography and Study. By A. W. JACKSON, A.M., of Concord, Massachusetts. With 2 Portraits. 8vo, 12s. 6d.

Max Müller (F.)
MY AUTOBIOGRAPHY: a Fragment. With 6 Portraits, 8vo, 12s. 6d.
AULD LANG SYNE. Second Series. 8vo, 10s. 6d.
CHIPS FROM A GERMAN WORK-SHOP. Vol. II. Biographical Essays. Crown 8vo, 5s.

Meade.—GENERAL SIR RICHARD MEADE AND THE FEUDATORY STATES OF CENTRAL AND SOUTHERN INDIA. By THOMAS HENRY THORNTON. With Portrait, Map and Illustrations. 8vo, 10s. 6d. net.

Morris.—THE LIFE OF WILLIAM MORRIS. By J. W. MACKAIL. With 2 Portraits and 8 other Illustrations by E. H. NEW, etc. 2 vols. Large Crown 8vo, 10s. net.

On the Banks of the Seine.—By A. M. F., Authoress of 'Foreign Courts and Foreign Homes'. Crown 8vo, 6s.

Paget.—MEMOIRS AND LETTERS OF SIR JAMES PAGET. Edited by STEPHEN PAGET, one of his sons. With 6 Portraits (3 Photogravures) and 4 other Illustrations. 8vo, 12s. 6d. net.

Pearson.—CHARLES HENRY PEARSON, Author of 'National Life and Character'. Memorials by Himself, his Wife and his Friends. Edited by WILLIAM STEBBING. With a Portrait. 8vo, 14s.

Place.—THE LIFE OF FRANCIS PLACE, 1771-1854. By GRAHAM WALLAS, M.A. With 2 Portraits. 8vo, 12s.

Powys.—PASSAGES FROM THE DIARIES OF MRS. PHILIP LYBBE POWYS, OF HARDWICK HOUSE, OXON. 1756-1808. Edited by EMILY J. CLIMENSON. 8vo, gilt top, 16s.

Râmakrishna : his Life and Sayings. By the Right Hon. F. MAX MÜLLER. Crown 8vo, 5s.

Rich. — MARY RICH, COUNTESS OF WARWICK (1625 - 1678) : Her Family and Friends. By C. FELL SMITH. With 7 Photogravure Portraits and 9 other Illustrations. 8vo, gilt top, 18s. net.

Romanes.—THE LIFE AND LETTERS OF GEORGE JOHN ROMANES, M.A., LL.D., F.R.S. Written and Edited by his WIFE. With Portrait and 2 Illustrations. Crown 8vo, 5s. net.

Russell. — SWALLOWFIELD AND ITS OWNERS. By CONSTANCE, Lady RUSSELL of Swallowfield Park. With 15 Photogravure Portraits and 36 other Illustrations. 4to, gilt edges, 42s. net.

Biography, Personal Memoirs, etc.—*continued*.

Seebohm.—THE OXFORD REFOR-MERS—JOHN COLET, ERASMUS, AND THOMAS MORE : a History of their Fellow-Work. By FREDERIC SEEBOHM. 8vo, 14s.

Shakespeare.—OUTLINES OF THE LIFE OF SHAKESPEARE. By J. O. HALLIWELL-PHILLIPPS. With Illustrations and Facsimiles. 2 vols. Royal 8vo, 21s.

Tales of my Father.—By A. M. F. Author of 'Foreign Courts and Foreign Homes.' and 'On the Banks of the Seine'. Crown 8vo, 6s.

Tallentyre.—THE WOMEN OF THE SALONS, and other French Portraits. By S. G. TALLENTYRE. With 11 Photogravure Portraits. 8vo, 10s. 6d. net.

Victoria, Queen, 1819-1901. By RICHARD R. HOLMES, M.V.O., F.S.A. Librarian to the Queen. With Photogravure Portrait. Cr. 8vo, gilt top, 5s. net.

Walpole. — SOME UNPUBLISHED LETTERS OF HORACE WALPOLE. Edited by Sir SPENCER WALPOLE, K.C.B. With 2 Portraits. Cr. 8vo, 4s. 6d. net.

Wellington.—LIFE OF THE DUKE OF WELLINGTON. By the Rev. G. R. GLEIG, M.A. Crown 8vo, 3s. 6d.

Travel and Adventure, the Colonies, etc.

Arnold.—SEAS AND LANDS. By Sir EDWIN ARNOLD. With 71 Illustrations. Crown 8vo, 3s. 6d.

Baker (Sir S. W.).

EIGHT YEARS IN CEYLON. With 6 Illustrations. Crown 8vo, 3s. 6d.

THE RIFLE AND THE HOUND IN CEYLON. With 6 Illustrations. Crown 8vo, 3s. 6d.

Ball (JOHN).

THE ALPINE GUIDE. Reconstructed and Revised on behalf of the Alpine Club by W. A. B. COOLIDGE.

Vol. I., THE WESTERN ALPS : the Alpine Region, South of the Rhone Valley, from the Col de Tenda to the Simplon Pass. With 9 New and Revised Maps. Crown 8vo, 12s. net.

HINTS AND NOTES, PRACTICAL AND SCIENTIFIC, FOR TRAVELLERS IN THE ALPS : being a revision of the General Introduction to the 'Alpine Guide'. Crown 8vo, 3s. net.

Bent.—THE RUINED CITIES OF MASHONALAND : being a Record of Excavation and Exploration in 1891. By J. THEODORE BENT. With 117 Illustrations. Crown 8vo, 3s. 6d.

Brassey (THE LATE LADY).

A VOYAGE IN THE 'SUNBEAM'; OUR HOME ON THE OCEAN FOR ELEVEN MONTHS.

Cabinet Edition. With Map and 66 Illustrations. Crown 8vo, gilt edges, 7s. 6d.

'Silver Library' Edition. With 66 Illustrations. Crown 8vo, 3s. 6d.

Popular Edition. With 60 Illustrations. 4to, 6d. sewed, 1s. cloth.

School Edition. With 37 Illustrations. Fcp., 2s. cloth, or 3s. white parchment.

SUNSHINE AND STORM IN THE EAST.

Popular Edition. With 103 Illustrations. 4to, 6d. sewed, 1s. cloth.

IN THE TRADES, THE TROPICS, AND THE 'ROARING FORTIES'.

Cabinet Edition. With Map and 220 Illustrations. Crown 8vo, gilt edges, 7s. 6d.

Crawford. — SOUTH AMERICAN SKETCHES. By ROBERT CRAWFORD, M.A. Crown 8vo, 6s.

Fountain.—THE GREAT DESERTS AND FORESTS OF NORTH AMERICA. By PAUL FOUNTAIN. With a Preface by W. H. HUDSON, Author of 'The Naturalist in La Plata,' etc. 8vo, 9s. 6d. net.

Travel and Adventure, the Colonies, etc.—*continued.*

Froude (JAMES A.).
OCEANA : or England and her Colonies. With 9 Illustrations. Crown 8vo, 3s. 6d.

THE ENGLISH IN THE WEST INDIES : or, the Bow of Ulysses. With 9 Illustrations. Crown 8vo, 2s. boards, 2s. 6d. cloth.

Grove. — SEVENTY - ONE DAYS' CAMPING IN MOROCCO. By Lady GROVE. With Photogravure Portrait and 32 Illustrations from Photographs. 8vo, 7s. 6d. net.

Haggard.— A WINTER PILGRIMAGE : Being an Account of Travels through Palestine, Italy and the Island of Cyprus, undertaken in the year 1900. By H. RIDER HAGGARD. With 31 Illustrations from Photographs. Crown 8vo, gilt top, 12s. 6d. net.

Heathcote.—ST. KILDA. By NORMAN HEATHCOTE. With 80 Illustrations from Sketches and Photographs of the People, Scenery and Birds, by the Author. 8vo, 10s. 6d. net.

Howitt.—VISITS TO REMARKABLE PLACES. Old Halls, Battlefields, Scenes, illustrative of Striking Passages in English History and Poetry. By WILLIAM HOWITT. With 80 Illustrations. Crown 8vo, 3s. 6d.

Knight (E. F.).
WITH THE ROYAL TOUR : a Narrative of the Recent Tour of the Duke and Duchess of Cornwall and York through Greater Britain. With 16 Illustrations and a Map. Crown 8vo, 5s. net.

THE CRUISE OF THE 'ALERTE'; the Narrative of a search for Treasure on the Desert Island of Trinidad. With 2 Maps and 23 Illustrations. Crown 8vo, 3s. 6d.

WHERE THREE EMPIRES MEET : a Narrative of Recent Travel in Kashmir, Western Tibet, Baltistan, Ladak, Gilgit, and the adjoining Countries. With a Map and 54 Illustrations. Crown 8vo, 3s. 6d.

THE 'FALCON' ON THE BALTIC : a Voyage from London to Copenhagen in a Three-Tonner. With 10 Full-page Illustrations. Cr. 8vo, 3s. 6d.

Lees.—PEAKS AND PINES : another Norway Book. By J. A. LEES. With 63 Illustrations and Photographs. Cr. 8vo, 6s.

Lees and Clutterbuck.—B.C. 1887 : A RAMBLE IN BRITISH COLUMBIA. By J. A. LEES and W. J. CLUTTERBUCK. With Map and 75 Illustrations. Crown 8vo, 3s. 6d.

Lynch. — ARMENIA : Travels and Studies. By H. F. B. LYNCH. With 197 Illustrations (some in tints) reproduced from Photographs and Sketches by the Author, 16 Maps and Plans, a Bibliography, and a Map of Armenia and adjacent countries. 2 vols. Medium 8vo, gilt top, 42s. net.

Nansen.—THE FIRST CROSSING OF GREENLAND. By FRIDTJOF NANSEN. With 143 Illustrations and a Map. Cr. 8vo, 3s. 6d.

Rice.—OCCASIONAL ESSAYS ON NATIVE SOUTH INDIAN LIFE. By STANLEY P. RICE, Indian Civil Service. 8vo, 10s. 6d.

Smith.—CLIMBING IN THE BRITISH ISLES. By W. P. HASKETT SMITH. With Illustrations and numerous Plans.
Part I. ENGLAND. 16mo, 3s. net.
Part II. WALES AND IRELAND. 16mo, 3s. net.

Spender.—TWO WINTERS IN NORWAY : being an Account of Two Holidays spent on Snow-shoes and in Sleigh Driving, and including an Expedition to the Lapps. By A. EDMUND SPENDER. With 40 Illustrations from Photographs. 8vo, 10s. 6d. net.

Stephen.—THE PLAYGROUND OF EUROPE (The Alps). By LESLIE STEPHEN. With 4 Illustrations. Cr. 8vo, 3s. 6d.

Three in Norway.—By Two of them. With a Map and 59 Illustrations. Cr. 8vo, 2s. boards, 2s. 6d. cloth.

Tyndall (JOHN).
THE GLACIERS OF THE ALPS : With 61 Illustrations. Crown 8vo, 6s. 6d. net.

HOURS OF EXERCISE IN THE ALPS. With 7 Illustrations. Cr. 8vo, 6s. 6d. net.

Sport and Pastime.
THE BADMINTON LIBRARY.
Edited by His Grace the (Eighth) DUKE OF BEAUFORT, K.G., and
A. E. T. WATSON.

ARCHERY. By C. J. Longman and Col. H. Walrond. With Contributions by Miss Legh, Viscount Dillon, etc. With 2 Maps, 23 Plates, and 172 Illustrations in the Text. Crown 8vo. cloth, 6s. net ; half-bound, with gilt top, 9s. net.

ATHLETICS. By Montague Shearman. With Chapters on Athletics at School by W. Beacher Thomas; Athletic Sports in America by C. H. Sherrill : a Contribution on Paperchasing by W. Rye, and an Introduction by Sir Richard Webster (Lord Alverstone). With 12 Plates and 37 Illustrations in the Text. Crown 8vo, cloth, 6s. net ; half-bound, with gilt top, 9s. net.

BIG GAME SHOOTING. By Clive Phillipps-Wolley.
Vol. I. Africa and America. With Contributions by Sir Samuel W. Baker, W. C. Oswell, F. C. Selous, etc. With 20 Plates and 57 Illustrations in the Text. Crown 8vo, cloth, 6s. net ; half-bound, with gilt top, 9s. net.
Vol. II. Europe, Asia, and the Arctic Regions. With Contributions by Lieut.-Colonel R. Heber Percy, Major Algernon C. Heber Percy, etc. With 17 Plates and 56 Illustrations in the Text. Crown 8vo, cloth, 6s. net ; half-bound, with gilt top, 9s. net.

BILLIARDS. By Major W. Broadfoot, R.E. With Contributions by A. H. Boyd, Sydenham Dixon, W. J. Ford, etc. With 11 Plates, 19 Illustrations in the Text, and numerous Diagrams. Crown 8vo, cloth, 6s. net ; half-bound, with gilt top, 9s. net.

COURSING AND FALCONRY. By Harding Cox, Charles Richardson, and the Hon. Gerald Lascelles. With 20 Plates and 55 Illustrations in the Text. Crown 8vo, cloth, 6s. net ; half-bound, with gilt top, 9s. net.

CRICKET. By A. G. Steel and the Hon. R. H. Lyttelton. With Contributions by Andrew Lang, W. G. Grace, F. Gale, etc. With 13 Plates and 52 Illustrations in the Text. Crown 8vo, cloth, 6s. net ; half-bound, with gilt top, 9s. net.

CYCLING. By the Earl of Albemarle and G. Lacy Hillier. With 19 Plates and 44 Illustrations in the Text. Crown 8vo, cloth, 6s. net ; half-bound, with gilt top, 9s. net.

DANCING. By Mrs. Lilly Grove. With contributions by Miss Middleton, The Hon. Mrs. Armytage, etc. With Musical Examples, and 38 Full-page Plates and 93 Illustrations in the Text. Cr. 8vo, cloth, 6s. net; half-bound, with gilt top, 9s. net.

DRIVING. By His Grace the (Eighth) Duke of Beaufort, K.G. With Contributions by A. E. T. Watson, The Earl of Onslow, etc. With 12 Plates and 54 Illustrations in the Text. Crown 8vo, cloth, 6s. net ; half-bound, with gilt top, 9s. net.

FENCING, BOXING AND WRESTLING. By Walter H. Pollock, F. C. Grove, C. Prevost, E. B. Mitchell, and Walter Armstrong. With 18 Plates and 24 Illustrations in the Text. Crown 8vo, cloth, 6s. net ; half-bound, with gilt top, 9s. net.

FISHING. By H. Cholmondeley-Pennell.
Vol. I.—Salmon and Trout. With Contributions by H. R. Francis, Major John P. Traherne, etc. With 9 Plates and numerous Illustrations of Tackle, etc. Crown 8vo, 6s. net ; half-bound, with gilt top, 9s. net.
Vol. II.—Pike and Other Coarse Fish. With Contributions by the Marquis of Exeter, William Senior, G. Christopher Davis, etc. With 7 Plates and numerous Illustrations of Tackle, etc. Cr. 8vo, cloth, 6s. net ; half-bound, with gilt top, 9s. net.

FOOTBALL.—History, by Montague Shearman ; The Association Game, by W. J. Oakley and G. O. Smith; The Rugby Union Game, by Frank Mitchell. With other Contributions by R. E. Macnaghten, M. C. Kemp, J. E. Vincent, Walter Camp and A. Sutherland. With 19 Plates and 35 Illustrations in the Text. Crown 8vo, cloth, 6s. net ; half-bound, with gilt top, 9s. net.

GOLF. By Horace G. Hutchinson. With Contributions by the Rt. Hon. A. J. Balfour, M.P., Sir Walter Simpson, Bart., Andrew Lang, etc. With 34 Plates and 56 Illustrations in the Text. Crown 8vo, cloth, 6s. net ; half-bound, with gilt top, 9s. net.

Sport and Pastime—*continued.*
THE BADMINTON LIBRARY—*continued.*
Edited by HIS GRACE THE (EIGHTH) DUKE OF BEAUFORT, K.G., and
A. E. T. WATSON.

HUNTING. By His Grace the (Eighth) DUKE OF BEAUFORT, K.G., and MOW-BRAY MORRIS. With Contributions by the EARL OF SUFFOLK AND BERKSHIRE, Rev. E. W. L. DAVIES, G. H. LONGMAN, etc. With 5 Plates and 54 Illustrations in the Text. Crown 8vo, cloth, 6s. net ; half-bound, with gilt top, 9s. net.

MOTORS AND MOTOR-DRIVING. By ALFRED C. HARMSWORTH, the MARQUIS DE CHASSELOUP-LAUBAT, the Hon. JOHN SCOTT-MONTAGU, R. J. MECREDY, the Hon. C. S. ROLLS, Sir DAVID SALOMONS, Bart., etc. With 13 Plates and 136 Illustrations in the Text. Crown 8vo, cloth, 9s. net ; half-bound, 12s. net. A Cloth Box for use when Motoring, price 2s. net.

MOUNTAINEERING. By C. T. DENT. With Contributions by the Right Hon. J. BRYCE, M.P., Sir MARTIN CONWAY, D. W. FRESHFIELD, C. E. MATTHEWS, etc. With 13 Plates and 91 Illustrations in the Text. Crown 8vo, cloth, 6s. net ; half-bound, with gilt top, 9s. net.

POETRY OF SPORT (THE). Selected by HEADLEY PEEK. With a Chapter on Classical Allusions to Sport by ANDREW LANG, and a Special Preface to the BADMINTON LIBRARY by A. E. T. WATSON. With 32 Plates and 74 Illustrations in the Text. Cr. 8vo, cloth, 6s. net ; half-bound, with gilt top, 9s. net.

RACING AND STEEPLE-CHASING. By the EARL OF SUFFOLK AND BERK-SHIRE, W. G. CRAVEN, the Hon. F. LAWLEY, ARTHUR COVENTRY, and A. E. T. WATSON. With Frontispiece and 56 Illustrations in the Text. Cr. 8vo, cloth, 6s. net ; half-bound, with gilt top, 9s. net.

RIDING AND POLO. By Captain ROBERT WEIR, J. MORAY BROWN, T. F. DALE, the late DUKE OF BEAUFORT, the EARL OF SUFFOLK AND BERKSHIRE, etc. With 18 Plates and 41 Illustrations in the Text. Crown 8vo, cloth, 6s. net ; half-bound, with gilt top, 9s. net.

ROWING. By R. P. P. ROWE and C. M. PITMAN. With Chapters on Steering by C. P. SEROCOLD and F. C. BEGG ; Metropolitan Rowing by S. LE BLANC SMITH ; and on PUNTING by P. W. SQUIRE. With 75 Illustrations. Crown 8vo, cloth, 6s. net ; half-bound, with gilt top, 9s. net.

SEA FISHING. By JOHN BICKERDYKE, Sir H. W. GORE-BOOTH, ALFRED C. HARMSWORTH, and W. SENIOR. With 22 Full-page Plates and 175 Illustrations in the Text. Crown 8vo, cloth, 6s. net ; half-bound, with gilt top, 9s. net.

SHOOTING.
Vol. I.—FIELD AND COVERT. By LORD WALSINGHAM and Sir RALPH PAYNE-GALLWEY, Bart. With Contributions by the Hon. GERALD LASCELLES and A. J. STUART-WORTLEY. With 11 Plates and 95 Illustrations in the Text. Crown 8vo, cloth, 6s. net : half-bound, with gilt top, 9s. net.

Vol. II.—MOOR AND MARSH. By LORD WALSINGHAM and Sir RALPH PAYNE-GALLWEY, Bart. With Contributions by LORD LOVAT and LORD CHARLES LENNOX KERR. With 8 Plates and 57 Illustrations in the Text. Crown 8vo, cloth, 6s. net ; half-bound, with gilt top, 9s. net.

SKATING, CURLING, TOBOGGANING. By J. M. HEATHCOTE, C. G. TEBBUTT, T. MAXWELL WITHAM, Rev. JOHN KERR, ORMOND HAKE, HENRY A. BUCK, etc. With 12 Plates and 272 Illustrations in the Text. Crown 8vo, cloth, 6s. net ; half-bound, with gilt top, 9s. net.

SWIMMING. By ARCHIBALD SINCLAIR and WILLIAM HENRY, Hon. Secs. of the Life-Saving Society. With 13 Plates and 112 Illustrations in the Text. Cr. 8vo, cloth, 6s. net ; half-bound, with gilt top, 9s. net.

TENNIS, LAWN TENNIS, RACKETS AND FIVES. By J. M. and C. G. HEATHCOTE, E. O. PLEYDELL-BOUVERIE, and A. C. AINGER. With Contributions by the Hon. A. LYTTELTON, W. C. MARSHALL, Miss L. DOD, etc. With 12 Plates and 67 Illustrations in the Text. Crown 8vo, cloth, 6s. net ; half-bound, with gilt top, 9s. net.

YACHTING.
Vol. I.—CRUISING, CONSTRUCTION OF YACHTS, YACHT RACING RULES, FITTING-OUT, etc. By Sir EDWARD SULLIVAN, Bart., the EARL OF PEMBROKE, LORD BRASSEY, K.C.B., C. E. SETH-SMITH, C.B., G. L. WATSON, R. T. PRITCHETT, E. F. KNIGHT, etc. With 21 Plates and 93 Illustrations in the Text. Crown 8vo, cloth, 6s. net ; half-bound, with gilt top, 9s. net.

Vol. II.—YACHT CLUBS, YACHTING IN AMERICA AND THE COLONIES, YACHT RACING, etc. By R. T. PRITCHETT, the MARQUIS OF DUFFERIN AND AVA, K.P., the EARL OF ONSLOW, JAMES McFERRAN, etc. With 35 Plates and 160 Illustrations in the Text. Crown 8vo, cloth, 6s. net ; half-bound, with gilt top, 9s. net.

Sport and Pastime—*continued.*

FUR, FEATHER, AND FIN SERIES.

Edited by A. E. T. WATSON.

Crown 8vo, price 5s. each Volume, cloth.

*** *The Volumes are also issued half-bound in Leather, with gilt top. The price can be had from all Booksellers.*

THE PARTRIDGE. NATURAL HISTORY, by the Rev. H. A. MACPHERSON; SHOOTING, by A. J. STUART-WORTLEY; COOKERY, by GEORGE SAINTSBURY. With 11 Illustrations and various Diagrams in the Text. Crown 8vo, 5s.

THE GROUSE. NATURAL HISTORY, by the Rev. H. A. MACPHERSON; SHOOTING, by A. J. STUART-WORTLEY; COOKERY, by GEORGE SAINTSBURY. With 13 Illustrations and various Diagrams in the Text. Crown 8vo, 5s.

THE PHEASANT. NATURAL HISTORY, by the Rev. H. A. MACPHERSON; SHOOTING, by A. J. STUART-WORTLEY; COOKERY, by ALEXANDER INNES SHAND. With 10 Illustrations and various Diagrams. Crown 8vo, 5s.

THE HARE. NATURAL HISTORY, by the Rev. H. A. MACPHERSON; SHOOTING, by the Hon. GERALD LASCELLES; COURSING, by CHARLES RICHARDSON; HUNTING, by J. S. GIBBONS and G. H. LONGMAN; COOKERY, by Col. KENNEY HERBERT. With 9 Illustrations. Crown 8vo, 5s.

RED DEER. NATURAL HISTORY, by the Rev. H. A. MACPHERSON; DEER STALKING, by CAMERON OF LOCHIEL; STAG HUNTING, by Viscount EBRINGTON; COOKERY, by ALEXANDER INNES SHAND. With 10 Illustrations. Crown 8vo, 5s.

THE SALMON. By the Hon. A. E. GATHORNE-HARDY. With Chapters on the Law of Salmon Fishing by CLAUD DOUGLAS PENNANT; COOKERY, by ALEXANDER INNES SHAND. With 8 Illustrations. Crown 8vo, 5s.

THE TROUT. By the MARQUESS OF GRANBY. With Chapters on the Breeding of Trout by Col. H. CUSTANCE; and COOKERY, by ALEXANDER INNES SHAND. With 12 Illustrations. Crown 8vo, 5s.

THE RABBIT. By JAMES EDMUND HARTING. COOKERY, by ALEXANDER INNES SHAND. With 10 Illustrations. Crown 8vo, 5s.

PIKE AND PERCH. By WILLIAM SENIOR ('Redspinner,' Editor of the *Field*). With Chapters by JOHN BICKERDYKE and W. H. POPE. COOKERY, by ALEXANDER INNES SHAND. With 12 Illustrations. Crown 8vo, 5s.

Alverstone and Alcock.—SURREY CRICKET: Its History and Associations. Edited by the Right Hon. LORD ALVERSTONE, L.C.J., President, and C. W. ALCOCK, Secretary, of the Surrey County Cricket Club. With 48 Illustrations. 8vo, 16s. net.

Bickerdyke.—DAYS OF MY LIFE ON WATER, FRESH AND SALT: and other papers. By JOHN BICKERDYKE. With Photo-Etching Frontispiece and 8 Full-page Illustrations. Crown 8vo, 3s. 6d.

Blackburne.—MR. BLACKBURNE'S GAMES AT CHESS. Selected, Annotated and Arranged by Himself. Edited, with a Biographical Sketch and a brief History of Blindfold Chess, by P. ANDERSON GRAHAM. With Portrait of Mr. Blackburne. 8vo, 7s. 6d. net.

Cawthorne and Herod.—ROYAL ASCOT: its History and its Associations. By GEORGE JAMES CAWTHORNE and RICHARD S. HEROD. With 32 Plates and 106 Illustrations in the Text. Demy 4to, £1 11s. 6d. net.

Dead Shot (The): or, Sportsman's Complete Guide. Being a Treatise on the use of the Gun, with Rudimentary and Finishing Lessons in the Art of Shooting Game of all kinds. Also Game-driving, Wildfowl and Pigeon-Shooting, Dog-breaking, etc. By MARKSMAN. With numerous Illustrations. Crown 8vo, 10s. 6d.

Ellis.—CHESS SPARKS; or, Short and Bright Games of Chess. Collected and Arranged by J. H. ELLIS, M.A. 8vo, 4s. 6d.

Sport and Pastime—*continued.*

Folkard.—THE WILD-FOWLER: A Treatise on Fowling, Ancient and Modern, descriptive also of Decoys and Flight-ponds, Wild-fowl Shooting, Gunning-punts, Shooting-yachts, etc. Also Fowling in the Fens and in Foreign Countries, Rock-fowling, etc., etc. By H. C. FOLKARD. With 13 Engravings on Steel, and several Woodcuts. 8vo, 12s. 6d.

Ford. — MIDDLESEX COUNTY CRICKET CLUB, 1864-1899. Written and Compiled by W. J. FORD (at the request of the Committee of the County C.C.). With Frontispiece Portrait of Mr. V. E. Walker. 8vo, 10s. net.

Ford.—THE THEORY AND PRACTICE OF ARCHERY. By HORACE FORD. New Edition, thoroughly Revised and Rewritten by W. BUTT, M.A. With a Preface by C. J. LONGMAN, M.A. 8vo, 14s.

Francis.—A BOOK ON ANGLING: or, Treatise on the Art of Fishing in every Branch ; including full illustrated List of Salmon Flies. By FRANCIS FRANCIS. With Portrait and Coloured Plates. Crown 8vo, 15s.

Fremantle.—THE BOOK OF THE RIFLE. By the Hon. T. F. FREMANTLE, V.D., Major, 1st Bucks V.R.C. With 54 Plates and 107 Diagrams in the Text. 8vo, 12s. 6d. net.

Gathorne-Hardy.—AUTUMNS IN ARGYLESHIRE WITH ROD AND GUN. By the Hon. A. E. GATHORNE-HARDY. With 8 Photogravure Illustrations by ARCHIBALD THORBURN. 8vo, 6s. net.

Graham. — COUNTRY PASTIMES FOR BOYS. By P. ANDERSON GRAHAM. With 252 Illustrations from Drawings and Photographs. Crown 8vo, gilt edges, 3s. net.

Hutchinson.—THE BOOK OF GOLF AND GOLFERS. By HORACE G. HUTCHINSON. With Contributions by Miss AMY PASCOE, H. H. HILTON, J. H. TAYLOR, H. J. WHIGHAM and Messrs. SUTTON & SONS. With 71 Portraits from Photographs. Large Crown 8vo, gilt top, 7s. 6d. net.

Lang.—ANGLING SKETCHES. By ANDREW LANG. With 20 Illustrations. Crown 8vo, 3s. 6d.

Lillie (ARTHUR).
CROQUET: its History, Rules and Secrets. With 4 Full-page Illustrations, 15 Illustrations in the Text, and 27 Diagrams. Crown 8vo, 6s.

CROQUET UP TO DATE. Containing the Ideas and Teachings of the Leading Players and Champions. With Contributions by Lieut.-Col. the Hon. H. NEEDHAM, C. D. LOCOCK, etc. With 19 Illustrations (15 Portraits) and numerous Diagrams. 8vo, 10s. 6d. net.

Locock.—SIDE AND SCREW: being Notes on the Theory and Practice of the Game of Billiards. By C. D. LOCOCK. With Diagrams. Crown 8vo, 5s. net.

Longman.—CHESS OPENINGS. By FREDERICK W. LONGMAN. Fcp. 8vo, 2s. 6d.

Mackenzie.—NOTES FOR HUNTING MEN. By Captain CORTLANDT GORDON MACKENZIE. Crown 8vo, 2s. 6d. net.

Madden.—THE DIARY OF MASTER WILLIAM SILENCE: a Study of Shakespeare and of Elizabethan Sport. By the Right Hon. D. H. MADDEN, Vice-Chancellor of the University of Dublin. 8vo, gilt top, 16s.

Maskelyne.—SHARPS AND FLATS: a Complete Revelation of the Secrets of Cheating at Games of Chance and Skill. By JOHN NEVIL MASKELYNE, of the Egyptian Hall. With 62 Illustrations. Crown 8vo, 6s.

Millais. — THE WILD-FOWLER IN SCOTLAND. By JOHN GUILLE MILLAIS, F.Z.S., etc. With a Frontispiece in Photogravure by Sir J. E. MILLAIS, Bart., P.R.A., 8 Photogravure Plates, 2 Coloured Plates, and 50 Illustrations from the Author's Drawings and from Photographs. Royal 4to, gilt top, 30s. net.

Modern Bridge.—By 'Slam'. With a Reprint of the Laws of Bridge, as adopted by the Portland and Turf Clubs. 18mo, gilt edges, 3s. 6d. net.

Park.—THE GAME OF GOLF. By WILLIAM PARK, Jun., Champion Golfer, 1887-89. With 17 Plates and 26 Illustrations in the Text. Crown 8vo, 7s. 6d.

Sport and Pastime—*continued.*

Payne-Gallwey (Sir RALPH, Bart.).

LETTERS TO YOUNG SHOOTERS (First Series). On the choice and Use of a Gun. With 41 Illustrations. Crown 8vo, 7s. 6d.

LETTERS TO YOUNG SHOOTERS (Second Series). On the Production, Preservation, and Killing of Game. With Directions in Shooting Wood-Pigeons and Breaking-in Retrievers. With Portrait and 103 Illustrations. Crown 8vo, 12s. 6d.

LETTERS TO YOUNG SHOOTERS (Third Series). Comprising a Short Natural History of the Wildfowl that are Rare or Common to the British Islands, with Complete Directions in Shooting Wildfowl on the Coast and Inland. With 200 Illustrations. Cr. 8vo. 18s.

Pole.—THE THEORY OF THE MODERN SCIENTIFIC GAME OF WHIST. By WILLIAM POLE, F.R.S. Fcp. 8vo, gilt edges, 2s. net.

Proctor.—HOW TO PLAY WHIST: with the Laws and Etiquette of Whist. By RICHARD A. PROCTOR. Crown 8vo, gilt edges, 3s. net.

Ronalds.—THE FLY-FISHER'S ENTOMOLOGY. By ALFRED RONALDS. With 20 Coloured Plates. 8vo, 14s.

Selous. — SPORT AND TRAVEL, EAST AND WEST. By FREDERICK COURTENEY SELOUS. With 18 Plates and 35 Illustrations in the Text. Medium 8vo, 12s. 6d. net.

Mental, Moral and Political Philosophy.

LOGIC, RHETORIC, PSYCHOLOGY, ETC.

Abbott.—THE ELEMENTS OF LOGIC. By T. K. ABBOTT, B.D. 12mo, 3s.

Aristotle.

THE ETHICS: Greek Text, Illustrated with Essay and Notes. By Sir ALEXANDER GRANT, Bart. 2 vols. 8vo, 32s.

AN INTRODUCTION TO ARISTOTLE'S ETHICS. Books I.-IV. (Book X., c. vi.-ix. in an Appendix.) With a continuous Analysis and Notes. By the Rev. E. MOORE, D.D. Crown 8vo, 10s. 6d.

Bacon (FRANCIS).

COMPLETE WORKS. Edited by R. L. ELLIS, JAMES SPEDDING and D. D. HEATH. 7 vols. 8vo, £3 13s. 6d.

Bacon (FRANCIS)—*continued.*

LETTERS AND LIFE, including all his occasional Works. Edited by JAMES SPEDDING. 7 vols. 8vo, £4 4s.

THE ESSAYS: With Annotations. By RICHARD WHATELY, D.D. 8vo, 10s. 6d.

THE ESSAYS: With Notes by F. STORR and C. H. GIBSON. Crown 8vo, 3s. 6d.

THE ESSAYS: With Introduction, Notes and Index. By E. A. ABBOTT, D.D. 2 vols. Fcp. 8vo, 6s. The Text and Index only, without Introduction and Notes, in one volume. Fcp. 8vo, 2s. 6d.

Mental, Moral and Political Philosophy—*continued.*

Bain (ALEXANDER).

MENTAL AND MORAL SCIENCE: a Compendium of Psychology and Ethics. Crown 8vo, 10s. 6d.
Or Separately,
Part I. PSYCHOLOGY AND HIS-
TORY OF PHILOSOPHY. Crown 8vo, 6s. 6d.
Part II. THEORY OF ETHICS AND ETHICAL SYSTEMS. Cr. 8vo, 4s. 6d.

LOGIC. Part I. DEDUCTION. Crown 8vo, 4s. Part II. INDUCTION. Crown 8vo, 6s. 6d.

THE SENSES AND THE INTELLECT. 8vo, 15s.

THE EMOTIONS AND THE WILL. 8vo, 15s.

PRACTICAL ESSAYS. Cr. 8vo, 2s.

Bray.—THE PHILOSOPHY OF NE-
CESSITY: or, Law in Mind as in Matter. By CHARLES BRAY. Cr. 8vo, 5s.

Brooks.—THE ELEMENTS OF MIND: being an Examination into the Nature of the First Division of the Elementary Substances of Life. By H. JAMYN BROOKS. 8vo, 10s. 6d. net.

Crozier (JOHN BEATTIE).

CIVILIZATION AND PROGRESS: being the Outlines of a New System of Political, Religious and Social Philosophy. 8vo, 14s.

HISTORY OF INTELLECTUAL DE-
VELOPMENT: on the Lines of Mod-
ern Evolution.
Vol. I. 8vo, 14s.
Vol. II. (*In preparation.*)
Vol. III. 8vo, 10s. 6d.

Davidson.—THE LOGIC OF DE-
FINITION, Explained and Applied. By WILLIAM L. DAVIDSON, M.A. Cr. 8vo, 6s.

Green (THOMAS HILL).—THE WORKS OF. Edited by R. L. NETTLESHIP.
Vols. I. and II. Philosophical Works. 8vo, 16s. each.
Vol. III. Miscellanies. With Index to the three Volumes, and Memoir. 8vo, 21s.

LECTURES ON THE PRINCIPLES OF POLITICAL OBLIGATION. With Preface by BERNARD BOSAN-
QUET. 8vo, 5s.

Gurnhill.—THE MORALS OF SUI-
CIDE. By the Rev. J. GURNHILL, B.A. Crown 8vo, 6s.

Hodgson (SHADWORTH H.).

TIME AND SPACE: a Metaphysical Essay. 8vo, 16s.

THE THEORY OF PRACTICE: an Ethical Inquiry. 2 vols. 8vo, 24s.

THE PHILOSOPHY OF REFLEC-
TION. 2 vols. 8vo, 21s.

THE METAPHYSIC OF EXPERI-
ENCE. Book I. General Analysis of Experience; Book II. Positive Science; Book III. Analysis of Conscious Action; Book IV. The Real Universe. 4 vols. 8vo, 36s. net.

Hume. — THE PHILOSOPHICAL WORKS OF DAVID HUME. Edited by T. H. GREEN and T. H. GROSE. 4 vols. 8vo, 28s. Or separately. Essays. 2 vols. 14s. Treatise of Human Nature. 2 vols. 14s.

James.—THE WILL TO BELIEVE, and Other Essays in Popular Philosophy. By WILLIAM JAMES, M.D., LL.D., etc. Crown, 8vo, 7s. 6d.

Justinian.—THE INSTITUTES OF JUSTINIAN: Latin Text, chiefly that of Huschke, with English Introduction, Translation, Notes and Summary. By THOMAS C. SANDARS, M.A. 8vo, 18s.

Kant (IMMANUEL).

CRITIQUE OF PRACTICAL REASON, AND OTHER WORKS ON THE THEORY OF ETHICS. Translated by T. K. ABBOTT, B.D. With Memoir. 8vo, 12s. 6d.

FUNDAMENTAL PRINCIPLES OF THE METAPHYSIC OF ETHICS. Translated by T. K. ABBOTT, B.D. Crown 8vo, 3s.

INTRODUCTION TO LOGIC, AND HIS ESSAY ON THE MISTAKEN SUBTILITY OF THE FOUR FIGURES. Translated by T. K. ABBOTT. 8vo, 6s.

Mental, Moral and Political Philosophy—*continued.*

Kelly.—GOVERNMENT OR HUMAN EVOLUTION. By EDMOND KELLY, M.A., F.G.S. Vol. I. Justice. Crown 8vo, 7s. 6d. net. Vol. II. Collectivism and Individualism. Cr. 8vo, 10s. 6d. net.

Killick.—HANDBOOK TO MILL'S SYSTEM OF LOGIC. By Rev. A. H. KILLICK, M.A. Crown 8vo, 3s. 6d.

Ladd (GEORGE TRUMBULL).

PHILOSOPHY OF CONDUCT : a Treatise of the Facts, Principles and Ideals of Ethics. 8vo, 21s.

ELEMENTS OF PHYSIOLOGICAL PSYCHOLOGY. 8vo, 21s.

OUTLINES OF DESCRIPTIVE PSY-CHOLOGY : a Text-Book of Mental Science for Colleges and Normal Schools. 8vo, 12s.

OUTLINES OF PHYSIOLOGICAL PSYCHOLOGY. 8vo, 12s.

PRIMER OF PSYCHOLOGY. Crown 8vo, 5s. 6d.

Lecky.—THE MAP OF LIFE: Conduct and Character. By WILLIAM EDWARD HARTPOLE LECKY. Library Edition, 8vo, 10s. 6d. Cabinet Edition, Crown 8vo, 5s. net.

Leighton. — TYPICAL MODERN CONCEPTIONS OF GOD ; or, The Absolute of German Romantic Idealism and of English Evolutionary Agnosticism. With a Constructive Essay. By JOSEPH ALEXANDER LEIGHTON. Crown 8vo, 3s. 6d. net.

Lutoslawski.—THE ORIGIN AND GROWTH OF PLATO'S LOGIC. With an Account of Plato's Style and of the Chronology of his Writings. By WINCENTY LUTOSLAWSKI. 8vo, 21s.

Max Müller (F.).

THE SCIENCE OF THOUGHT. 8vo, 21s.

THE SIX SYSTEMS OF INDIAN PHILOSOPHY. 8vo, 18s.

THREE LECTURES ON THE VEDANTA PHILOSOPHY. Cr. 8vo, 5s.

Mill (JOHN STUART).

A SYSTEM OF LOGIC. Cr. 8vo, 3s. 6d.

ON LIBERTY. Crown 8vo, 1s. 4d.

CONSIDERATIONS ON REPRESEN-TATIVE GOVERNMENT. Crown 8vo, 2s.

UTILITARIANISM. 8vo, 2s. 6d.

EXAMINATION OF SIR WILLIAM HAMILTON'S PHILOSOPHY. 8vo, 16s.

NATURE, THE UTILITY OF RE-LIGION AND THEISM. Three Essays. 8vo, 5s.

Monck.—AN INTRODUCTION TO LOGIC. By WILLIAM HENRY S. MONCK, M.A. Crown 8vo, 5s.

Pierce—STUDIES IN AUDITORY AND VISUAL SPACE PERCEPTION : Essays on Experimental Psychology. By A. H. PIERCE. Cr. 8vo, 6s. 6d. net.

Richmond. — THE MIND OF A CHILD. By ENNIS RICHMOND. Crown 8vo, 3s. 6d. net.

Romanes.—MIND AND MOTION AND MONISM. By GEORGE JOHN ROMANES. Crown 8vo, 4s. 6d.

Sully (JAMES).

THE HUMAN MIND : a Text-book of Psychology. 2 vols. 8vo, 21s.

OUTLINES OF PSYCHOLOGY. Cr. 8vo, 9s.

THE TEACHER'S HANDBOOK OF PSYCHOLOGY. Crown 8vo, 6s. 6d.

STUDIES OF CHILDHOOD. 8vo, 10s. 6d.

CHILDREN'S WAYS: being Selections from the Author's 'Studies of Childhood'. With 25 Illustrations. Crown 8vo, 4s. 6d.

Sutherland.—THE ORIGIN AND GROWTH OF THE MORAL IN-STINCT. By ALEXANDER SUTHERLAND, M.A. 2 vols. 8vo, 28s.

Swinburne.—PICTURE LOGIC : an Attempt to Popularise the Science of Reasoning. By ALFRED JAMES SWIN-BURNE, M.A. With 23 Woodcuts. Crown 8vo, 2s. 6d.

Mental, Moral and Political Philosophy—continued.

Thomas. — INTUITIVE SUGGES-
TION. By J. W. THOMAS, Author of
'Spiritual Law in the Natural World,'
etc. Crown 8vo, 3s. 6d. net.

Webb.—THE VEIL OF ISIS; a Series
of Essays on Idealism. By THOMAS E.
WEBB, LL.D., Q.C. 8vo, 10s. 6d.

Weber.—HISTORY OF PHILOSO-
PHY. By ALFRED WEBER, Professor
in the University of Strasburg. Translated by FRANK THILLY, Ph.D. 8vo, 16s.

Whately (ARCHBISHOP).
BACON'S ESSAYS. With Annotations.
8vo, 10s. 6d.
ELEMENTS OF LOGIC. Crown 8vo,
4s. 6d.
ELEMENTS OF RHETORIC. Crown
8vo, 4s. 6d.

Zeller (Dr. EDWARD).
THE STOICS, EPICUREANS, AND
SCEPTICS. Translated by the R——
O. J. REICHEL, M.A. Crown 8vo, 15s.
OUTLINES OF THE HISTORY OF
GREEK PHILOSOPHY. Translated
by SARAH F. ALLEYNE and EVELYN
ABBOTT, M.A., LL.D. Cr. 8vo, 10s. 6d.
PLATO AND THE OLDER ACA-
DEMY. Translated by SARAH F.
ALLEYNE and ALFRED GOODWIN, B.A.
Crown 8vo, 18s.
SOCRATES AND THE SOCRATIC
SCHOOLS. Translated by the Rev.
O. J. REICHEL, M.A. Cr. 8vo, 10s. 6d.
ARISTOTLE AND THE EARLIER
PERIPATETICS. Translated by B.
F. C. COSTELLOE, M.A., and J. H.
MUIRHEAD, M.A. 2 vols. Cr. 8vo, 24s.

STONYHURST PHILOSOPHICAL SERIES.

A MANUAL OF POLITICAL ECO-
NOMY. By C. S. DEVAS, M.A.
Crown 8vo, 7s. 6d.

FIRST PRINCIPLES OF KNOW-
LEDGE. By JOHN RICKABY, S.J.
Crown 8vo, 5s.

GENERAL METAPHYSICS. By JOHN
RICKABY, S.J. Crown 8vo, 5s.

LOGIC. By RICHARD F. CLARKE, S.J.
Crown 8vo, 5s.

MORAL PHILOSOPHY (ETHICS
AND NATURAL LAW). By JOSEPH
RICKABY, S.J. Crown 8vo, 5s.

NATURAL THEOLOGY. By BERNARD
BOEDDER, S.J. Crown 8vo, 6s. 6d.

PSYCHOLOGY. By MICHAEL MAHER,
S.J., D.Litt., M.A. (Lond.). Crown
8vo, 6s. 6d.

History and Science of Language, etc.

Davidson.—LEADING AND IM-
PORTANT ENGLISH WORDS : Ex-
plained and Exemplified. By WILLIAM
L. DAVIDSON, M.A. Fcp. 8vo, 3s. 6d.

Farrar.—LANGUAGE AND LAN-
GUAGES. By F. W. FARRAR, D.D.,
Dean of Canterbury. Crown 8vo, 6s.

Graham. — ENGLISH SYNONYMS,
Classified and Explained : with Practical
Exercises. By G. F. GRAHAM. Fcp.
8vo, 6s.

Max Müller (F.).

THE SCIENCE OF LANGUAGE.
2 vols. Crown 8vo, 10s.

Max Müller (F.)—continued.
BIOGRAPHIES OF WORDS, AND
THE HOME OF THE ARYAS.
Crown 8vo, 5s.
CHIPS FROM A GERMAN WORK-
SHOP. Vol. III. ESSAYS ON
LANGUAGE AND LITERATURE.
Crown 8vo, 5s.
LAST ESSAYS. First Series. Essays
on Language, Folklore and other
Subjects. Crown 8vo, 5s.

Roget.—THESAURUS OF ENGLISH
WORDS AND PHRASES. Classified
and Arranged so as to Facilitate the
Expression of Ideas and Assist in Lite-
rary Composition. By PETER MARK
ROGET, M.D., F.R.S. With full Index.
Cr. 8vo, 9s. net.

Political Economy and Economics.

Ashley (W. J.).
ENGLISH ECONOMIC HISTORY AND THEORY. Crown 8vo, Part I., 5s. Part II., 10s. 6d.
SURVEYS, HISTORIC AND ECONO-MIC. Crown 8vo, 9s. net.

Bagehot.—ECONOMIC STUDIES. By WALTER BAGEHOT. Crown 8vo. 3s. 6d.

Barnett. — PRACTICABLE SOCIAL-ISM. Essays on Social Reform. By SAMUEL A. and HENRIETTA BARNETT. Crown 8vo, 6s.

Devas.—A MANUAL OF POLITICAL ECONOMY. By C. S. DEVAS, M.A. Crown 8vo, 7s. 6d. (*Stonyhurst Philo-sophical Series.*)

Lawrence. — LOCAL VARIATIONS IN WAGES. By F. W. LAWRENCE, M.A. With Index and 18 Maps and Diagrams. 4to, 8s. 6d.

Leslie. — ESSAYS ON POLITICAL ECONOMY. By T. E. CLIFFE LESLIE, Hon. LL.D., Dubl. 8vo, 10s. 6d.

Macleod (HENRY DUNNING).
ECONOMICS FOR BEGINNERS. Cr. 8vo, 2s.
THE ELEMENTS OF ECONOMICS. 2 vols. Crown 8vo, 3s. 6d. each.
BIMETALLISM. 8vo, 5s. net.
THE ELEMENTS OF BANKING. Cr. 8vo, 3s. 6d.
THE THEORY AND PRACTICE OF BANKING. Vol. I. 8vo, 12s. Vol. II. 14s.

Macleod (HENRY DUNNING)—cont.
THE THEORY OF CREDIT. 8vo. In 1 vol. 30s. net; or separately, Vol. I., 10s. net. Vol. II., Part I., 10s. net. Vol. II., Part II., 10s. net.
INDIAN CURRENCY. 8vo, 2s. 6d. net.

Mill.—POLITICAL ECONOMY. By JOHN STUART MILL.
Popular Edition. Crown 8vo, 3s. 6d.
Library Edition. 2 vols. 8vo, 30s.

Mulhall. — INDUSTRIES AND WEALTH OF NATIONS. By MICH-AEL G. MULHALL, F.S.S. With 32 Diagrams. Crown 8vo, 8s. 6d.

Spahr. — AMERICA'S WORKING PEOPLE. By CHARLES B. SPAHR. Crown 8vo, 5s. net.

Symes.—POLITICAL ECONOMY: a Short Textbook of Political Economy. With Problems for solution, Hints for Supplementary Reading, and a Supple-mentary chapter on Socialism. By J. E. SYMES, M.A. Crown 8vo, 2s. 6d.

Toynbee.—LECTURES ON THE IN-DUSTRIAL REVOLUTION OF THE 18TH CENTURY IN ENGLAND. By ARNOLD TOYNBEE. 8vo, 10s. 6d.

Webb (SIDNEY and BEATRICE).
THE HISTORY OF TRADE UNION-ISM. With Map and Bibliography. 8vo, 7s. 6d. net.
INDUSTRIAL DEMOCRACY: a Study in Trade Unionism. 2 vols. 8vo, 12s. net.
PROBLEMS OF MODERN INDUS-TRY: Essays. 8vo, 7s. 6d.

Evolution, Anthropology, etc.

Clodd (EDWARD).
THE STORY OF CREATION: a Plain Account of Evolution. With 77 Il-lustrations. Crown 8vo, 3s. 6d.
A PRIMER OF EVOLUTION: being a Popular Abridged Edition of 'The Story of Creation'. With Illustra-tions. Fcp. 8vo, 1s. 6d.

Lubbock.—THE ORIGIN OF CIVIL-ISATION, and the Primitive condition of Man. By Sir J. LUBBOCK, Bart., M.P. (Lord Avebury). With 5 Plates and 20 Illustrations. 8vo, 18s.

Evolution, Anthropology, etc.—*continued.*

Packard.—LAMARCK, THE FOUN-
DER OF EVOLUTION : his Life and
Work, with Translations of his Writ-
ings on Organic Evolution. By ALPHEUS
S. PACKARD. M.D., LL.D., Professor of
Zoology and Geology in Brown Univer-
sity. With 10 Portrait and other Illus-
trations. Large Crown 8vo, 9s. net.

Romanes (GEORGE JOHN).
ESSAYS. Edited by C. LLOYD MOR-
GAN. Crown 8vo, 5s. net.
AN EXAMINATION OF WEISMANN-
ISM. Crown 8vo, 6s.

Romanes (GEORGE JOHN)—*continued.*
DARWIN, AND AFTER DARWIN :
an Exposition of the Darwinian
Theory, and a Discussion on Post-
Darwinian Questions.
Part I. THE DARWINIAN THEORY.
With Portrait of Darwin and 125
Illustrations. Crown 8vo, 10s. 6d.
Part II. POST-DARWINIAN QUES-
TIONS : Heredity and Utility. With
Portrait of the Author and 5 Illus-
trations. Crown 8vo, 10s. 6d.
Part III. POST-DARWINIAN QUES-
TIONS : Isolation and Physiological
Selection. Crown 8vo, 5s.

The Science of Religion, etc.

Balfour.—THE FOUNDATIONS OF
BELIEF : being Notes Introductory to
the Study of Theology. By the Right
Hon. ARTHUR JAMES BALFOUR. Crown
8vo, 6s. net.

Baring-Gould.—THE ORIGIN AND
DEVELOPMENT OF RELIGIOUS
BELIEF. By the Rev. S. BARING-
GOULD. 2 vols. Crown 8vo, 3s. 6d. each.

Campbell.—RELIGION IN GREEK
LITERATURE. By the Rev. LEWIS
CAMPBELL, M.A., LL.D. 8vo, 15s.

Davidson.—THEISM, as Grounded in
Human Nature, Historically and Critic-
ally Handled. Being the Burnett
Lectures for 1892 and 1893, delivered at
Aberdeen. By W. L. DAVIDSON, M.A.,
LL.D. 8vo, 15s.

Lang (ANDREW).
MAGIC AND RELIGION. 8vo, 10s. 6d.
CUSTOM AND MYTH : Studies of
Early Usage and Belief. With 15
Illustrations. Crown 8vo, 3s. 6d.
MYTH, RITUAL AND RELIGION.
2 vols. Crown 8vo, 7s.
MODERN MYTHOLOGY : a Reply to
Professor Max Müller. 8vo, 9s.
THE MAKING OF RELIGION. Cr.
8vo, 5s. net.

Max Müller (The Right Hon. F.).
CHIPS FROM A GERMAN WORK-
SHOP. Vol. IV. Essays on Mytho-
logy and Folk Lore. Crown 8vo, 5s.
THE SIX SYSTEMS OF INDIAN
PHILOSOPHY. 8vo, 18s.
CONTRIBUTIONS TO THE SCIENCE
OF MYTHOLOGY. 2 vols. 8vo, 32s.

Max Müller (The Rt. Hon. F.)—*contd.*
THE ORIGIN AND GROWTH OF RE-
LIGION,as illustrated by the Religions
of India. The Hibbert Lectures, de-
livered at the Chapter House, West-
minster Abbey, in 1878. Cr. 8vo, 5s.
INTRODUCTION TO THE SCIENCE
OF RELIGION : Four Lectures de-
livered at the Royal Institution.
Crown 8vo, 5s.
NATURAL RELIGION. The Gifford
Lectures, delivered before the Uni-
versity of Glasgow in 1888. Cr. 8vo, 5s.
PHYSICAL RELIGION. The Gifford
Lectures, delivered before the Univer-
sity of Glasgow in 1890. Cr. 8vo, 5s.
ANTHROPOLOGICAL RELIGION.
The Gifford Lectures, delivered before
the University of Glasgow in 1891.
Crown 8vo, 5s.
THEOSOPHY ; or, PSYCHOLOGICAL
RELIGION. The Gifford Lectures,
delivered before the University of
Glasgow in 1892. Crown 8vo, 5s.
THREE LECTURES ON THE
VEDANTA PHILOSOPHY, de-
livered at the Royal Institution in
March, 1894. Crown 8vo, 5s.
LAST ESSAYS. Second Series—Essays
on the Science of Religion. Cr. 8vo, 5s.

Wood-Martin (W. G.).
TRACES OF THE ELDER FAITHS
OF IRELAND : a Folklore Sketch.
A Handbook of Irish Pre-Christian
Traditions. With 192 Illustrations.
2 vols. 8vo, 30s. net.
PAGAN IRELAND : an Archæological
Sketch. A Handbook of Irish Pre-
Christian Antiquities. With 512 Illus-
trations. 8vo, 15s.

Classical Literature, Translations, etc.

Abbott.—HELLENICA. A Collection of Essays on Greek Poetry, Philosophy, History and Religion. Edited by EVELYN ABBOTT, M.A., LL.D. Crown 8vo, 7s. 6d.

Æschylus. — EUMENIDES OF ÆSCHYLUS. With Metrical English Translation. By J. F. DAVIES. 8vo, 7s.

Aristophanes.—THE ACHARNIANS OF ARISTOPHANES, translated into English Verse. By R. Y. TYRRELL. Crown 8vo, 1s.

Becker (W. A.). Translated by the Rev. F. METCALFE, B.D.

GALLUS: or, Roman Scenes in the Time of Augustus. With Notes and Excursuses. With 26 Illustrations. Crown 8vo, 3s. 6d.

CHARICLES: or, Illustrations of the Private Life of the Ancient Greeks. With Notes and Excursuses. With 26 Illustrations. Crown 8vo, 3s. 6d.

Campbell.—RELIGION IN GREEK LITERATURE. By the Rev. LEWIS CAMPBELL, M.A., LL.D., Emeritus Professor of Greek, University of St. Andrews. 8vo, 15s.

Cicero. — CICERO'S CORRESPONDENCE. By R. Y. TYRRELL. Vols. I., II., III., 8vo, each 12s. Vol. IV., 15s. Vol. V., 14s. Vol. VI., 12s. Vol. VII., Index, 7s. 6d.

Harvard Studies in Classical Philology. Edited by a Committee of the Classical Instructors of Harvard University. Vols. XI. and XII. 1900 and 1901. 8vo, 6s. 6d. net.

Hime. — LUCIAN, THE SYRIAN SATIRIST. By Lieut.-Colonel HENRY W. L. HIME (late) Royal Artillery. 8vo, 5s. net.

Homer.

THE ILIAD OF HOMER. Freely rendered into English Prose for the use of those who cannot read the original. By SAMUEL BUTLER. Crown 8vo, 7s. 6d.

Homer—*continued.*

THE ODYSSEY. Rendered into English Prose, for the use of those who cannot read the original. By SAMUEL BUTLER. With 4 Maps and 7 Illustrations. 8vo, 7s. 6d.

THE ODYSSEY OF HOMER. Done into English Verse. By WILLIAM MORRIS. Crown 8vo, 6s.

Horace.—THE WORKS OF HORACE, rendered into English Prose. With Life, Introduction and Notes. By WILLIAM COUTTS, M.A. Crown 8vo, 5s. net.

Keller. — HOMERIC SOCIETY : a Sociological Study of the 'Iliad' and 'Odyssey'. By ALBERT GALLOWAY KELLER Ph.D. Crown 8vo, 5s. net.

Lucan.—THE PHARSALIA OF LUCAN, Translated into Blank Verse. By Sir EDWARD RIDLEY. 8vo, 14s.

Lucian.—TRANSLATIONS FROM LUCIAN. By AUGUSTA M. CAMPBELL DAVIDSON, M.A. Edin. Crown 8vo, 5s. net.

Mackail.—SELECT EPIGRAMS FROM THE GREEK ANTHOLOGY. By J. W. MACKAIL. Edited with a Revised Text, Introduction, Translation, and Notes. 8vo, 16s.

Ogilvie.—HORAE LATINAE: Studies in Synonyms and Syntax. By the late ROBERT OGILVIE, M.A., LL.D., H.M. Chief Inspector of Schools for Scotland. Edited by ALEXANDER SOUTER, M.A. With a Memoir by JOSEPH OGILVIE, M.A., LL.D. 8vo, 12s. 6d. net.

Rich.—A DICTIONARY OF ROMAN AND GREEK ANTIQUITIES. By A. RICH, B.A. With 2000 Woodcuts. Crown 8vo, 6s. net.

Sophocles.—Translated into English Verse. By ROBERT WHITELAW, M.A., Assistant Master in Rugby School. Cr. 8vo, 8s. 6d.

Tyrrell.—DUBLIN TRANSLATIONS INTO GREEK AND LATIN VERSE. Edited by R. Y. TYRRELL. 8vo, 6s.

Classical Literature, Translations, etc.—*continued*.

Virgil.

THE POEMS OF VIRGIL. Translated into English Prose by JOHN CONINGTON. Crown 8vo, 6s.

THE ÆNEID OF VIRGIL. Translated into English Verse by JOHN CONINGTON. Crown 8vo, 6s.

THE ÆNEIDS OF VIRGIL. Done into English Verse. By WILLIAM MORRIS. Crown 8vo, 6s.

THE ÆNEID OF VIRGIL, freely translated into English Blank Verse. By W. J. THORNHILL. Crown 8vo, 6s. net.

Virgil—*continued*.

THE ÆNEID OF VIRGIL. Translated into English Verse by JAMES RHOADES. Books I.-VI. Crown 8vo, 5s. Books VII.-XII. Crown 8vo, 5s.

THE ECLOGUES AND GEORGICS OF VIRGIL. Translated into English Prose by J. W. MACKAIL, Fellow of Balliol College, Oxford. 16mo, 5s.

Wilkins.—THE GROWTH OF THE HOMERIC POEMS. By G. WILKINS. 8vo, 6s.

Poetry and the Drama.

Arnold.—THE LIGHT OF THE WORLD; or, the Great Consummation. By Sir EDWIN ARNOLD. With 14 Illustrations after HOLMAN HUNT. Crown 8vo, 5s. net.

Bell (Mrs. HUGH).
CHAMBER COMEDIES: a Collection of Plays and Monologues for the Drawing-room. Crown 8vo, 5s. net.
FAIRY TALE PLAYS, AND HOW TO ACT THEM. With 91 Diagrams and 52 Illustrations. Crown 8vo, 3s. net.
RUMPELSTILTZKIN: a Fairy Play in Five Scenes (Characters, 7 Male; 1 Female). From 'Fairy Tale Plays and How to Act Them'. With Illustrations, Diagrams and Music. Crown 8vo, sewed, 6d.

Bird.—RONALD'S FAREWELL, and other Verses. By GEORGE BIRD, M.A., Vicar of Bradwell, Derbyshire. Fcp. 8vo, 4s. 6d. net.

Dabney.—THE MUSICAL BASIS OF VERSE: a Scientific Study of the Principles of Poetic Composition. By J. P. DABNEY. Crown 8vo, 6s.6d. net.

Goethe.—THE FIRST PART OF THE TRAGEDY OF FAUST IN ENGLISH. By THOS. E. WEBB, LL.D., sometime Fellow of Trinity College; Professor of Moral Philosophy in the University of Dublin, etc. New and Cheaper Edition, with THE DEATH OF FAUST, from the Second Part. Crown 8vo, 6s.

Ingelow (JEAN).
POETICAL WORKS. Complete in One Volume. Crown 8vo, gilt top, 6s. net.
LYRICAL AND OTHER POEMS. Selected from the Writings of JEAN INGELOW. Fcp. 8vo, 2s. 6d. cloth plain, 3s. cloth gilt.

Lang (ANDREW).
GRASS OF PARNASSUS. Fcp. 8vo, 2s. 6d. net.
THE BLUE POETRY BOOK. Edited by ANDREW LANG. With 100 Illustrations. Crown 8vo, gilt edges, 6s.

Lecky.—POEMS. By the Right Hon. W. E. H. LECKY. Fcp. 8vo, 5s.

Lytton (THE EARL OF), (OWEN MEREDITH).
THE WANDERER. Cr. 8vo, 10s. 6d.
LUCILE. Crown 8vo, 10s. 6d.
SELECTED POEMS. Cr. 8vo, 10s. 6d.

Macaulay.—LAYS OF ANCIENT ROME, WITH 'IVRY' AND 'THE ARMADA'. By Lord MACAULAY. Illustrated by G. SCHARF. Fcp. 4to, 10s. 6d.
——————— Bijou Edition, 18mo, 2s. 6d., gilt top.
——————— Popular Edition, Fcp. 4to, 6d. sewed, 1s. cloth.
Illustrated by J. R. WEGUELIN. Cr. 8vo, 3s. net.
Annotated Edition. Fcp. 8vo, 1s. sewed, 1s. 6d. cloth.

Poetry and the Drama—*continued.*

MacDonald.—A BOOK OF STRIFE, IN THE FORM OF THE DIARY OF AN OLD SOUL: Poems. By GEORGE MacDONALD, LL.D. 18mo, 6s.

Moon.—POEMS OF LOVE AND HOME. By GEORGE WASHINGTON MOON, Hon. F.R.S.L. With Portrait. 16mo, 2s. 6d.

Morris (WILLIAM).

POETICAL WORKS—LIBRARY EDITION.
Complete in 11 volumes. Crown 8vo, price 5s. net each.

THE EARTHLY PARADISE. 4 vols. Crown 8vo, 5s. net each.

THE LIFE AND DEATH OF JASON. Crown 8vo, 5s. net.

THE DEFENCE OF GUENEVERE, and other Poems. Crown 8vo, 5s. net.

THE STORY OF SIGURD THE VOLSUNG, AND THE FALL OF THE NIBLUNGS. Crown 8vo, 5s. net.

POEMS BY THE WAY, AND LOVE IS ENOUGH. Crown 8vo, 5s. net.

THE ODYSSEY OF HOMER. Done into English Verse. Crown 8vo, 5s. net.

THE ÆNEIDS OF VIRGIL. Done into English Verse. Crown 8vo, 5s. net.

THE TALE OF BEOWULF, SOME-TIME KING OF THE FOLK OF THE WEDERGEATS. Translated by WILLIAM MORRIS and A. J. WYATT. Crown 8vo, 5s. net.

Certain of the POETICAL WORKS may also be had in the following Editions :—

THE EARTHLY PARADISE.
Popular Edition. 5 Vols. 12mo, 25s. ; or 5s. each, sold separately.
The same in Ten Parts, 25s. ; or 2s. 6d. each, sold separately.
Cheap Edition, in 1 vol. Crown 8vo, 6s. net.

POEMS BY THE WAY. Square crown 8vo, 6s.

*** For Mr. William Morris's other Works, see pp. 27, 37, 38, 40.

Morte Arthur: an Alliterative Poem of the Fourteenth Century. Edited from the Thornton MS., with Introduction, Notes and Glossary. By MARY MACLEOD BANKS. Fcp. 8vo, 3s. 6d.

Nesbit.—LAYS AND LEGENDS. By E. NESBIT (Mrs. HUBERT BLAND). First Series. Crown 8vo, 3s. 6d. Second Series. With Portrait. Crown 8vo, 5s.

Ramal.—SONGS OF CHILDHOOD. By WALTER RAMAL. With a Frontispiece from a Drawing by RICHARD DOYLE. Fcp. 8vo, 3s. 6d. net.

Riley. — OLD-FASHIONED ROSES : Poems. By JAMES WHITCOMBE RILEY. 12mo, gilt top, 5s.

Romanes.—A SELECTION FROM THE POEMS OF GEORGE JOHN ROMANES, M.A., LL.D., F.R.S. With an Introduction by T. HERBERT WARREN, President of Magdalen College, Oxford. Crown 8vo, 4s. 6d.

Savage-Armstrong.--BALLADS OF DOWN. By G. F. SAVAGE-ARMSTRONG. M.A., D.Litt. Crown 8vo, 7s. 6d.

Shakespeare.

BOWDLER'S FAMILY SHAKE-SPEARE. With 36 Woodcuts. 1 vol. 8vo, 14s. Or in 6 vols. Fcp. 8vo, 21s.

THE SHAKESPEARE BIRTHDAY BOOK. By MARY F. DUNBAR. 32mo, 1s. 6d.

Stevenson.—A CHILD'S GARDEN OF VERSES. By ROBERT LOUIS STEVENSON. Fcp. 8vo, gilt top, 5s.

Wagner. — THE NIBELUNGEN RING. Done into English Verse by REGINALD RANKIN, B.A., of the Inner Temple, Barrister-at-Law.
Vol. I. Rhine Gold, The Valkyrie. Fcp. 8vo, gilt top, 4s. 6d.
Vol. II. Siegfried, The Twilight of the Gods. Fcp. 8vo, gilt top, 4s. 6d.

Fiction, Humour, etc.

Anstey (F.).

VOCES POPULI. (Reprinted from *Punch*.)

First Series. With 20 Illustrations by J. BERNARD PARTRIDGE. Crown 8vo, gilt top, 3s. net.

Second Series. With 25 Illustrations by J. BERNARD PARTRIDGE. Crown 8vo, gilt top, 3s. net.

THE MAN FROM BLANKLEY'S, and other Sketches. (Reprinted from *Punch*.)· With 25 Illustrations by J. BERNARD PARTRIDGE. Crown 8vo, gilt top, 3s. net.

Bailey.—MY LADY OF ORANGE: a Romance of the Netherlands in the Days of Alva. By H. C. BAILEY. With 8 Illustrations. Crown 8vo, 6s.

Beaconsfield (THE EARL OF).

NOVELS AND TALES. Complete in 11 vols. Crown 8vo, 1s. 6d. each, or in sets, 11 vols., gilt top, 15s. net.

Vivian Grey.	Sybil.
The Young Duke, etc.	Henrietta Temple.
Alroy, Ixion, etc.	Venetia.
Contarini, Fleming, etc.	Coningsby.
	Lothair.
Tancred.	Endymion.

NOVELS AND TALES. THE HUGHENDEN EDITION. With 2 Portraits and 11 Vignettes. 11 vols. Crown 8vo, 42s.

Churchill.—SAVROLA : a Tale of the Revolution in Laurania. By WINSTON SPENCER CHURCHILL, M.P. Crown 8vo, 6s.

Crawford.—THE AUTOBIOGRAPHY OF A TRAMP. By J. H. CRAWFORD. With a Photogravure Frontispiece 'The Vagrants,' by FRED. WALKER, and 8 other Illustrations. Crown 8vo, 5s. net.

Creed.—THE VICAR OF ST. LUKE'S. By SIBYL CREED. Cr. 8vo, 6s.

Dougall.—BEGGARS ALL. By L. DOUGALL. Crown 8vo, 3s. 6d.

Doyle (A. CONAN).

MICAH CLARKE: a Tale of Monmouth's Rebellion. With 10 Illustrations. Crown 8vo, 3s. 6d.

THE REFUGEES : a Tale of the Huguenots. With 25 Illustrations. Crown 8vo, 3s. 6d.

THE STARK MUNRO LETTERS. Crown 8vo, 3s. 6d.

THE CAPTAIN OF THE POLESTAR, and other Tales. Crown 8vo, 3s. 6d.

Dyson.—THE GOLD-STEALERS : a Story of Waddy. By EDWARD DYSON, Author of 'Rhymes from the Mines,' etc. Crown 8vo, 6s.

Farrar (F. W., DEAN OF CANTERBURY).

DARKNESS AND DAWN : or, Scenes in the Days of Nero. An Historic Tale. Crown 8vo, gilt top, 6s. net.

GATHERING CLOUDS : a Tale of the Days of St. Chrysostom. Crown 8vo, gilt top, 6s. net.

Fowler (EDITH H.).

THE YOUNG PRETENDERS. A Story of Child Life. With 12 Illustrations by Sir PHILIP BURNE-JONES, Bart. Crown 8vo, 6s.

THE PROFESSOR'S CHILDREN. With 24 Illustrations by ETHEL KATE BURGESS. Crown 8vo, 6s.

Francis (M. E.).

FIANDER'S WIDOW. Crown 8vo, 6s.

YEOMAN FLEETWOOD. With Frontispiece. Crown 8vo, 3s. net.

PASTORALS OF DORSET. With 8 Illustrations. Crown 8vo, 6s.

Froude.—THE TWO CHIEFS OF DUNBOY: an Irish Romance of the Last Century. By JAMES A. FROUDE. Crown 8vo, 3s. 6d.

Fiction, Humour, etc.—*continued.*

Gurdon.—M E M O R I E S   A N D
FANCIES : Suffolk Tales and other
Stories ; Fairy Legends ; Poems ; Mis-
cellaneous Articles. By the late Lady
CAMILLA GURDON.   Crown 8vo, 5s.

Haggard (H. RIDER).

ALLAN QUATERMAIN.   With 31
Illustrations.   Crown 8vo. 3s. 6d.

ALLAN'S WIFE. With 34 Illustrations.
Crown 8vo, 3s. 6d.

BEATRICE. With Frontispiece and
Vignette. Crown 8vo, 3s. 6d.

BLACK   HEART   AND   WHITE
HEART, and other Stories.   With 33
Illustrations. Crown 8vo, 6s.

CLEOPATRA. With 29 Illustrations.
Crown 8vo, 3s. 6d.

COLONEL QUARITCH, V.C.   With
Frontispiece and Vignette.   Crown
8vo, 3s. 6d.

DAWN. With 16 Illustrations. Crown
8vo, 3s. 6d.

DOCTOR THERNE.   Cr. 8vo, 3s. 6d.

ERIC BRIGHTEYES.   With 51 Illustrations. Crown 8vo, 3s. 6d.

HEART OF THE WORLD. With 15
Illustrations. Crown 8vo, 3s. 6d.

JOAN HASTE.   With 20 Illustrations.
Crown 8vo, 3s. 6d.

LYSBETH.   With   26   Illustrations.
Crown 8vo, 6s.

MAIWA'S REVENGE. Cr. 8vo, 1s. 6d.

MONTEZUMA'S DAUGHTER.   With
24 Illustrations. Crown 8vo, 3s. 6d.

MR. MEESON'S WILL.   With 16
Illustrations. Crown 8vo, 3s. 6d.

NADA THE LILY. With 23 Illustrations. Crown 8vo, 3s. 6d.

Haggard (H. RIDER)—*continued.*

SHE. With 32 Illustrations.   Crown
8vo, 3s. 6d.

SWALLOW : a Tale of the Great Trek.
With 8 Illustrations.   Crown 8vo
3s. 6d.

THE PEOPLE OF THE MIST. With
16 Illustrations. Crown 8vo, 3s. 6d.

THE WITCH'S HEAD.   With 16
Illustrations. Crown 8vo, 3s. 6d.

Haggard   and   Lang. — T H E
WORLD'S DESIRE. By H. RIDER
HAGGARD and ANDREW LANG.   With
27 Illustrations. Crown 8vo, 3s. 6d.

Harte. — IN   THE   CARQUINEZ
WOODS.   By BRET HARTE.   Crown
8vo, 3s. 6d.

Hope.—THE HEART OF PRINCESS
OSRA. By ANTHONY HOPE. With 9
Illustrations. Crown 8vo, 3s. 6d.

Howard (Lady MABEL).

THE UNDOING OF JOHN BREW-
STER. Crown 8vo, 6s.

THE FAILURE OF SUCCESS. Crown
8vo, 6s.

Jerome.—SKETCHES   IN   LAVEN-
DER : BLUE AND GREEN.   By
JEROME K. JEROME, Author of 'Three
Men in a Boat,' etc. Crown 8vo, 3s. 6d.

Joyce.—OLD   CELTIC   ROMANCES.
Twelve of the most beautiful of the
Ancient Irish Romantic Tales. Trans-
lated from the Gaelic. By P. W. JOYCE,
LL.D. Crown 8vo, 3s. 6d.

Lang.—A MONK OF FIFE ; a Story of
the Days of Joan of Arc. By ANDREW
LANG. With 13 Illustrations by SELWYN
IMAGE. Crown 8vo, 3s. 6d.

Fiction, Humour, etc.—*continued*.

Lyall (EDNA).

THE HINDERERS. Crown 8vo, 2s. 6d.

THE AUTOBIOGRAPHY OF A SLANDER. Fcp. 8vo, 1s. sewed.

Presentation Edition. With 20 Illustrations by LANCELOT SPEED. Cr. 8vo, 2s. 6d. net.

THE AUTOBIOGRAPHY OF A TRUTH. Fcp. 8vo, 1s. sewed, 1s. 6d. cloth.

DOREEN. The Story of a Singer. Crown 8vo, 6s.

WAYFARING MEN. Crown 8vo, 6s.

HOPE THE HERMIT : a Romance of Borrowdale. Crown 8vo, 6s.

Marchmont.—IN THE NAME OF A WOMAN : a Romance. By ARTHUR W. MARCHMONT. With 8 Illustrations. Crown 8vo, 6s.

Mason and Lang.—PARSON KELLY. By A. E. W. MASON and ANDREW LANG. Crown 8vo, 3s. 6d.

Max Müller.—DEUTSCHE LIEBE (GERMAN LOVE) : Fragments from the Papers of an Alien. Collected by F. MAX MÜLLER. Translated from the German by G. A. M. Crown 8vo, gilt top, 5s.

Melville (G. J. WHYTE).

The Gladiators.	Holmby House.
The Interpreter.	Kate Coventry.
Good for Nothing.	Digby Grand.
The Queen's Maries.	General Bounce.

Crown 8vo, 1s. 6d. each.

Merriman.—FLOTSAM : A Story of the Indian Mutiny. By HENRY SETON MERRIMAN. With Frontispiece and Vignette by H. G. MASSEY. Crown 8vo, 3s. 6d.

Morris (WILLIAM).

THE SUNDERING FLOOD. Crown 8vo, 7s. 6d.

THE WATER OF THE WONDROUS ISLES. Crown 8vo, 7s. 6d.

THE WELL AT THE WORLD'S END. 2 vols. 8vo, 28s.

THE WOOD BEYOND THE WORLD. Crown 8vo, 6s. net.

THE STORY OF THE GLITTERING PLAIN, which has been also called The Land of the Living Men, or The Acre of the Undying. Square post 8vo, 5s. net.

THE ROOTS OF THE MOUNTAINS, wherein is told somewhat of the Lives of the Men of Burgdale, their Friends, their Neighbours, their Foemen, and their Fellows-in-Arms. Written in Prose and Verse. Square cr. 8vo, 8s.

A TALE OF THE HOUSE OF THE WOLFINGS, and all the Kindreds of the Mark. Written in Prose and Verse. Square crown 8vo, 6s.

A DREAM OF JOHN BALL, AND A KING'S LESSON. 12mo, 1s. 6d.

NEWS FROM NOWHERE : or, An Epoch of Rest. Being some Chapters from an Utopian Romance. Post 8vo, 1s. 6d.

THE STORY OF GRETTIR THE STRONG. Translated from the Icelandic by EIRÍKR MAGNÚSSON and WILLIAM MORRIS. Crown 8vo, 5s. net.

THREE NORTHERN LOVE STORIES, and other Tales. Translated from the Icelandic by EIRÍKR MAGNÚSSON and WILLIAM MORRIS. Crown 8vo, 6s. net.

** For Mr. William Morris's other Works, see pp. 24, 37, 38 and 40.

Fiction, Humour, etc.—*continued.*

Newman (CARDINAL).

LOSS AND GAIN : The Story of a Convert. Crown 8vo, 3s. 6d.

CALLISTA : a Tale of the Third Century. Crown 8vo, 3s. 6d.

Phillipps-Wolley.—SNAP : A Legend of the Lone Mountain. By C. PHILLIPPS-WOLLEY. With 13 Illustrations. Crown 8vo, 3s. 6d.

Raymond.—TWO MEN O' MENDIP. By WALTER RAYMOND. Crown 8vo, 6s.

Ridley.—ANNE MAINWARING. By ALICE RIDLEY, Author of 'The Story of Aline'. Crown 8vo, 6s.

Sewell (ELIZABETH M.).

A Glimpse of the World.	Amy Herbert.
Laneton Parsonage.	Cleve Hall.
Margaret Percival.	Gertrude.
Katherine Ashton.	Home Life.
The Earl's Daughter.	After Life.
The Experience of Life.	Ursula. Ivors.

Crown 8vo, cloth plain, 1s. 6d. each ; cloth extra, gilt edges, 2s. 6d. each.

Sheehan.—LUKE DELMEGE. By the Rev. P. A. SHEEHAN, P.P., Author of 'My New Curate'. Crown 8vo, 6s.

Somerville (E. Œ.) and **Ross** (MARTIN).

SOME EXPERIENCES OF AN IRISH R.M. With 31 Illustrations by E. Œ. SOMERVILLE. Crown 8vo, 6s.

THE REAL CHARLOTTE. Crown 8vo, 3s. 6d.

THE SILVER FOX. Crown 8vo, 3s. 6d.

Stebbing. — RACHEL WULFSTAN, and other Stories. By W. STEBBING, author of 'Probable Tales'. Crown 8vo, 4s. 6d.

Stevenson (ROBERT LOUIS).

THE STRANGE CASE OF DR. JEKYLL AND MR. HYDE. Fcp. 8vo, 1s. sewed, 1s. 6d. cloth.

THE STRANGE CASE OF DR. JEKYLL AND MR. HYDE, WITH OTHER FABLES. Cr. 8vo, bound in buckram, with gilt top, 5s. net. *'Silver Library' Edition.* Crown 8vo, 3s. 6d.

MORE NEW ARABIAN NIGHTS —THE DYNAMITER. By ROBERT LOUIS STEVENSON and FANNY VAN DE GRIFT STEVENSON. Crown 8vo, 3s. 6d.

THE WRONG BOX. By ROBERT LOUIS STEVENSON and LLOYD OSBOURNE. Crown 8vo, 3s. 6d.

Suttner.—LAY DOWN YOUR ARMS (*Die Waffen Nieder*) : The Autobiography of Martha von Tilling. By BERTHA VON SUTTNER. Translated by T. HOLMES. Crown 8vo, 1s. 6d.

Swan.—BALLAST. By MYRA SWAN. Crown 8vo, 6s.

Trollope (ANTHONY).

THE WARDEN. Crown 8vo, 1s. 6d.

BARCHESTER TOWERS. Crown 8vo, 1s. 6d.

Walford (L. B.).

CHARLOTTE. Crown 8vo, 6s.

ONE OF OURSELVES. Cr. 8vo, 6s.

THE INTRUDERS. Cr. 8vo, 2s. 6d.

LEDDY MARGET. Cr. 8vo, 2s. 6d.

IVA KILDARE : a Matrimonial Problem. Crown 8vo, 2s. 6d.

MR. SMITH : a Part of his Life. Cr. 8vo, 2s. 6d.

THE BABY'S GRANDMOTHER. Crown 8vo, 2s. 6d.

Fiction, Humour, etc.—*continued.*

Walford (L. B.)—*continued.*

COUSINS. Crown 8vo, 2s. 6d.

TROUBLESOME DAUGHTERS. Cr. 8vo, 2s. 6d.

PAULINE. Crown 8vo, 2s. 6d.

DICK NETHERBY. Cr. 8vo, 2s. 6d.

THE HISTORY OF A WEEK. Cr. 8vo, 2s. 6d.

A STIFF-NECKED GENERATION. Crown 8vo, 2s. 6d.

NAN, and other Stories. Crown 8vo, 2s. 6d.

THE MISCHIEF OF MONICA. Cr. 8vo, 2s. 6d.

THE ONE GOOD GUEST. Crown 8vo, 2s. 6d.

'PLOUGHED,' and other Stories. Cr. 8vo, 2s. 6d.

THE MATCHMAKER. Crown 8vo, 2s. 6d.

Ward.—ONE POOR SCRUPLE. By Mrs. WILFRID WARD. Crown 8vo, 6s.

West.—EDMUND FULLESTON : or, The Family Evil Genius. By B. B. WEST, Author of ' Half Hours with the Millionaires,' etc. Crown 8vo, 6s.

Weyman (STANLEY).

THE HOUSE OF THE WOLF. With Frontispiece and Vignette. Crown 8vo, 3s. 6d.

A GENTLEMAN OF FRANCE. With Frontispiece and Vignette. Crown 8vo, 6s.

THE RED COCKADE. With Frontispiece and Vignette. Crown 8vo, 6s.

SHREWSBURY. With 24 Illustrations by CLAUDE A. SHEPPERSON. Cr. 8vo, 6s.

SOPHIA. With Frontispiece. Crown 8vo, 6s.

Yeats (S. LEVETT).

THE CHEVALIER D'AURIAC. Cr. 8vo, 3s. 6d.

THE TRAITOR'S WAY. Crown 8vo, 6s.

Popular Science (Natural History, etc.).

Butler. — OUR HOUSEHOLD IN-SECTS. An Account of the Insect-Pests found in Dwelling-Houses. By EDWARD A. BUTLER, B.A., B.Sc. (Lond.). With 113 Illustrations. Cr. 8vo, 3s. 6d.

Furneaux (W.).

THE OUTDOOR WORLD; or, The Young Collector's Handbook. With 18 Plates (16 of which are coloured), and 549 Illustrations in the Text. Crown 8vo, gilt edges, 6s. net.

Furneaux (W.)—*continued.*

BUTTERFLIES AND MOTHS (British). With 12 coloured Plates and 241 Illustrations in the Text. Crown 8vo, gilt edges, 6s. net.

LIFE IN PONDS AND STREAMS. With 8 coloured Plates and 331 Illustrations in the Text. Cr. 8vo, gilt edges, 6s. net.

Popular Science (Natural History, etc.)—*continued.*

Hartwig (GEORGE).

THE SEA AND ITS LIVING WON-
DERS. With 12 Plates and 303
Woodcuts. 8vo, gilt top, 7s. net.

THE TROPICAL WORLD. With 8
Plates and 172 Woodcuts. 8vo, gilt
top, 7s. net.

THE POLAR WORLD. With 3 Maps,
8 Plates and 85 Woodcuts. 8vo, gilt
top, 7s. net.

THE SUBTERRANEAN WORLD.
With 3 Maps and 80 Woodcuts. 8vo.
gilt top. 7s. net.

Helmholtz.—POPULAR LECTURES
ON SCIENTIFIC SUBJECTS. By
HERMANN VON HELMHOLTZ. With 68
Woodcuts. 2 vols. Cr. 8vo, 3s. 6d.
each.

Hudson (W. H.).

BIRDS AND MAN. Large Crown
8vo, 6s. net.

NATURE IN DOWNLAND. With 12
Plates and 14 Illustrations in the
Text, by A. D. McCORMICK. 8vo,
10s. 6d. net.

BRITISH BIRDS. With a Chapter on
Structure and Classification by FRANK
E. BEDDARD, F.R.S. With 16 Plates
(8 of which are Coloured), and over
100 Illustrations in the Text. Crown
8vo, gilt edges, 6s. net.

BIRDS IN LONDON. With 17 Plates
and 15 Illustrations in the Text, by
BRYAN HOOK, A. D. McCORMICK,
and from Photographs from Nature,
by R. B. LODGE. 8vo, 12s.

Millais.—THE NATURAL HISTORY
OF THE BRITISH SURFACE-FEED-
ING DUCKS. By JOHN GUILLE
MILLAIS, F.Z.S., etc. With 6 Photo-
gravures and 66 Plates (41 in Colours)
from Drawings by the Author, ARCHI-
BALD THORBURN, and from Photographs.
Royal 4to, £6 6s.

Proctor (RICHARD A.).

LIGHT SCIENCE FOR LEISURE
HOURS. Familiar Essays on Scientific Subjects. Crown 8vo, 3s. 6d.

ROUGH WAYS MADE SMOOTH.
Familiar Essays on Scientific Subjects.
Crown 8vo, 3s. 6d.

PLEASANT WAYS IN SCIENCE.
Crown 8vo, 3s. 6d.

NATURE STUDIES. By R. A. PROC-
TOR. GRANT ALLEN, A. WILSON, T.
FOSTER and E. CLODD. Cr. 8vo, 3s. 6d.

LEISURE READINGS. By R. A.
PROCTOR, E. CLODD, A. WILSON, T.
FOSTER and A. C. RANYARD. Crown
8vo, 3s. 6d.

*** *For Mr. Proctor's other books see
pp. 16 and 35 and Messrs. Longmans &
Co.'s Catalogue of Scientific Works.*

Stanley.—A FAMILIAR HISTORY
OF BIRDS. By E. STANLEY, D.D.,
formerly Bishop of Norwich. With 160
Illustrations. Crown 8vo, 3s. 6d.

Wood (Rev. J. G.).

HOMES WITHOUT HANDS: A Description of the Habitations of Animals,
classed according to their Principle of
Construction. With 140 Illustrations.
8vo, gilt top, 7s. net.

INSECTS AT HOME: A Popular
Account of British Insects, their
Structure, Habits and Transforma-
tions. With 700 Illustrations. 8vo,
gilt top, 7s. net.

OUT OF DOORS: a Selection of
Original Articles on Practical Natural
History. With 11 Illustrations. Cr.
8vo, 3s. 6d.

PETLAND REVISITED. With 33
Illustrations. Crown 8vo, 3s. 6d.

STRANGE DWELLINGS: a Description of the Habitations of Animals,
abridged from 'Homes without
Hands'. With 60 Illustrations. Cr.
8vo, 3s. 6d.

Works of Reference.

Gwilt.—AN ENCYCLOPÆDIA OF ARCHITECTURE. By JOSEPH GWILT, F.S.A. With 1700 Engravings. Revised (1888), with alterations and Considerable Additions by WYATT PAPWORTH. 8vo, 21s. net.

Maunder (SAMUEL).

BIOGRAPHICAL TREASURY. With Supplement brought down to 1889. By Rev. JAMES WOOD. Fcp. 8vo, 6s.

TREASURY OF GEOGRAPHY, Physical, Historical, Descriptive and Political. With 7 Maps and 16 Plates. Fcp. 8vo, 6s.

THE TREASURY OF BIBLE KNOWLEDGE. By the Rev. J. AYRE, M.A. With 5 Maps, 15 Plates, and 300 Woodcuts. Fcp. 8vo, 6s.

TREASURY OF KNOWLEDGE AND LIBRARY OF REFERENCE. Fcp. 8vo, 6s.

HISTORICAL TREASURY. Fcp. 8vo, 6s.

Maunder (SAMUEL)—*continued.*

THE TREASURY OF BOTANY. Edited by J. LINDLEY, F.R.S., and T. MOORE, F.L.S. With 274 Woodcuts and 20 Steel Plates. 2 vols. Fcp. 8vo, 12s.

Roget.—THESAURUS OF ENGLISH WORDS AND PHRASES. Classified and Arranged so as to Facilitate the Expression of Ideas and assist in Literary Composition. By PETER MARK ROGET, M.D., F.R.S. Recomposed throughout, enlarged and improved, partly from the Author's Notes, and with a full Index, by the Author's Son, JOHN LEWIS ROGET. Crown 8vo, 9s. net.

Willich.—POPULAR TABLES for giving information for ascertaining the value of Lifehold, Leasehold, and Church Property, the Public Funds, etc. By CHARLES M. WILLICH. Edited by H. BENCE JONES. Crown 8vo, 10s. 6d.

Children's Books.

Adelborg. — CLEAN PETER AND THE CHILDREN OF GRUBBYLEA. By OTTILIA ADELBORG. Translated from the Swedish by Mrs. GRAHAM WALLAS. With 23 Coloured Plates. Oblong 4to, boards, 3s. 6d. net.

Brown.—THE BOOK OF SAINTS AND FRIENDLY BEASTS. By ABBIE FARWELL BROWN. With 8 Illustrations by FANNY Y. CORY. Cr. 8vo, 4s. 6d. net.

Buckland.—TWO LITTLE RUNAWAYS. Adapted from the French of LOUIS DESNOYERS. By JAMES BUCKLAND. With 110 Illustrations by CECIL ALDIN. Crown 8vo, 6s.

Corbin and Going.—URCHINS OF THE SEA. By MARIE OVERTON CORBIN and CHARLES BUXTON GOING. With Drawings by F. I. BENNETT. Oblong 4to, 3s. 6d.

Crake (Rev. A. D.).

EDWY THE FAIR; or, The First Chronicle of Æscenduue. Crown 8vo, silver top, 2s. net.

ALFGAR THE DANE: or, The Second Chronicle of Æscendune. Crown 8vo, silver top, 2s. net.

THE RIVAL HEIRS: being the Third and last Chronicle of Æscendune. Crown 8vo, silver top, 2s. net.

THE HOUSE OF WALDERNE. A Tale of the Cloister and the Forest in the Days of the Barons' Wars. Cr. 8vo, silver top, 2s. net.

BRIAN FITZ-COUNT. A Story of Wallingford Castle and Dorchester Abbey. Crown 8vo, silver top, 2s. net.

Children's Books—*continued.*

Henty (G. A.).—Edited by.

YULE LOGS: A Story Book for Boys. By VARIOUS AUTHORS. With 61 Illustrations. Cr. 8vo, gilt edges, 3s. net.

YULE-TIDE YARNS: a Story Book for Boys. By VARIOUS AUTHORS. With 45 Illustrations. Crown 8vo, gilt edges, 3s. net.

Lang (ANDREW).—Edited by.

THE VIOLET FAIRY BOOK. With 8 Coloured Plates and 54 other Illustratious. Crown 8vo, gilt edges, 6s.

THE BLUE FAIRY BOOK. With 138 Illustrations. Crown 8vo, gilt edges, 6s.

THE RED FAIRY BOOK. With 100 Illustrations. Crown 8vo, gilt edges, 6s.

THE GREEN FAIRY BOOK. With 99 Illustrations. Crown 8vo, gilt edges, 6s.

THE GREY FAIRY BOOK. With 65 Illustrations. Crown 8vo, gilt edges, 6s.

THE YELLOW FAIRY BOOK. With 104 Illustrations. Crown 8vo, gilt edges, 6s.

THE PINK FAIRY BOOK. With 67 Illustrations. Crown 8vo, gilt edges, 6s.

THE BLUE POETRY BOOK. With 100 Illustrations. Crown 8vo, gilt edges, 6s.

THE TRUE STORY BOOK. With 66 Illustrations. Crown 8vo, gilt edges, 6s.

THE RED TRUE STORY BOOK. With 100 Illustrations. Cr. 8vo, gilt edges, 6s.

THE ANIMAL STORY BOOK. With 67 Illustrations. Crown 8vo, gilt edges, 6s.

THE RED BOOK OF ANIMAL STORIES. With 65 Illustrations. Crown 8vo, gilt edges, 6s.

THE ARABIAN NIGHTS ENTERTAINMENTS. With 66 Illustrations. Crown 8vo, gilt edges, 6s.

Meade (L. T.).

DADDY'S BOY. With 8 Illustrations. Crown 8vo, gilt edges, 3s. net.

DEB AND THE DUCHESS. With 7 Illustrations. Crown 8vo, gilt edges, 3s. net.

THE BERESFORD PRIZE. With 7 Illustrations. Crown 8vo, gilt edges, 3s. net.

THE HOUSE OF SURPRISES. With 6 Illustrations. Crown 8vo, gilt edges, 3s. net.

Murray.—FLOWER LEGENDS FOR CHILDREN. By HILDA MURRAY (the Hon. Mrs. MURRAY of Elibank). Pictured by J. S. ELAND. With numerous Coloured and other Illustrations. Oblong 4to, 6s.

Praeger (ROSAMOND).

THE ADVENTURES OF THE THREE BOLD BABES: HECTOR, HONORIA AND ALISANDER. A Story in Pictures. With 24 Coloured Plates and 24 Outline Pictures. Oblong 4to, 3s. 6d.

THE FURTHER DOINGS OF THE THREE BOLD BABES. With 24 Coloured Pictures and 24 Outline Pictures. Oblong 4to, 3s. 6d.

Smith.—THE ADVENTURES OF CAPTAIN JOHN SMITH: Captain of Two Hundred and Fifty Horse, and sometime President of Virginia. Edited by E. P. ROBERTS. Crown 8vo.

Stevenson.—A CHILD'S GARDEN OF VERSES. By ROBERT LOUIS STEVENSON. Fcp. 8vo, gilt top, 5s.

Tappan.—OLD BALLADS IN PROSE. By EVA MARCH TAPPAN. With 4 Illustrations by FANNY Y. CORY. Crown 8vo, gilt top, 4s. 6d. net.

Children's Books—*continued.*

Upton (FLORENCE K. and BERTHA).

THE ADVENTURES OF TWO DUTCH DOLLS AND A 'GOLLIWOGG'. With 31 Coloured Plates and numerous Illustrations in the Text. Oblong 4to, 6s.

THE GOLLIWOGG'S BICYCLE CLUB. With 31 Coloured Plates and numerous Illustrations in the Text. Oblong 4to, 6s.

THE GOLLIWOGG AT THE SEA-SIDE. With 31 Coloured Plates and numerous Illustrations in the Text. Oblong 4to, 6s.

Upton (FLORENCE K. and BERTHA)—*continued.*

THE GOLLIWOGG IN WAR. With 31 Coloured Plates. Oblong 4to, 6s.

THE GOLLIWOGG'S POLAR ADVENTURES. With 31 Coloured Plates. Oblong 4to, 6s.

THE GOLLIWOGG'S AUTO-GO-CART. With 31 Coloured Plates and numerous Illustrations in the Text. Oblong 4to, 6s.

THE VEGE-MEN'S REVENGE. With 31 Coloured Plates and numerous Illustrations in the Text. Oblong 4to, 6s.

THE SILVER LIBRARY.

Crown 8vo, 3s. 6d. EACH VOLUME.

Arnold's (Sir Edwin) Seas and Lands. With 17 Illustrations. 3s. 6d.

Bagehot's (W.) Biographical Studies. .3s. 6d.

Bagehot's (W.) Economic Studies. 3s. 6d.

Bagehot's (W.) Literary Studies. With Portrait. 3 vols. 3s. 6d. each.

Baker's (Sir S. W.) Eight Years in Ceylon. With 6 Illustrations. 3s. 6d.

Baker's (Sir S. W.) Rifle and Hound in Ceylon. With 6 Illustrations. 3s. 6d.

Baring-Gould's (Rev. S.) Curious Myths of the Middle Ages. 3s. 6d.

Baring-Gould's (Rev. S.) Origin and Development of Religious Belief. 2 vols. 3s. 6d. each.

Becker's (W. A.) Gallus: or, Roman Scenes in the Time of Augustus. With 26 Illustrations. 3s. 6d.

Becker's (W. A.) Charicles: or, Illustrations of the Private Life of the Ancient Greeks. With 26 Illustrations. 3s. 6d.

Bent's (J. T.) The Ruined Cities of Mashonaland. With 117 Illustrations. 3s. 6d.

Brassey's (Lady) A Voyage in the 'Sunbeam'. With 66 Illustrations. 3s. 6d.

Churchill's (W. Spencer) The Story of the Malakand Field Force, 1897. With 6 Maps and Plans. 3s. 6d.

Clodd's (E.) Story of Creation: a Plain Account of Evolution. With 77 Illustrations. 3s. 6d.

Conybeare (Rev. W. J.) and Howson's (Very Rev. J. S.) Life and Epistles of St. Paul. With 46 Illustrations. 3s. 6d.

Dougall's (L.) Beggars All; a Novel. 3s. 6d.

Doyle's (A. Conan) Micah Clarke. A Tale of Monmouth's Rebellion. With 10 Illustrations. 3s. 6d.

Doyle's (A. Conan) The Captain of the Polestar, and other Tales. 3s. 6d.

Doyle's (A. Conan) The Refugees: A Tale of the Huguenots. With 25 Illustrations. 3s. 6d.

Doyle's (A. Conan) The Stark Munro Letters. 3s. 6d.

Froude's (J. A.) The History of England, from the Fall of Wolsey to the Defeat of the Spanish Armada. 12 vols. 3s. 6d. each.

Froude's (J. A.) The English in Ireland. 3 vols. 10s. 6d.

Froude's (J. A.) The Divorce of Catherine of Aragon. 3s. 6d.

Froude's (J. A.) The Spanish Story of the Armada, and other Essays. 3s. 6d.

Froude's (J. A.) English Seamen in the Sixteenth Century. 3s. 6d.

Froude's (J. A.) Short Studies on Great Subjects. 4 vols. 3s. 6d. each.

Froude's (J. A.) Oceana, or England and her Colonies. With 9 Illustrations. 3s. 6d.

Froude's (J. A.) The Council of Trent. 3s. 6d.

THE SILVER LIBRARY—*continued.*

Froude's (J. A.) The Life and Letters of Erasmus. 3*s.* 6*d.*

Froude's (J. A.) Thomas Carlyle: a History of his Life. 1795-1835. 2 vols. 7*s.* 1834-1881. 2 vols. 7*s.*

Froude's (J. A.) Cæsar : a Sketch. 3*s.* 6*d.*

Froude's (J. A.) The Two Chiefs of Dunboy : an Irish Romance of the Last Century. 3*s.* 6*d.*

Froude's (J. A.) Writings, Selections from. 3*s.* 6*d.*

Gleig's (Rev. G. R.) Life of the Duke of Wellington. With Portrait. 3*s.* 6*d.*

Greville's (C. C. F.) Journal of the Reigns of King George IV., King William IV., and Queen Victoria. 8 vols. 3*s.* 6*d.* each.

Haggard's (H. R.) She: A History of Adventure. With 32 Illustrations. 3*s.* 6*d.*

Haggard's (H. R.) Allan Quatermain. With 20 Illustrations. 3*s.* 6*d.*

Haggard's (H. R.) Colonel Quaritch, V.C.: a Tale of Country Life. With Frontispiece and Vignette. 3*s.* 6*d.*

Haggard's (H. R.) Cleopatra. With 29 Illustrations. 3*s.* 6*d.*

Haggard's (H. R.) Eric Brighteyes. With 51 Illustrations. 3*s.* 6*d.*

Haggard's (H. R.) Beatrice. With Frontispiece and Vignette. 3*s.* 6*d.*

Haggard's (H. R.) Allan's Wife. With 34 Illustrations. 3*s.* 6*d.*

Haggard's (H. R.) Heart of the World. With 15 Illustrations. 3*s.* 6*d.*

Haggard's (H. R.) Montezuma's Daughter. With 25 Illustrations. 3*s.* 6*d.*

Haggard's (H. R.) Swallow: a Tale of the Great Trek. With 8 Illustrations. 3*s.* 6*d.*

Haggard's (H. R.) The Witch's Head. With 16 Illustrations. 3*s.* 6*d.*

Haggard's (H. R.) Mr. Meeson's Will. With 16 Illustrations. 3*s.* 6*d.*

Haggard's (H. R.) Nada the Lily. With 23 Illustrations. 3*s.* 6*d.*

Haggard's (H. R.) Dawn. With 16 Illustrations. 3*s.* 6*d.*

Haggard's (H. R.) The People of the Mist. With 16 Illustrations. 3*s.* 6*d.*

Haggard's (H. R.) Joan Haste. With 20 Illustrations. 3*s.* 6*d.*

Haggard (H. R.) and Lang's (A.) The World's Desire. With 27 Illus. 3*s.* 6*d.*

Harte's (Bret) In the Carquinez Woods, and other Stories. 3*s.* 6*d.*

Helmholtz's (Hermann von) Popular Lectures on Scientific Subjects. With 68 Illustrations. 2 vols. 3*s.* 6*d.* each.

Hope's (Anthony) The Heart of Princess Osra. With 9 Illustrations. 3*s.* 6*d.*

Howitt's (W.) Visits to Remarkable Places. With 80 Illustrations. 3*s.* 6*d.*

Jefferies' (R.) The Story of My Heart: My Autobiography. With Portrait. 3*s.* 6*d.*

Jefferies' (R.) Field and Hedgerow. With Portrait. 3*s.* 6*d.*

Jefferies' (R.) Red Deer. With 17 Illustrations. 3*s.* 6*d.*

Jefferies' (R.) Wood Magic: a Fable. With Frontispiece and Vignette by E. V. B. 3*s.* 6*d.*

Jefferies' (R.) The Toilers of the Field. With Portrait from the Bust in Salisbury Cathedral. 3*s.* 6*d.*

Kaye (Sir J.) and Malleson's (Colonel) History of the Indian Mutiny of 1857-8. 6 vols. 3*s.* 6*d.* each.

Knight's (E. F.) The Cruise of the 'Alerte': the Narrative of a Search for Treasure on the Desert Island of Trinidad. With 2 Maps and 23 Illustrations. 3*s.* 6*d.*

Knight's (E. F.) Where Three Empires Meet: a Narrative of Recent Travel in Kashmir, Western Tibet, Baltistan, Gilgit. With a Map and 54 Illustrations. 3*s.* 6*d.*

Knight's (E. F.) The 'Falcon' on the Baltic : a Coasting Voyage from Hammersmith to Copenhagen in a Three-Ton Yacht. With Map and 11 Illustrations. 3*s.* 6*d.*

THE SILVER LIBRARY—*continued.*

Köstlin's (J.) Life of Luther. With 62 Illustrations and 4 Facsimiles of MSS. 3*s.* 6*d.*

Lang's (A.) Angling Sketches. With 20 Illustrations. 3*s.* 6*d.*

Lang's (A.) Custom and Myth: Studies of Early Usage and Belief. 3*s.* 6*d.*

Lang's (A.) Cock Lane and Common-Sense. 3*s.* 6*d.*

Lang's (A.) The Book of Dreams and Ghosts. 3*s.* 6*d.*

Lang's (A.) A Monk of Fife: a Story of the Days of Joan of Arc. With 13 Illustrations. 3*s.* 6*d.*

Lang's (A.) Myth, Ritual and Religion. 2 vols. 7*s.*

Lees (J. A.) and Clutterbuck's (W.J.) B.C. 1887, A Ramble in British Columbia. With Maps and 75 Illustrations. 3*s.* 6*d.*

Levett-Yeats' (S.) The Chevalier D'Auriac. 3*s.* 6*d.*

Macaulay's (Lord) Complete Works. 'Albany' Edition. With 12 Portraits. 12 vols. 3*s.* 6*d.* each.

Macaulay's (Lord) Essays and Lays of Ancient Rome, etc. With Portrait and 4 Illustrations to the 'Lays'. 3*s.* 6*d.*

Macleod's (H. D.) Elements of Banking. 3*s.* 6*d.*

Marshman's (J. C.) Memoirs of Sir Henry Havelock. 3*s.* 6*d.*

Mason (A. E. W.) and Lang's (A.) Parson Kelly. 3*s.* 6*d.*

Merivale's (Dean) History of the Romans under the Empire. 8 vols. 3*s.* 6*d.* each.

Merriman's (H. S.) Flotsam: a Tale of the Indian Mutiny. 3*s.* 6*d.*

Mill's (J. S.) Political Economy. 3*s.* 6*d.*

Mill's (J. S.) System of Logic. 3*s.* 6*d.*

Milner's (Geo.) Country Pleasures: the Chronicle of a year chiefly in a Garden. 3*s.* 6*d.*

Nansen's (F.) The First Crossing of Greenland. With 142 Illustrations and a Map. 3*s.* 6*d.*

Phillipps-Wolley's (C.) Snap: a Legend of the Lone Mountain. With 13 Illustrations. 3*s.* 6*d.*

Proctor's (R. A.) The Orbs Around Us. 3*s.* 6*d.*

Proctor's (R. A.) The Expanse of Heaven. 3*s.* 6*d.*

Proctor's (R. A.) Light Science for Leisure Hours. First Series. 3*s.* 6*d.*

Proctor's (R. A.) The Moon. 3*s.* 6*d.*

Proctor's (R. A.) Other Worlds than Ours. 3*s.* 6*d.*

Proctor's (R. A.) Our Place among Infinities: a Series of Essays contrasting our Little Abode in Space and Time with the Infinities around us. 3*s.* 6*d.*

Proctor's (R. A.) Other Suns than Ours. 3*s.* 6*d.*

Proctor's (R. A.) Rough Ways made Smooth. 3*s.* 6*d.*

Proctor's (R. A.) Pleasant Ways in Science. 3*s.* 6*d.*

Proctor's (R. A.) Myths and Marvels of Astronomy. 3*s.* 6*d.*

Proctor's (R. A.) Nature Studies. 3*s.* 6*d.*

Proctor's (R. A.) Leisure Readings. By R. A. PROCTOR, EDWARD CLODD, ANDREW WILSON, THOMAS FOSTER and A. C. RANYARD. With Illustrations. 3*s.* 6*d.*

Rossetti's (Maria F.) A Shadow of Dante. 3*s.* 6*d.*

Smith's (R. Bosworth) Carthage and the Carthaginians. With Maps, Plans, etc. 3*s.* 6*d.*

Stanley's (Bishop) Familiar History of Birds. With 160 Illustrations. 3*s.* 6*d.*

THE SILVER LIBRARY—*continued.*

Stephen's (L.) The Playground of Europe (The Alps). With 4 Illustrations. 3s. 6d.

Stevenson's (R. L.) The Strange Case of Dr. Jekyll and Mr. Hyde; with other Fables. 3s. 6d.

Stevenson (R. L.) and Osbourne's (Ll.) The Wrong Box. 3s. 6d.

Stevenson (Robt. Louis) and Stevenson's (Fanny van de Grift) More New Arabian Nights. — The Dynamiter. 3s. 6d.

Trevelyan's (Sir G. O.) The Early History of Charles James Fox. 3s. 6d.

Weyman's (Stanley J.) The House of the Wolf: a Romance. 3s. 6d.

Wood's (Rev. J. G.) Petland Revisited. With 33 Illustrations. 3s. 6d.

Wood's (Rev. J. G.) Strange Dwellings. With 60 Illustrations. 3s. 6d.

Wood's (Rev. J. G.) Out of Doors. With 11 Illustrations. 3s. 6d.

Cookery, Domestic Management, etc.

Acton.—MODERN COOKERY. By ELIZA ACTON. With 150 Woodcuts. Fcp. 8vo, 4s. 6d.

Angwin. — SIMPLE HINTS ON CHOICE OF FOOD, with Tested and Economical Recipes. For Schools, Homes and Classes for Technical Instruction. By M. C. ANGWIN, Diplomate (First Class) of the National Union for the Technical Training of Women, etc. Crown 8vo, 1s.

Ashby.—HEALTH IN THE NURSERY. By HENRY ASHBY, MD., F.R.C.P., Physician to the Manchester Children's Hospital. With 25 Illustrations. Cr. 8vo, 3s. net.

Bull (THOMAS, M.D.).
HINTS TO MOTHERS ON THE MANAGEMENT OF THEIR HEALTH DURING THE PERIOD OF PREGNANCY. Fcp. 8vo, sewed, 1s. 6d. ; cloth, gilt edges, 2s. net.
THE MATERNAL MANAGEMENT OF CHILDREN IN HEALTH AND DISEASE. Fcp. 8vo, sewed, 1s. 6d. ; cloth, gilt edges, 2s. net.

De Salis (MRS.).
A LA MODE COOKERY : UP-TO-DATE RECIPES. With 24 Plates (16 in Colours). Crown 8vo, 5s. net.
CAKES AND CONFECTIONS À LA MODE. Fcp. 8vo, 1s. 6d.
DOGS : A Manual for Amateurs. Fcp. 8vo, 1s. 6d.
DRESSED GAME AND POULTRY À LA MODE. Fcp. 8vo, 1s. 6d.
DRESSED VEGETABLES À LA MODE. Fcp. 8vo, 1s. 6d.
DRINKS À LA MODE. Fcp. 8vo, 1s. 6d.

De Salis (MRS.)—*continued.*
ENTREES À LA MODE. Fcp. 8vo, 1s. 6d.
FLORAL DECORATIONS. Fcp. 8vo, 1s. 6d.
GARDENING À LA MODE. Fcp. 8vo, Part I., Vegetables, 1s. 6d. Part II., Fruits, 1s. 6d.
NATIONAL VIANDS À LA MODE. Fcp. 8vo, 1s. 6d.
NEW-LAID EGGS. Fcp. 8vo, 1s. 6d.
OYSTERS À LA MODE. Fcp. 8vo, 1s. 6d.
PUDDINGS AND PASTRY À LA MODE. Fcp. 8vo, 1s. 6d.
SAVOURIES À LA MODE. Fcp. 8vo, 1s. 6d.
SOUPS AND DRESSED FISH À LA MODE. Fcp. 8vo, 1s. 6d.
SWEETS AND SUPPER DISHES À LA MODE. Fcp. 8vo, 1s. 6d.
TEMPTING DISHES FOR SMALL INCOMES. Fcp. 8vo, 1s. 6d.
WRINKLES AND NOTIONS FOR EVERY HOUSEHOLD. Crown 8vo, 1s. 6d.

Lear.—MAIGRE COOKERY. By H. L. SIDNEY LEAR. 16mo, 2s.

Poole.—COOKERY FOR THE DIABETIC. By W. H. and Mrs. POOLE. With Preface by Dr. PAVY. Fcp. 8vo, 2s. 6d.

Rotheram. — HOUSEHOLD COOKERY RECIPES. By M. A. ROTHERAM, First Class Diplomée, National Training School of Cookery, London ; Instructress to the Bedfordshire County Council. Crown 8vo, 2s.

The Fine Arts and Music.

Burns and Colenso. — LIVING ANATOMY. By CECIL L. BURNS, R.B.A., and ROBERT J. COLENSO, M.A., M.D. 40 Plates, 11¼ × 8¾ in., each Plate containing Two Figures—(*a*) A Natural Male or Female Figure ; (*b*) The same Figure Anatomised. In a Portfolio. 7*s*. 6*d*. net.

Hamlin.—A TEXT-BOOK OF THE HISTORY OF ARCHITECTURE. By A. D. F. HAMLIN, A.M. With 229 Illustrations. Crown 8vo, 7*s*. 6*d*.

Haweis (Rev. H. R.).

MUSIC AND MORALS. With Portrait of the Author, and Numerous Illustrations, Facsimiles and Diagrams. Crown 8vo, 6*s*. net.

MY MUSICAL LIFE. With Portrait of Richard Wagner and 3 Illustrations. Crown 8vo, 6*s*. net.

Huish, Head and Longman.— SAMPLERS AND TAPESTRY EMBROIDERIES. By MARCUS B. HUISH, LL.B. ; also 'The Stitchery of the Same,' by Mrs. HEAD ; and 'Foreign Samplers,' by Mrs. C. J. LONGMAN. With 30 Reproductions in Colour and 40 Illustrations in Monochrome. 4to, £2 2*s*. net.

Hullah.—THE HISTORY OF MODERN MUSIC. By JOHN HULLAH. 8vo, 8*s*. 6*d*.

Jameson (Mrs. ANNA).

SACRED AND LEGENDARY ART, containing Legends of the Angels and Archangels, the Evangelists, the Apostles, the Doctors of the Church, St. Mary Magdalene, the Patron Saints, the Martyrs, the Early Bishops, the Hermits and the Warrior-Saints of Christendom, as represented in the Fine Arts. With 19 Etchings and 187 Woodcuts. 2 vols. 8vo, 20*s*. net.

LEGENDS OF THE MONASTIC ORDERS, as represented in the Fine Arts, comprising the Benedictines and Augustines, and Orders derived from their rules, the Mendicant Orders, the Jesuits, and the Order of the Visitation of St. Mary. With 11 Etchings and 88 Woodcuts. 1 vol, 8vo, 10*s*, net.

Jameson (Mrs. ANNA)—*continued.*

LEGENDS OF THE MADONNA, OR BLESSED VIRGIN MARY. Devotional with and without the Infant Jesus, Historical from the Annunciation to the Assumption, as represented in Sacred and Legendary Christian Art. With 27 Etchings and 165 Woodcuts. 1 vol. 8vo, 10*s*. net.

THE HISTORY OF OUR LORD, as exemplified in Works of Art, with that of His Types, St. John the Baptist, and other persons of the Old and New Testament. Commenced by the late Mrs. JAMESON ; continued and completed by LADY EASTLAKE. With 31 Etchings and 281 Woodcuts. 2 vols. 8vo, 20*s*. net.

Kingsley.—A HISTORY OF FRENCH ART, 1100-1899. By ROSE G. KINGSLEY. 8vo, 12*s*. 6*d*. net.

Kristeller.—ANDREA MANTEGNA. By PAUL KRISTELLER. English Edition by S. ARTHUR STRONG, M.A., Librarian to the House of Lords, and at Chatsworth. With 26 Photogravure Plates and 162 Illustrations in the Text. 4to, gilt top, £3 10*s*. net.

Macfarren.—LECTURES ON HARMONY. By Sir GEORGE A. MACFARREN. 8vo, 12*s*.

Morris (WILLIAM).

HOPES AND FEARS FOR ART. Five Lectures delivered in Birmingham, London, etc., in 1878-1881. Crown 8vo, 4*s*. 6*d*.

AN ADDRESS DELIVERED AT THE DISTRIBUTION OF PRIZES TO STUDENTS OF THE BIRMINGHAM MUNICIPAL SCHOOL OF ART ON 21ST FEBRUARY, 1894. 8vo, 2*s*. 6*d*. net. (*Printed in 'Golden' Type.*)

ART AND THE BEAUTY OF THE EARTH. A Lecture delivered at Burslem Town Hall on 13th October, 1881. 8vo, 2*s*. 6*d*. net. (*Printed in 'Golden' Type.*)

SOME HINTS ON PATTERN - DESIGNING : a Lecture delivered at the Working Men's College, London, on 10th December, 1881. 8vo, 2*s*. 6*d*. net. (*Printed in 'Golden' Type.*)

The Fine Arts and Music—*continued.*

Morris (WILLIAM)—*continued.*

ARTS AND ITS PRODUCERS (1888) AND THE ARTS AND CRAFTS OF TO-DAY (1889). 8vo, 2s. 6d. net. (*Printed in 'Golden' Type.*)

ARCHITECTURE AND HISTORY, AND WESTMINSTER ABBEY. Two Papers read before the Society for the Protection of Ancient Buildings. 8vo, 2s. 6d. net. (*Printed in 'Golden' Type.*)

ARTS AND CRAFTS ESSAYS BY MEMBERS OF THE ARTS AND CRAFTS EXHIBITION SOCIETY. With a Preface by WILLIAM MORRIS. Crown 8vo, 2s. 6d. net.

*** *For Mr. William Morris's other works see pp.* 24, 27 *and* 40.

Van Dyke.—A TEXT-BOOK ON THE HISTORY OF PAINTING. By JOHN C. VAN DYKE. With 110 Illustrations. Crown 8vo, 6s.

Willard.—HISTORY OF MODERN ITALIAN ART. By ASHTON ROLLINS WILLARD. With Photogravure Frontispiece and 28 full-page Illustrations. 8vo, 18s. net.

Wellington.—A DESCRIPTIVE AND HISTORICAL CATALOGUE OF THE COLLECTIONS OF PICTURES AND SCULPTURE AT APSLEY HOUSE, LONDON. By EVELYN, Duchess of Wellington. Illustrated by 52 Photo-Engravings, specially executed by BRAUN, CLÉMENT & Co., of Paris. 2 vols. Royal 4to, £6 6s. net.

Miscellaneous and Critical Works.

Annals of Mathematics (under the Auspices of Harvard University). Issued Quarterly. 4to, 2s. net each number.

Bagehot.—LITERARY STUDIES. By WALTER BAGEHOT. With Portrait. 3 vols. Crown 8vo, 3s. 6d. each.

Baker.—EDUCATION AND LIFE: Papers and Addresses. By JAMES H. BAKER, M.A., LL.D. Crown 8vo, 4s. 6d.

Baring-Gould.—CURIOUS MYTHS OF THE MIDDLE AGES. By Rev. S. BARING-GOULD. Crown 8vo, 3s. 6d.

Baynes.—SHAKESPEARE STUDIES, and other Essays. By the late THOMAS SPENCER BAYNES, LL.B., LL.D. With a Biographical Preface by Professor LEWIS CAMPBELL. Crown 8vo, 7s. 6d.

Charities Register, THE ANNUAL, AND DIGEST; being a Classified Register of Charities in or available in the Metropolis. 8vo, 4s.

Christie.—SELECTED ESSAYS. By RICHARD COPLEY CHRISTIE, M.A. Oxon., Hon. LL.D. Vict. With 2 Portraits and 3 other Illustrations. 8vo, 12s. net.

Dickinson.—KING ARTHUR IN CORNWALL. By W. HOWSHIP DICKINSON, M.D. With 5 Illustrations. Crown 8vo, 4s. 6d.

Essays in Paradox. By the Author of 'Exploded Ideas' and 'Times and Days'. Crown 8vo, 5s.

Evans.—THE ANCIENT STONE IMPLEMENTS, WEAPONS AND ORNAMENTS OF GREAT BRITAIN. By Sir JOHN EVANS, K.C.B. With 537 Illustrations. 8vo, 28s.

Exploded Ideas, AND OTHER ESSAYS. By the Author of 'Times and Days'. Crown 8vo, 5s.

Frost.—A MEDLEY BOOK. By GEO. FROST. Crown 8vo, 3s. 6d. net.

Geikie. — THE VICAR AND HIS FRIENDS. By CUNNINGHAM GEIKIE, D.D., LL.D. Crown 8vo, 5s. net.

Haggard. — A FARMER'S YEAR: being his Commonplace Book for 1898. By H. RIDER HAGGARD. With 36 Illustrations. Crown 8vo, 7s. 6d. net.

Hodgson.—OUTCAST ESSAYS AND VERSE TRANSLATIONS. By SHADWORTH H. HODGSON, LL.D. Crown 8vo, 8s. 6d.

Hoenig.—INQUIRIES CONCERNING THE TACTICS OF THE FUTURE. By FRITZ HOENIG. With 1 Sketch in the Text and 5 Maps. Translated by Captain H. M. BOWER. 8vo, 15s. net.

Hutchinson.—DREAMS AND THEIR MEANINGS. By HORACE G. HUTCHINSON. 8vo, gilt top, 9s. 6d. net.

Miscellaneous and Critical Works—*continued.*

Jefferies (RICHARD).

FIELD AND HEDGEROW. With Portrait. Crown 8vo, 3s. 6d.

THE STORY OF MY HEART: my Autobiography. Crown 8vo, 3s. 6d.

RED DEER. With 17 Illustrations. Crown 8vo, 3s. 6d.

THE TOILERS OF THE FIELD. Cr. 8vo, 3s. 6d.

WOOD MAGIC : a Fable. Crown 8vo, 3s. 6d.

Jekyll (GERTRUDE).

HOME AND GARDEN : Notes and Thoughts, Practical and Critical, of a Worker in both. With 53 Illustrations from Photographs. 8vo, 10s. 6d. net.

WOOD AND GARDEN : Notes and Thoughts, Practical and Critical, of a Working Amateur. With 71 Illustrations. 8vo, 10s. 6d. net.

Johnson (J. & J. H.).

THE PATENTEE'S MANUAL : a Treatise on the Law and Practice of Letters Patent. 8vo, 10s. 6d.

AN EPITOME OF THE LAW AND PRACTICE CONNECTED WITH PATENTS FOR INVENTIONS. With a Reprint of the Patents Acts of 1883, 1885, 1886 and 1888. Crown 8vo, 2s. 6d.

Joyce.—THE ORIGIN AND HISTORY OF IRISH NAMES OF PLACES. By P. W. JOYCE, LL.D. 2 vols. Crown 8vo, 5s. each.

Lang (ANDREW).

LETTERS TO DEAD AUTHORS. Fcp. 8vo, 2s. 6d. net.

BOOKS AND BOOKMEN. With 2 Coloured Plates and 17 Illustrations. Fcp. 8vo, 2s. 6d. net.

OLD FRIENDS. Fcp. 8vo, 2s. 6d. net.

LETTERS ON LITERATURE. Fcp. 8vo, 2s. 6d. net.

ESSAYS IN LITTLE. With Portrait of the Author. Crown 8vo, 2s. 6d.

COCK LANE AND COMMON-SENSE. Crown 8vo, 3s. 6d.

THE BOOK OF DREAMS AND GHOSTS. Crown 8vo, 3s. 6d.

Maryon.— HOW THE GARDEN GREW. By MAUD MARYON. With 4 Illustrations. Crown 8vo, 5s. net.

Matthews.—NOTES ON SPEECH-MAKING. By BRANDER MATTHEWS. Fcp. 8vo, 1s. 6d. net.

Max Müller (The Right Hon. F.).

COLLECTED WORKS. 18 vols. Cr. 8vo, 5s. each.

Vol. I. NATURAL RELIGION : the Gifford Lectures, 1888.

Vol. II. PHYSICAL RELIGION : the Gifford Lectures, 1890.

Vol. III. ANTHROPOLOGICAL RELIGION : the Gifford Lectures, 1891.

Vol. IV. THEOSOPHY ; or, Psychological Religion : the Gifford Lectures, 1892.

CHIPS FROM A GERMAN WORKSHOP.

Vol. V. Recent Essays and Addresses.

Vol. VI. Biographical Essays.

Vol. VII. Essays on Language and Literature.

Vol. VIII. Essays on Mythology and Folk-lore.

Vol. IX. THE ORIGIN AND GROWTH OF RELIGION, as illustrated by the Religions of India : the Hibbert Lectures, 1878.

Vol. X. BIOGRAPHIES OF WORDS, AND THE HOME OF THE ARYAS.

Vols. XI., XII. THE SCIENCE OF LANGUAGE : Founded on Lectures delivered at the Royal Institution in 1861 and 1863. 2 vols. 10s.

Vol. XIII. INDIA : What can it Teach Us ?

Vol. XIV. INTRODUCTION TO THE SCIENCE OF RELIGION. Four Lectures, 1870.

Vol. XV. RÁMAKRISHNA : his Life and Sayings.

Vol. XVI. THREE LECTURES ON THE VEDÁNTA PHILOSOPHY, 1894.

Vol. XVII. LAST ESSAYS. First Series. Essays on Language, Folk-lore, etc.

Vol. XVIII. LAST ESSAYS. Second Series. Essays on the Science of Religion.

Miscellaneous and Critical Works—*continued.*

Milner. — COUNTRY PLEASURES: the Chronicle of a Year chiefly in a Garden. By GEORGE MILNER. Crown 8vo, 3s. 6d.

Morris.—SIGNS OF CHANGE. Seven Lectures delivered on various Occasions. By WILLIAM MORRIS. Post 8vo, 4s. 6d.

Parker and Unwin.—THE ART OF BUILDING A HOME: a Collection of Lectures and Illustrations. By BARRY PARKER and RAYMOND UNWIN. With 68 Full-page Plates. 8vo, 10s. 6d. net.

Pollock.—JANE AUSTEN: her Contemporaries and Herself. By WALTER HERRIES POLLOCK. Crown 8vo, 3s. 6d. net.

Poore (GEORGE VIVIAN, M.D.).

ESSAYS ON RURAL HYGIENE. With 13 Illustrations. Crown 8vo, 6s. 6d.

THE DWELLING HOUSE. With 36 Illustrations. Crown 8vo, 3s. 6d.

THE MILROY LECTURES ON THE EARTH IN RELATION TO THE PRESERVATION AND DESTRUC-TION OF CONTAGIA, together with other Papers on Public Health. Cr. 8vo.

Rossetti.—A SHADOW OF DANTE: being an Essay towards studying Himself, his World, and his Pilgrimage. By MARIA FRANCESCA ROSSETTI. Crown 8vo, 3s. 6d.

Soulsby (LUCY H. M.).

STRAY THOUGHTS ON READING. Fcp. 8vo, 2s. 6d. net.

STRAY THOUGHTS FOR GIRLS. 16mo, 1s. 6d. net.

STRAY THOUGHTS FOR MOTHERS AND TEACHERS. Fcp. 8vo, 2s. 6d. net.

10,000/5/02.

Soulsby (LUCY H. M.)—*continued.*

STRAY THOUGHTS FOR INVALIDS. 16mo, 2s. net.

STRAY THOUGHTS ON CHARAC-TER. Fcp. 8vo, 2s. 6d. net.

Southey.—THE CORRESPONDENCE OF ROBERT SOUTHEY WITH CAROLINE BOWLES. Edited by EDWARD DOWDEN. 8vo, 14s.

Stevens.—ON THE STOWAGE OF SHIPS AND THEIR CARGOES. With Information regarding Freights, Charter-Parties, etc. By ROBERT WHITE STEVENS. 8vo, 21s.

Sutherland. — TWENTIETH CEN-TURY INVENTIONS: A FORECAST. By GEORGE SUTHERLAND, M.A. Crown 8vo, 4s. 6d. net.

Turner and Sutherland. — THE DEVELOPMENT OF AUSTRALIAN LITERATURE. By HENRY GYLES TURNER and ALEXANDER SUTHERLAND. With Portraits and Illustrations. Crown 8vo, 5s.

Warwick.—PROGRESS IN WOMEN'S EDUCATION IN THE BRITISH EMPIRE: being the Report of Confer-ences and a Congress held in connection with the Educational Section, Victorian Era Exhibition. Edited by the COUN-TESS OF WARWICK. Crown 8vo, 6s.

Weathers.—A PRACTICAL GUIDE TO GARDEN PLANTS. By JOHN WEATHERS, F.R.H.S. With 159 Dia-grams. 8vo, 21s. net.

Webb.—THE MYSTERY OF WIL-LIAM SHAKESPEARE: A Summary of Evidence. By his Honour Judge T. WEBB, sometime Regius Professor of Laws and Public Orator in the Univer-sity of Dublin. 8vo, 10s. 6d. net.

Whittall.—FREDERIC THE GREAT ON KINGCRAFT, from the Original Manuscript; with Reminiscences and Turkish Stories. By Sir J. WILLIAM WHITTALL, President of the British Chamber of Commerce of Turkey. 8vo, 7s. 6d. net.

1184571R0

Printed in Great Britain by
Amazon.co.uk, Ltd.,
Marston Gate.